19.⁰⁰

THE CULT OF ALIEN GODS

THE CULT OF ALIEN GODS
H. P. LOVECRAFT
AND EXTRATERRESTRIAL POP CULTURE

J A S O N   C O L A V I T O

Prometheus Books

59 John Glenn Drive
Amherst, New York 14228-2197

Published 2005 by Prometheus Books

Inquiries should be addressed to
Prometheus Books
59 John Glenn Drive
Amherst, New York 14228–2197
VOICE: 716–691–0133, ext. 207
FAX: 716–564–2711
WWW.PROMETHEUSBOOKS.COM

09 08 07 06 05   5 4 3 2 1

Library of Congress Cataloging-in-Publication Data

Colavito, Jason.
   The cult of alien gods : H. P. Lovecraft and extraterrestrial pop culture / by Jason Colavito.
       p. cm.
   Includes bibliographical references (p.   ) and index.
   ISBN 1–59102–352–1 (pbk.: alk. paper)
   1. Lovecraft, H. P. (Howard Philips), 1890–1937—Criticism and interpretation. 2. Lovecraft, H. P. (Howard Philips), 1890–1937—Appreciation—United States. 3. Lovecraft, H. P. (Howard Philips), 1890–1937—Influence. 4. Popular culture—United States—History—20th century. 5. Horror tales, American—History and criticism. 6. Life on other planets in literature. 7. Human-alien encounters in literature. 8. Cthulhu (Fictitious character) 9. Gods in literature. I. Title.

PS3523.O833Z575 2005
813'.52—dc22

                                                                      2005020527

Printed in the United States of America on acid-free paper

CONTENTS

INTERLUDE: THE VIEW FROM 1976

PART FOUR: FROM SIRIUS TO ORION AND BEYOND

PART FIVE: HUMAN CLONES FROM THE TWELFTH PLANET

CONCLUSION

ACKNOWLEDGMENTS

This book exists today largely because my parents indulged my childhood passion for reading, and it is because of them that I was able to read widely and broadly enough to gather the materials that later became the work you hold in your hands. This book exists too because of a number of friends who tolerated my penchant for talking (perhaps they would say lecturing) at length on various odd topics. These talks eventually helped me make the connections that came together here. To all of them (you know who you are), I give my thanks.

I also want to thank Dr. Jack Rossen and Dr. Michael Malpass, my former college professors who persuaded me to study archaeology at school and who taught me most of what I know about its methods. Any mistakes I have made in describing the field are entirely my fault.

Thanks too to Dr. Thomas E. "Eddie" Bullard, who read my manuscript in rough form and offered useful criticism and feedback. Though we differ in our opinions, his comments were on target and made my book stronger. I also wish to thank Dr. Michael Shermer, publisher of *Skeptic* magazine, for giving my theory its first professional airing in the pages of his journal.

Thanks should also go to the individuals who consented to answer my strange questions for this book: Graham Hancock, Laurence Gardner, Alan Alford, Ricky Roehr, and Joseph Trainor. Also thanks to those who kindly let me reproduce their wonderful photographs and art: Jon Bodsworth, John W. Anderson, Pat Linse, and Frances Laurent.

Finally, I have to acknowledge the tremendous debt I owe to H. P. Lovecraft, whose work is responsible for what literary success I have had. *Iä! Cthulhu fhtagn!*

PRELUDE

1

THE CROSSROADS
OF FACT AND FICTION

H. P. Lovecraft, known to the aficionados of the occult—demonology, witchcraft—as a master storyteller, is responsible for our first selection in this museum of the frequently morbid. To you connoisseurs of the black arts, you'll probably recognize it. It's a painting that tells the story of a young artist who recruits his models from odd places. And the models are very odd indeed. The painter's name, incidentally, is Pickman. The title is "Pickman's Model." And where else would you see a story like this except in the *Night Gallery*?
—Rod Serling, *Night Gallery*, December 1, 1971[1]

In the early 1970s, everyone knew Rod Serling, the charismatic and affable host of the science fiction show *The Twilight Zone*. Nearing age fifty, Serling had presided over much of the golden age of television, from his work on the pioneering *Playhouse 90* to his current gig, hosting an anthology show of horror stories, *The Night Gallery*. On his programs, Serling often presented a strange and remarkable world where the inexplicable was commonplace, and the impossible happened each week. More often than not, the cause of these strange occurrences came from the depths of outer space.

"Rod Serling freely admitted that he was unabashedly a

great devotee of tales of horror, fantasy, and the supernatural," his wife, Carol, remembered.[2] Serling had grown up at the height of the pulp fiction era, reading classic and modern horror stories in sensational magazines like *Weird Tales* and *Astounding Stories*. His favorite authors were Edgar Allan Poe, whose terrifying nineteenth-century tales spoke of macabre minds, and H. P. Lovecraft, whose Depression-era stories of cosmic horror hinted that buried in man's past was archaeological evidence that humanity had once been visited by extraterrestrials. By the time Serling entered television, Lovecraft had become something of a cult figure, inspiring a devoted following of fans.

Lovecraft's influence clearly showed in Serling's work. In *The Night Gallery* anthology series, several of the episodes were based on Lovecraft's stories, including "Pickman's Model," where the monster in a painting is not just a figment of the artist's imagination. In *The Twilight Zone*, occasional hints of cosmic horror surfaced amid the out-and-out science fiction. Most impressively, in Serling's best-loved film, *Planet of the Apes*, which he wrote, archaeological anomalies revealed a dark secret about an alien world. No one can forget the startling vision of the ruined Statue of Liberty in the film's famous closing scene, or even the hints of Earth life in the apes' archaeological investigations. Serling had in effect reversed the Lovecraft premise: instead of humans finding evidence of aliens, it was the strange beings (the apes) finding evidence of us.

So the concept of archaeology revealing startling secrets was nothing new to Serling when in 1972 his producer, Alan Landsburg, called him on the phone to tell him of an amazing discovery he made.

"Rod," Landsburg told him, "I think it's real. I think I can prove that Earth was visited by intelligent life from outer space."[3]

Serling was not terribly amused at first, but Landsburg presented seemingly miraculous evidence that man had in fact been visited. He claimed to have seen the runways where their crafts had landed and cryptic signals built by the visitors. Further, he had seen the actual remains of structures they had made while they were here. What made Landsburg's revelations particularly shocking was the remarkable claim that the aliens had not come today or yesterday but had come thousands of years ago.

Called either the "ancient-astronaut hypothesis" or Paleo-SETI after the Search for Extraterrestrial Intelligence conducted by NASA, the theory held that in the remote past aliens had come to Earth and ancient humans mistook them for gods. These visitors wowed the natives with their technological prowess, and they left traces of their coming in ancient myths and monuments.

Sitting across the table from Serling, Landsburg pulled out series of photographs of things that should not be. He showed him snapshots of millennia-old batteries and ancient drawings of spaceships, radios, and airports—all dating back to the darkest and most remote epoch of humanity's ancient past. These were things that should not be, but they were here; they existed. Truly, if these things were real, then humanity's earliest gods were extraterrestrials whose amazing technology had given them the aura of the supernatural. This would be the story of the century, and Rod Serling was there.

"Had it been anyone else," Serling later wrote, "showing the objects and pictures to me, I might have said 'Mountebank!'"[4] But Serling trusted that the talented television producer was on to something: "He had more than the amateur's command of the fields of archaeology, biology and related scientific investigation. By the time we were finished I had seen enough evidence to convince me that we had entered a new and fascinating field of research."[5]

Yet it seems impossible that Serling could not be at least a little troubled by the odd similarity between this amazing new research and those Lovecraft stories he had read in his youth. Might there be some connection between the horror author's tales of alien gods and this seemingly miraculous proof? Serling must have held his doubts and decided that the connection just wasn't there or never put the pieces together.

Much of Alan Landsburg's interest in the subject had come from a fiery and outrageous best-seller called *Chariots of the Gods?* written originally in German in 1968 by a Swiss hotelier named Erich von Däniken. In that book, von Däniken had shockingly claimed that alien beings from another world had descended to Earth in the remote past, genetically engineered humanity, built the greatest monuments of the past, and then left with a promise to return. Von Däniken blasted conventional archaeology for ignoring what was clearly evidence of humanity's alien heritage, and his words struck a cord with Landsburg and with many people living through the heady days of cultural upheaval and the wholesale rejection of convention in the late 1960s.

In 1972, Landsburg made his call to Serling to share von Däniken's shocking claims. After Serling had become convinced that the theory held water, he and Landsburg plotted their next move. This information was too sensational, too amazing to be kept to themselves. If archaeology were ignoring, or worse attacking, these theories, then they would bring them directly to the people. The two men worked together to bring *Chariots* to the small screen in the form of a television documentary. Titled *In Search of Ancient Astronauts*, the 1973 NBC special outlined the major points in von Däniken's thesis, taking the viewer around the world to survey the incredible evidence for alien intervention: the impossibly large pyramids around the world, the haunting statues of Easter Island, the alien runways at Nazca in South America. Rod Serling's credibility and celebrity helped to give weight to this seemingly impossible idea. The documentary was a huge success and catapulted the ancient-astronaut hypothesis from the intellectual fringe right into Middle America.

"It brought together on film," Landsburg wrote, "some of the visible signs that Earth might have been visited long ago by astronauts from some other world—visitors whom the awed Earthmen would probably have taken for gods."[6]

With Serling's distinctive voice intoning questions about how mere mortals could construct the colossal bulk of Egypt's Great Pyramid or how the Nasca people could have laid out an airport in the deserts of Chile,[7] millions of Americans were exposed for the first time to the idea that the wonders of the past were monuments to extraterrestrials. And many of those viewers became convinced that something was amiss with the textbook view of the ancient past.

In the year after *In Search of Ancient Astronauts* aired, von Däniken's little book became an overnight sensation in the United States. While it had run as a six-part serial in the *National Enquirer* three years earlier, it now sped through thirty-seven printings. By the beginning of 1974, four million copies were in print, and the sequels *Gods from Outer Space* and *Gold of the Gods* were selling rapidly. Other authors quickly jumped on the bandwagon, including Alan Landsburg, who, along with his wife, released *In Search of Ancient Mysteries* and its follow-up, *The Outer Space Connection*, providing a still larger compendium of ancient mysteries. Ancient astronauts became a literary genre, and its authors now claimed that the aliens had initiated a cult of immortality and that aliens may even have had a hand in manipulating human evolution or genetically engineering humanity.

While the idea that aliens were our ancestors quickly came under attack from scientists as impossible and false, it continued to garner impressive numbers of followers. Von Däniken would go on to write more than twenty-five books expounding his claims, and his imitators and followers each wrote several more. Mainstream science began to take note, and archaeologists had to insert comments refuting alien intervention in their books, articles, and documentaries, if only to show that they thought nothing of the idea.

Rod Serling remained convinced until his death that something was going on in humanity's past that could not be explained. Yet he confessed in his preface to *The Outer Space Connection*, "I was engrossed in a world more clearly the province of the fiction writer than the journalist."[8] Perhaps when he wrote that he had in mind the strange tales of the Providence, Rhode Island, author H. P. Lovecraft, who forty years earlier had written all of it as fiction. If so, he never said. Serling died in 1975 still believing that aliens had come to Earth in the distant past. If only he had known just how uncanny his words were. . . .

I came to the theory of ancient astronauts a bit late. Not born until after the initial craze had faded away, I never experienced the first wave of alien ancestor frenzy. My first contact with the world of the strange came from television. In countless hours spent watching the Discovery Channel and A&E, I encountered this strange idea of prehistoric visitation buried in the sensational documentaries that I could not have then known were less than faithful to the facts. In reruns of Leonard Nimoy's classic series *In Search Of*. . . (for which Serling's documentary was the pilot) and in episodes of his then-current show *Ancient Mysteries*, so-called experts proclaimed that aliens had come to Earth, had created its ancient wonders, and were still coming today.

When I was young and in full intellectual rebellion against my schooling, I found this idea seductive and believed wholeheartedly in the theory of ancient visitors, convinced that the powers that be were concealing a fabulous past from me. I wanted to believe and I needed to believe. Always a bright child, I had advanced beyond my studies quite quickly, and this theory seemed to provide the intellectual stimulation that my endless thirst for knowledge needed. Yet even as I adopted wholesale these amazing ideas, I did not possess the intellectual tools needed to critically evaluate them. Still seduced by the idea that something was right because an authority figure told me so, how could I doubt what the glowing box told me each Saturday afternoon, or what the cumulative weight of the ancient histories seemed to say?

Yet in the back of my mind, there still existed the seeds of doubt: If the television shows kept insisting that the "orthodox" archaeologists were wrong, how could I be sure that the television was right? In other words, if the proponents of the Paleo-SETI hypothesis claimed that authority figures were wrong, and they were right, how could I then accept their authority? I had quiet doubts that something was wrong.

Nevertheless, I bravely soldiered on.

Being a voracious reader and as indiscriminate in my choice of books as I was in documentaries, I had absorbed all the classics of the ancient alien genre. My father had been taken by von Däniken's musings during the theory's early heyday, and he had a worn and tattered copy of *Gold of the Gods*, which I read and loved. Unable to satisfy my lust for ancient mysteries with just one book, *Gold* inspired me to seek out more "forbidden" knowledge. I devoured all the books of the preceding decades, including von Däniken's collected works and several strange tomes on pyramidology.

I was intrigued by the subject. The pyramids were an endlessly fascinating topic, and history had always been something I loved. It seemed for all the world that von Däniken was right, that he must be right, for his theories seemed to make so much sense on an emotional level. Besides, how could the book companies and television documentary people ever let these theories get through if they were not true? After all, was there not corroborating evidence in the many tales of UFO sightings and abductions, strange crafts, and intimate probing?

I was particularly susceptible to this line of reasoning. One hot summer day in my early teens, my brother came running alongside the house. He called for the whole family to come outside, shouting, "Look up there!" When I looked up, I saw a round, shiny disc hovering in the sky. It stayed up there for a few minutes before vanishing. Despite my best efforts to locate an explanation, it remains unexplained. If I had seen a UFO, then clearly something had to be going on.

In the year that followed, I read everything I could on extra-terrestrials, UFOs, alien abductions, and such. I read about the terrifying abduction of Betty and Barney Hill, a couple who claimed under hypnosis to have been taken by space aliens and to have had bizarre procedures performed on them. Theirs was the first widely reported case of forcible alien abduction and set the template for all that followed. I studied the so-called Roswell Incident, where a flying saucer was supposed to have crashed in 1947 in the New Mexico desert, and I read the original FBI cables about the flying discs recovered there and spirited to Ohio and then the forbidden Area 51, where they became the basis for the Stealth fighter jets.

But I quickly realized that this was nothing more than a modern myth. The original FBI cable had said the disc was small and at the end of a balloon (something so-called ufologists ignore when trumpeting the case). I thought, why would space aliens need a balloon? If they could cross galaxies, why not New Mexico? Then I found out that the celebrated abduction of Betty and Barney Hill almost certainly descended from the movie *Invaders from Mars* and an episode of *The Outer Limits* television series that aired only days before the "abduction." Key to the case: The Hill abduction featured the now-stereotypical bug-eyed aliens unknown in 1960s Hollywood. Yet that *Outer Limits* episode featured aliens fitting the exact description the Hills gave. In other words, the Hills' description of the aliens was ripped right from the television shows they had just finished watching.

After I found out how many UFO photographs were faked (and badly!), suddenly UFOs seemed a lot less interesting to me. As I learned more about physics and the complications of space travel, alien arrivals seemed less likely. Soon enough I came to the conclusion that aliens probably were not visiting Earth since it would take millennia to transverse the infinities between star systems.

So what about the evidence for ancient aliens?

In 1996, I found what seemed to be a logical answer on an episode of A&E's *Ancient Mysteries* where *Star Trek's* Leonard Nimoy introduced me to Graham Hancock, whose book *Fingerprints of the Gods* (1995) allowed all the anomalous evidence for ancient aliens to stand intact without the need for extraterrestrial visitation. Hancock proposed that a great lost civilization had existed before the end of the last Ice Age and that traces it left behind worldwide led to similarities in the great works of ancient cultures. The lost civilization's ambassadors were remembered as gods, and the ancient anomalies were their fingerprints. All the stories about higher beings that von Däniken had interpreted as evidence of aliens now became tales of the representatives of an advanced lost civilization. What could make more intuitive sense?

In the last months before the Internet revolution transformed bookselling, the local bookstore was the only place to seek out titles of interest. Late in 1996 I went to Barnes & Noble looking for a copy of *Fingerprints*, but there was none to be had. The clerk told me that the book was so immensely popular that the store could not keep it in stock. I had the store order me one, and six weeks later I plunged into a rip-roaring adventure in the style of Indiana Jones. Hancock's book was magical and, for me, the only training in mythology and ancient history I had received, thanks to a failing public school system more intent on indoctrinating political correctness than teaching much of anything. And with a monstrous set of endnotes and book-length bibliography, how could I doubt the veracity of the formidable volume?

In short order I read Hancock's sequel, *Message of the Sphinx* (1996), and his original exploration of an ancient mystery, *The Sign and the Seal* (1992), which probed the origins of the story of the Ark of the Covenant and where the relic, if it exists, might rest today. To this day, I find *The Sign and the Seal* a fascinating and imposing work of journalism, if not history.

Intrigued by the material presented uncritically before me, I devoured every book on the subject that I could find. I read classics in the genre like Gerald Hawkins's *Beyond Stonehenge* (1973) and more recent works like Robert Bauval's *Orion Mystery* (1994), which claimed that the pyramids at Giza were laid out to represent on the ground the three distinctive belt stars of the constellation Orion. Then I explored Robert Temple's unique vision of the world by reading *The Sirius Mystery* (1998 revised edition). The almost scholarly ethnographic analysis of the descent of Africa's Dogon tribe from ancient Egyptian stock made perfect sense to an uncritical layman, even if Temple's claim that they ultimately originated as amphibious aliens from Sirius did not. I can put it down only as the folly of youth that I had not thrown away the book just on the basis that amphibians from Sirius were treated as a serious revelation. *The Sirius Mystery* had argued that ancient Egyptian science was highly advanced and a legacy from a higher culture not of this world. Their special knowledge that Sirius was two stars instead of one (a binary system) had passed to the Dogon tribe through a long, documented line of descent. French anthropologists Marcel Griaule and Germaine Dieterlen had discovered this latent tradition intact during their research in 1935. The Dogon should not have known this cosmic fact because Western science had discovered it only in the preceding decades.

Yet no matter how successful the theories about prehistoric aliens or a lost civilization became, something just didn't feel right to me about the ideas, even as I embraced them as best-case scenarios in my youthful wish fulfillment. My unease had nothing to do with the evidence, which I was then not qualified to evaluate, knowing almost nothing about archaeology other than what the ancient-astronaut books had told me. No, my doubts were something different, even if surveys found that anywhere from a third to half of my college-age peers believed.[9]

Underlying the grand edifice of the ancient-astronaut theory was a small seed of doubt that would pop up time and again: Wasn't there something vaguely *fictional* about the story? Didn't it sound just a little bit like something out of science fiction? Or, more to the point, hadn't I heard this all somewhere before?

My other favorite genre for reading material was horror. While I was never a big fan of Stephen King, nor had I the patience to read his long novels, I had developed, however, a taste for short horror fiction, inspired, in part, by other musty paperbacks from the early 1970s: the Fontana books of horror, Alfred Hitchcock's collections of gruesome tales, and above all cheap reprints of Edgar Allan Poe. I progressed to other anthologies, and there I discovered the works of H. P. Lovecraft, whom Stephen King called "the 20th century's dark and baroque prince."[10]

In Lovecraft's sixty-odd tales of "cosmic horror," I encountered an incredible landscape of terror, the likes of which I had never imagined. Lovecraft wrote in intricate detail about cosmic vistas and soul-shattering philosophies that were beyond comprehension. Truly he deserved his place as the greatest author of horror in the twentieth century, the worthy and acknowledged successor of Edgar Allan Poe. Lovecraft dreamed up monsters so amazing that they blew away the tiny terrors of Poe or the bloody inanities of Clive Barker. No, here was something special, something amazing, something . . . familiar.

In reading the 1926 story "Call of Cthulhu," I had a sense of déjà vu. In the story, a young man puts together the pieces of a sinister puzzle linking together a diabolical cult, ancient artifacts, and a blasphemous revelation. Only one of the cultists, a man named Castro, would speak of their beliefs:

> Old Castro remembered bits of hideous legend that paled the speculations of theosophists and made man and the world seem recent and transient indeed. There had been aeons when other Things ruled on the earth, and They had had great cities. Remains of Them, he said the deathless Chinamen had told him, were still to be found as Cyclopean stones on islands in the Pacific. They all died vast epochs of time before men came, but there were arts which could revive Them when the stars had come round again to the right positions in the cycle of eternity. They had, indeed, come themselves from the stars, and brought Their images with Them.[11]

Here was von Däniken's case outlined forty years earlier! How could this be? Initially I ascribed it to coincidence, for surely the ancient-astronaut theory must be true, and therefore this story could not be related. Yet as the years went by, I could not live with the strange and unsettling thoughts that questioned this belief. Eventually I would come to realize that H. P. Lovecraft was the seminal figure in the world of alternative archaeology, and it was from his imagination that nearly all of the strange theories and alternative explanations were channeled. Lovecraft towered above all the other figures of fact and fiction as the First Cause of the ancient-astronaut hypothesis, and it was from him that all subsequent tales of extraterrestrial gods and lost civilizations came. But this ultimate revelation, this understanding of Lovecraft's place, was a long time in coming. Piece by piece, the puzzle started to fall into place.

By the time I entered college, I had decided to seek a degree in anthropology because these books on ancient mysteries and the stories of Lovecraft had so inspired me. Along the way I began to develop a broad understanding of the historical process and the evolution of society over the course of centuries. At last I came to the conclusion that Western civilization was in terminal decay. Inspired by Jacques Barzun's peerless *From Dawn to Decadence*, I began to see that the civilization born with Charlemagne had run its course, that the revolutions of the eighteenth century had marked the beginning of the end, and that the decline and rot had set in shortly after. Still awesome in its sweeping grandeur, the old world order continued on, pained by revolution, challenge, and change until the epic disasters of the two world wars destroyed forever the old ways. I saw now that the cold war and what followed was the twilight world akin to the strange days between Rome's fourth-century collapse and the early medieval genesis of a new civilization. I saw then that a great change had begun, but the new order had not yet arrived, so in this twilight of the West with the old cultural authorities overthrown and broken, it was no wonder that so many had come to reject science, which was nothing if not the defining characteristic of the West.

I began to understand what had gone wrong with the West, and soon I had even more evidence confirming my hypothesis.

I read a study conducted by anthropologist Walter van Beek, who tried to confirm the Dogon Sirius lore (double star, amphibious aliens, etc.) reported by Griaule decades earlier. Van Beek talked to the Dogon about Sirius, but his conclusions were disturbing to those who had believed what Robert Temple had written: "All agree . . . that they learned about the star from Griaule."[12] Here it was, the smoking gun: the Dogon had no special knowledge; in fact, they were only repeating what Griaule himself had told them. It was all a lie, and a bad one at that. Sure enough, no other anthropologist could duplicate Griaule's work. There was no Sirius mystery after all. I had already known that the alien-ancestor hypothesis was plainly ridiculous, but if the whole of *The Sirius Mystery* was built on a bed of lies, then what of those books that followed it? I knew, for example, that the engineer Robert Bauval, who was making a name for himself with his theories about Egypt and the stars, was inspired to write *The Orion Mystery* because of the Temple book. As Bauval himself said:

> In 1979, at London-Heathrow airport I bought a book called *The Sirius Mystery* by Robert Temple [which] explored aspects of Ancient Egyptian astronomy, and as I was both an amateur Egyptologist and a keen student of Ancient Egyptian astronomy, it seemed like a good book to take to the Sudan. . . . Temple had uncovered a mystery worthy of further investigation. If the Dogon had inherited their knowledge of Sirius B from the Ancient Egyptians, what other knowledge might these ancients have had concerning the stars? . . . It seemed obvious to me that the place to look for evidence of this lost knowledge was not among the tribes of Mali but in Egypt itself.[13]

Temple had a further influence on the developing theory that the Egyptians modeled the Giza pyramids on Orion because Bauval followed Temple in claiming that the pyramids represented the stars important to the ancient Egyptians: "After all, the pyramids were built at the time Robert Temple believed the star religion to have been of the greatest importance. Perhaps then the two were linked."[14] Temple had postulated that cities in ancient Egypt and Greece were planned to resemble the constellation Argo. Bauval applied the star-mirroring idea to the pyramids and "discovered" that the three Giza pyramids represented the belt stars of the constellation Orion.

Shocked and appalled by this revelation, I logged on to Graham Hancock's Web site, where Robert Bauval often answered questions. I asked him about his connection to Temple and whether he believed what the author had written. Bauval told me in an online discussion, "[While] I also know

Robert Temple personally, it also does not mean that I support his ideas."[15] Yet I had the explicit evidence in his own words that he *did* in fact support Temple's thesis, and not only that, he used it to support his revolutionary Orion Correlation Theory. Since I knew that Temple was demonstrably wrong, I had no choice but to conclude that while the pyramids might possibly represent Orion, the basis for Bauval's theory relied so heavily on Temple's work that it must be discarded. Along with that, the work of Hancock and his predecessors fell, too, since all the books on ancient mysteries referred to one another as their sources and their research.

With that, I had to sadly conclude that I had been deceived. Even though I loved these books, I knew they were not true. Sure, there were anomalies worthy of investigation and even a possibility that somewhere in the distant past there may have been some sort of link between cultures or even a vanished civilization, but the evidence that those authors presented was not the answer. I had hoped that it was true; I had wanted it to be true. But I could not prove it, and neither could they.

But what I could prove was where these ideas had come from and how they ended up in my head. Surely it was no coincidence that H. P. Lovecraft had written stories of alien gods decades before other authors made his science fiction into their science fact. Surely Rod Serling was on to something when he mused that the ancient-astronaut theory (and by extension, the lost-civilization theory) read more like the work of a fiction writer than a scientist. It didn't take much to find the hidden connection or to prove my idea that Lovecraft stood behind those modern myths was absolutely and shockingly true.

This book, then, is the story of the alternative archaeology movement and the ancient-astronaut theory. But it is more than just that—it is also the chronicle of a unique moment in the cultural decline of the West. It is nothing less than an account of how the five-hundred-year advance of science and progress faltered and failed, and with this epic failure came the demise of the Western rationalist idea itself. This journey takes us from Lovecraft's sources in the science fiction and pseudoscience of the late nineteenth century through his own unparalleled fictional work to the various branches of pseudohistory that descended from him unto this very day. Along the way, we'll see the development of strange theories, ranging from ancient astronauts, to lost civilizations, to UFO cults. Somehow, some way, Lovecraft's scribbling bequeathed us an eerie legacy of pseudoscience, horror, and the bizarre. And in the end, we'll understand how Lovecraft's strange stories had dangerous and unintended consequences for science and for the world today.

PART ONE
PRECURSORS OF THE MYTH

2

SCIENCE AND PSEUDOSCIENCE IN LOVECRAFT'S TIME

Our story properly begins during the autumn of 1926. H. P. Lovecraft had just left New York City after a rocky two-year stay that had left him permanently embittered. He had arrived in 1924 to marry Sonia Greene, and the two lived together in her apartment in Brooklyn. While living in the city, Lovecraft failed to find work and sank into depression. He hated the city, he hated its people, and he hated that it was unkind to him. He began to write nasty stories about the unkempt foreigners who he believed were polluting America, and he began to long to go home. By 1926, Lovecraft had had enough of New York, cursed the city, and packed up for good. He moved back to his beloved hometown of Providence, Rhode Island, and took up residence with his aunt in a Victorian duplex.[1]

Now in the glorious days of a New England autumn, he sat hunched over his desk in Providence writing out a strange story in longhand from an outline he had composed during his last days in New York. Despite the ink blotches and the inconvenience of using a fountain pen, Lovecraft almost always wrote longhand because he hated to type. Of course he owned a typewriter, a used Remington he had acquired in the July of 1906, but he had never bothered to learn the art of typing largely because he considered mechanical writing to be beneath him.[2] That same old typewriter would serve him for life on those rare occasions when a typewritten manuscript could not be avoided.

But in September 1926, the typewriter sat untouched while Lovecraft wrote his stories. He wrote very fast and used a special pen that would flow freely to keep up with his quick pace. Often difficult to decipher, his spidery longhand worsened the older he got and the faster he wrote. One woman reading a letter from him wondered seriously whether it were written in Arabic.[3] Writing late at night to avoid distractions, Lovecraft sped his pen across the page, filling the blank space with a marvelous tale. To be titled "The Call of Cthulhu," the story told of an octopus-headed alien monster called Cthulhu that had come to Earth in the deepest recesses of time. Cthulhu was now trapped beneath the Pacific Ocean, imprisoned in a lost sunken continent amid the stone temples of its former world, but there were strange cults that worshiped him as a god. Lovecraft finished composing his tale in October, and it would earn him $165 when he finally sold it to *Weird Tales* in 1928.[4]

To add a layer of reality to his story, Lovecraft drew on pieces of existing myth and legend as well as the sensational claims of amateur historians and philosophers. Here he threw in a bit of the myth of Atlantis, there a dollop of Theosophical philosophy. He never believed any of it himself, committed as he was to science, reason, and materialism. However, he recognized that dropping in bits of dark legends made for a sensational story. To lend credence to his synthetic myths, Lovecraft tied them to the intellectual developments of the decades leading up to Cthulhu's creation.

To understand the intellectual backdrop against which H. P. Lovecraft first developed the fictional conceit that aliens were mistaken for gods, it is necessary to understand something of the intellectual climate into which the ancient-astronaut idea was born. For more than a century before the theory's creation, the West had been torn between two opposed ideological poles, between the Enlightenment's worship of reason and the Romantic worship of the irrational. While Lovecraft himself stood in awe of the eighteenth century, the Enlightenment, and pure reason, his anachronistic love of the past was itself a manifestation of the Romantic spirit. Lovecraft would often fantasize about living in the colonial world, and he adopted the mannerisms of an eighteenth-century Georgian gentleman, including such irritating verbal tricks as old-fashioned spellings, the long *f* for the letter *s*, and the use of archaic words like "shewed" and "ye."

The eighteenth-century thinkers harked back to the classical past, to Greece and to Rome, as the embodiments of the best in the Western tradition, as the great age of reason. Called the Enlightenment because it swept away much of the superstitious and religious folly of the medieval and Renaissance periods, the period from 1750 to around 1800 (or later in some areas) appealed to Greek philosophy and Roman pragmatism as its guiding lights. It was true in 1776 when historian Edward Gibbon observed in his classic *Decline and Fall of the Roman Empire* that mankind had never seen a more prosperous and happy day than under the Antonine emperors of second-century Rome, an age of prosperity not surpassed until the mid-nineteenth century. As embodied in their art and their architecture, like the Greco-Roman buildings of Washington, DC, the people of the Enlightenment sought to revive Greco-Roman greatness in their own day. Science and reason, they believed, would lead the way. If aristocracy and hereditary privilege could be swept away, then a world of order and reason could take their place. Nevertheless, that world of perfect order envisioned by the reasonable thinkers of the Enlightenment burned away in the fiery excesses of the French Revolution, when even the famous cathedral of Notre Dame de Paris was turned into a bloody Temple of Reason.

The aftermath of that revolt led to the Romantics and the worship of what they believed was a simpler, more natural time: the Middle Ages. Holding that the anarchy, chaos, and chivalry of the medieval period was the perfect culmination of mankind in his (always his; "her" would come later) most chivalrous and dignified state, the Romantic thinkers praised the codes and conduct of the Middle Ages and saw in its art and Gothic architecture the Western tradition in its most noble incarnation. This was a world of faith, of piety, and of belief. The imagination held sway over contemptible reason, and the unseen forces at work in the world were given their proper due. The Romantics tried to revive medieval culture in the West, placing renewed emphasis on medieval affectations like coats of arms, heraldry, and pointed Gothic arches. In their art and architecture they appealed to a renewed medieval worldview, and their colossal Victorian structures with their pointed arches, turrets, and castlelike towers recalled this vanished world.

These two opposing views spawned two different systems of belief. As nineteenth-century science marched forward under the Enlightenment's banner of materialism and evolution, pseudoscience emerged to champion spiritualism and special creation, especially the intervention of forces from the great Outside. There was a clear divide between science and superstition, between reason and religion. It was a cultural war, and the sides were beginning to form.[5] It was this conflict of ideas that compelled Lovecraft to seek out a way to harmonize them through fiction and to rectify the ironic contradiction of his Romantic love of the Enlightenment.

He had read all of the great works of the period, and he saw that the late nineteenth and early twentieth centuries were a hotbed of pseudoscientific beliefs of all kinds, and they competed, often successfully, against legitimate sciences for the public trust. Spurred on by the war over the controversial and soul-shattering Darwinian theory of evolution, forces for and against science fought many battles. Both sides hardened into armed camps, leaving the open inquiry of true science a casualty in the war for and against materialism, the belief that all that exists is what can be seen and measured.[6]

Far too often, the scientists had calcified their belief in materialism into scientism, the doctrine that a perfect and unchanging science holds all the answers and explains everything. They were quick to attack new and radical ideas, often without hearing evidence or proof. Those on the other side adopted all manner of irrational convictions, from belief in ghosts and spirits, to belief in visitations from angels and heavenly beings, to belief in lost civilizations. These people required no proof, and in their excess they credulously believed anything and everything. However, these people adopted the language of science to give a veneer of authority to their claims, becoming in effect pseudoscientists, using the trappings but not the methods of true science. In the realm of archaeology, these pseudoscientists were especially active right from the start, seeing in the past any number of controversial and sometimes bizarre ideas.

Compared with biology or physics, archaeology is not an old science mostly because society's attitude toward the past has varied greatly over time. For most of human history, the ruins of the past were not held in great reverence, and throughout history old buildings and artifacts were continuously destroyed and rebuilt into new things. Thus the Roman Coliseum was torn apart to provide the blocks for Renaissance Roman villas, and the ruins of the great Temple of Artemis at Ephesus were reused in a Christian monastery. Time also has not been kind to the works of the past that had not been kept up. For every still-complete ancient building like the Pantheon in Rome, several dozen ruins half stood, and several thousand more were completely gone.

As a result, the record of the past is often fragmented and

distorted by incomplete evidence. By the eighteenth century, most of the remnants of past societies had fallen into decay, and none could say who or what had built some of the fabulous ruins that explorers were discovering all around the world. The Spanish recorded that no one alive had seen the pre-Inca city of Tiwanaku except as a ruin, and the Egyptian pyramids had a thousand legends attached to their creation. Among the most incredible of the ancient structures in the continental United States were the mounds, a mysterious series of earthen constructions of then-uncertain age and origin. The largest of the mounds, Monk's Mound at Cahokia (near modern-day St. Louis), stood more than one hundred feet tall and covered sixteen acres. It sat in the midst of one hundred smaller mounds in a great city, and this was just one of countless groupings of great structures all across the East and Midwest. To early explorers, this and other mounds were a baffling work, and to the early Americans, they were evidence of a lost race of white mound builders. After all, how could the Indians, whom America was busy exterminating, have been responsible for these constructions? Were they not nearly animals, too uncivilized to have done great things?

Unconvinced by the legend of a lost race constructing the mounds, in 1782 Thomas Jefferson conducted the first true archaeological excavation, uncovering an Indian burial mound by Virginia's Rivanna River and scientifically examining its contents. His notes were so precisely done that they are considered a valid field report even by today's standards. Recorded in his *Notes on the State of Virginia*, Jefferson's excavation was the first to investigate a claim of pseudoscience, namely, the claim that a lost race had constructed the fabulous mounds dotting the North American landscape.

Ever since explorers came into contact with native peoples in what would become America, they held that the natives were semi-savages, or worse, wholly savage. They could not in good conscience hold the barbaric people they found as the coequals of the advanced European civilizations that they represented. Despite Jefferson's excavation, leading white American intellectuals during the Romantic period increasingly believed that the mounds littering the country were the work of any number of fabulous groups, from the pre-Jeffersonian "lost race" to Victorian speculations about Vikings, Druids, and wandering Irish monks. Anyone, in fact, except the Indians. How much of this was Romantic and how much was real politik justifying the wholesale removal or extermination of native peoples is left for history to judge. Nevertheless, the lost-race hypothesis was for decades considered the truth.

As archaeologist and historian Brian Fagan noted: "Such wild theories appealed to the romantically inclined, to people who believed that American Indians were incapable of building anything as elaborate as a burial mound."[7] It was, in fact, a battle being waged between the two great trends in Western intellectual thought: the Enlightenment versus the Romantic period. Throughout the nineteenth and early twentieth centuries, the battle to reconcile the demands of reason with the appeal of the irrational and Romantic led otherwise level-headed people to embrace every realm of fantastic belief.

It was only in 1894 that the myth of the mound builders finally died. In the 1880s the director of the Smithsonian's Bureau of American Ethnology, John Wesley Powell, decided to end the controversy once and for all. He appointed Cyrus Thomas to head a division that would use the five thousand dollars Congress had appropriated for annual mound excavation to debunk the myth of the lost race. Thomas initially believed in the lost-race theory, but after an extensive campaign of scientific excavations, the evidence told him a different story. The skeletons he uncovered were clearly Indian, and he did not find any artifacts that could *not* be associated with Native Americans, either through their own industry or through trade with colonists. He published his conclusions in 1894: there could be no doubt, he said; the mounds were the work of ancient Indians, not a lost race.

"With the publication of Thomas' great work," Fagan explained, "every serious scholar of North American archaeology accepted that the Moundbuilders were native Americans. All modern research into these peoples is based on this fact."[8] From then on, archaeology proceeded as a science, investigating claims and drawing conclusions based on evidence. While not every excavation met this high standard, the trend had definitely changed, moving more toward science and further from Romantic speculation.

The Mound Builders case had taught a tough lesson, that indigenous peoples were capable of great deeds and the cultures that archaeology studied were likely independent and unique developments. While these lessons took time to enter into mainstream thought, and to some degree were still being opposed a century later, eventually early twentieth-century archaeology came to the conclusion that the ancient world was not all that mysterious and could be explained with science and reason. Of course, these beliefs were susceptible to the same urge to scientism that had plagued the biological sciences. Free inquiry would sometimes yield to dogmatism, especially the dogmatic idea that ancient cultures were fully independent and never communicated with one another. Some of this dogma stemmed from early evidence, and some of it from the professional pride of early archaeologists who did not want their finds compromised by the thought that "their" newly discovered people or cultures were derivative of any other. More than any other idea, this belief in cultural isolation would give the most fodder to the pseudoscientists.

But there were others who were not to be convinced by archaeology's authoritative claims. While formal archaeology began to acquire the aspects of science to meet the growing needs of mound investigators, a group of pseudoscientists began to develop their own parallel and completely opposite views about ancient history. Their view would be inspired by intuition, revelation, speculation, and alternative ways of knowing. If science sought evidence to make a conclusion, this type of false science would seek evidence to fit a conclusion.

Perhaps the most famous work of this kind, the 1882 book *Atlantis: The Antediluvian World*, stands as the first and most influential book on a lost civilization ever written. In it, the author, former American congressman and Populist Party founder Ignatius Donnelly, describes the fabulous civilization of Atlantis, the lost continent, somewhere in the Atlantic Ocean.

Plato had written about Atlantis in two short dialogues more than two millennia earlier, stories designed to demonstrate the corruption of Athenian morals in his day by comparing them to a more glorious past that had been destroyed by the same moral laxity now invading Athens. He had written that Atlantis was an island kingdom lying out in the Atlantic ("beyond the pillars of Hercules"), a kingdom of fabulous wealth and grandeur. But the gods destroyed Atlantis in a single day and night, sinking it beneath the waves for its corruption and impiety.[9] Plato's Atlantis story had been dismissed as a mere allegory or legend since the Renaissance, and there was no evidence that a lost continent had ever existed in the Atlantic Ocean.

But then in 1871 the maverick archaeologist Heinrich Schliemann excavated the ruins of Troy. Reading Homer's account of the war that destroyed the city, *The Iliad*, had inspired him, and he followed the Homeric description to the letter, locating the site of what he believed would be the city destroyed by the Greeks during the Trojan War. His discoveries in the Turkish countryside proved beyond doubt that the legendary city of *The Iliad* had a real historical counterpart. In other words, he had proved that at least part of Greek mythology was true.

If Troy were real, then why not other pieces of mythology? Schliemann soon discovered the Greek commander Agamemnon's capital at Mycenae, and more discoveries were coming fast and furious right through the 1870s and 1880s.

To Ignatius Donnelly, it could not have seemed much of a stretch to believe that Atlantis, another legendary Greek city, could have a basis in fact. Donnelly single-handedly rescued the fabled continent from obscurity and developed a thesis based on the proposition that the story was true. Building on Plato's short description, Donnelly claimed to find evidence around the world supporting his thesis that the advanced culture of Atlantis was the mother of all civilizations, seeding the world with knowledge after the destruction of the island kingdom. Some of his parallels were bizarre (claiming, for example, that knowledge of painting was an Atlantean legacy), and some were at least plausible at the time (like the presence of mummification in Egypt and South America). He claimed that the Atlanteans themselves worshiped the sun, and this religion was shared in Egypt and in South America and around the world.

Significantly for Lovecraft and the astronaut-alien theory, in one passage Donnelly claimed that the kings of Atlantis were remembered in a distorted form as the classical gods of antiquity:

> The Greeks, too young to have shared in the religion of Atlantis, but preserving some memory of that great country and its history, proceeded to convert its kings into gods, and to depict Atlantis itself as the heaven of the human race. Thus we find a great solar or nature worship in the elder nations, while Greece has nothing but an incongruous jumble of gods and goddesses, who are born and eat and drink and make love and ravish and steal and die; and who are worshipped as immortal in presence of the very monuments that testify to their death.[10]

Though he seems to think little of Greek religion, Donnelly provided the seed for an important aspect of the ancient-astronaut hypothesis: that the gods were not mental creations but were once flesh-and-blood creatures, moreover, flesh-and-blood creatures who represented a lost civilization, one of enormous technological development.

Donnelly argued that there could be no dispute about the connection between the Greek gods and Atlantis, citing numerous cases famous in his day of primitive peoples encountering a technologically advanced group and declaring them gods, a kind of Victorian version of the famed anthropological "cargo cult" wherein native peoples in the twentieth century built mock airplanes of brush to persuade the gods to bring them more trade goods from the white trader "gods":

> The history of Atlantis is the key of the Greek mythology. There can be no question that these gods of Greece were human beings. The tendency to attach divine attributes to great earthly rulers is one deeply implanted in human nature. The savages who killed Captain Cook firmly believed that he was immortal, that he was yet alive, and would return to punish them. The highly civilized Romans made gods out of their dead emperors. Dr. Livingstone mentions that on one occasion, after talking to a Bushman for some time about the Deity, he found that the savage thought he was speaking of Sekomi, the principal chief of the district.[11]

Thus Donnelly was able to read into the legends of peoples around the world a record of Atlanteans colonizing the ancient peoples of earth. If the Greek gods were Atlantean kings, surely the gods of other peoples were but distorted memories of these fantastic visitors. Mexico, the Yucatán, and Peru, lands where the gods Quetzalcoatl, Kukulkán, and Viracocha came ashore to civilize barbaric humanity, became testimony to the great men of Atlantis leaving their home continent to bring civilization to the benighted natives.

Other evidence continued to compel Donnelly toward the conclusion that all civilization had a common source. He found tales of a global flood all over the world. Noah in his ark was not alone, and the same motif appeared with Utnapishtim in Mesopotamia, or Deucalian in Greece, and this reinforced for Donnelly the notion that civilization was a legacy of lost Atlantis, whose civilization Plato had said was destroyed when the gods sank the island kingdom beneath the waves.

Donnelly took full advantage of the lack of archaeological knowledge in 1882. Back then, there was no way to fix a building or an artifact at an absolute date in time. Guesswork was rampant, and many of the experts disagreed about how old monuments were. Absolute dating techniques like carbon dating were then unknown, and it was impossible to say for sure whether the pre-Inca cities were older or younger than their Egyptian counterparts. As a result, Donnelly was able to take similarities in building styles and extrapolate a common ancestor, assuming erroneously that the civilizations of the Old and New Worlds were roughly contemporaneous. He saw that both Mexico and Egypt had pyramids, and he deduced that the Atlanteans had taught pyramid building to both cultures. He even fit the Mound Builders into his scheme, comparing their mounds to those of Europe and Asia and arguing for a common influence. He could not have known that thousands of years separated them.

Atlantis: The Antediluvian World set the tone and tenor for all subsequent books on alternative histories. It was all here: the ancient mysteries, the cross-cultural comparisons, and the outrageous claims that similarities across cultures were the work of those from the Outside, since the natives were never believed to be intellectually capable of advanced culture. This subtle streak of subconscious racism, so prevalent in the Mound Builder myth and the legend of the antediluvian world, would continue to haunt alternative historians for a century to come.

At the same time, others were inventing their own lost continents and lost civilizations, populating the ancient earth with a startling array of mysterious cultures that were believed at one time or another to have given rise to the familiar civilizations of human history. Lovecraft would come to use all of them as props in his works. Among the most popular of these early island worlds was Lemuria.

A little bit before Donnelly, biologists had begun to embrace the idea of evolution and even the heretical notion that human beings were descended from the same ancestors as the apes. The search was on for the so-called Missing Link between man and ape, and biologists began to seek out the zero point where people evolved. But first, science would have to plausibly explain how monkeys, apes, and lemurs spread out across the world. Where they evolved was a paramount issue since it could lead science to the place where humanity itself had its genesis.

Confronted with the strange fact that the primitive lemurs, primates that looked more like raccoons than monkeys, existed on both sides of the Indian Ocean, in both Madagascar and India, some had begun to propose that a land bridge had linked the two lands. The English zoologist Philip L. Sclater named the lost land "Lemuria."[12] This was a reasonable speculation before science discovered plate tectonics and the fact that the continents could and did move very slowly across the earth's surface over millions of years. Just such a move eventually proved to be the cause of the lemurs' far-flung distribution, but this would not be known for almost a century to come. Nevertheless, the scientific speculation of a Lemurian land bridge quickly got adopted by a pseudoscientific movement with pretensions to religious status.

By the 1870s, the German scientist Ernst Haeckel introduced the idea that Lemuria might have been the home of humanity. Building on the ideas of evolution, Haeckel correctly noted that the primitive lemurs and the more complex apes seemed to be related. Further, large apes lived on both sides of the Indian Ocean, gorillas and chimps in Africa, and orang-utans in Indonesia. Therefore, he concluded, they must have originated at a central point, the Indian Ocean land of Lemuria. Since humans were related to apes, it stood to reason that humanity's cradle must also lie where the apes had their first home: Lemuria. Zoologist Karl Shuker, a researcher into the unexplained, noted the irony of Lemuria's history: "It is ironic that even though in reality Lemuria was never anything more substantial than an incorrect notion aired by some nineteenth-century zoologists, today its name is better known than those of many genuine ancient lands."[13]

This was due, almost completely, to Lemuria's hold on the mind of one particular occultist. The discovery of the fossils of human ancestors like *Homo erectus* on both the Indonesian island of Java and in East Africa lent credence to this strange notion in the minds of some scientists and more occultists. Several leading occultists then adopted this lost continent as part of their metaphysical schemes. The most prominent of them was a spiritualist who claimed an unimaginable Lemurian history.

Madame Helena Blavatsky was likely the most famous occultist of the last decades of the nineteenth century. A Russian by birth and claiming noble blood, Blavatsky immigrated to the United States, where she is said to have been the first Russian woman naturalized as a US citizen.[14] In the fall of 1875 she stayed in Ithaca, New York, writing her first book, *Isis Unveiled*, a book that claimed to be a history of magic, religion, and the esoteric.[15] By something of a cosmic coincidence, I, too, lived in Ithaca (while attending college), but the atmosphere of the uncanny in that open-minded community led me to deeply different conclusions.[16]

Always a foul-mouthed old woman prone to temper tantrums and invective, Blavatsky, along with lawyer Henry S. Olcott, founded the Theosophical Society in New York City in 1875 to impart the wisdom of the ages to her followers. Olcott remembered that the grand old lady seemed to be possessed of a different soul: "Putting aside [Blavatsky's] actions, habits of thought, masculine ways, her constant asseverations of the fact . . . putting these aside, I have pumped enough out of her to satisfy me that the theory long since communicated by me to you was correct—she is a man, a very old man, and a most learned and wonderful man."[17] Blavatsky was apparently believed to possess Spiritualist powers, making strange smells appear and materializing objects from thin air. These and other wonders were the stock-in-trade of the Spiritualist movement, and powers like Blavatsky's were successfully debunked by the Spiritualists' sworn enemy, the escape artist Harry Houdini. However, that was still to come. In the 1870s and 1880s Spiritualism was a force, and Blavatsky was riding a wave.

Isis Unveiled was published in 1877 to some degree of praise and garnered interest in the infant Theosophical Society. The society's stated goal was to meld the philosophies of the East and the West into a harmonious whole to prepare the world for universal brotherhood. Not content to confine her message solely to America, in 1879 Blavatsky picked up and moved to India. Three years later she moved the official headquarters of Theosophy to Adyar, India, where it remains to this day.[18] She then took up residence in England, where in 1888 she released in two large volumes her most infamous work, *The Secret Doctrine*.

Blavatsky's book claimed to channel the prehistoric *Book of Dzyan*, said to be older than mankind itself, though in fact it was an uncredited paraphrase of the Sanskrit Rig Veda, which, for interested parties, is believed to have been composed between 3000 and 2000 BCE.[19] In it, Blavatsky told the world that eighteen million years ago boneless, rubberlike vegetable creatures lived on Earth. They evolved into an intelligent race four million years ago, and this race was described as "gentle." Then three million years ago a race of androgynous giants developed and created monsters when they mated with animals, spawning, of course, Greek myths about minotaurs, centaurs, and other hybrids. But by this frantic mating the pure essence of intelligence became trapped into a fleshy cycle of reproduction.

Claiming to have received channeled celestial wisdom from the spirit world, Blavatsky contended that the ethereal spirits had revealed that Lemuria was the homeland of humanity, the place of the first creation. Further, there were to be seven Root Races ruling the Earth in succession, of which humanity today was only the fifth. The fourth of these races were the Atlanteans, who were destroyed by black magic. Lemuria would rise and fall to spawn new races until the Seventh Root Race, perfect in every way, would take its rightful place as master of the world. Lemuria, she said, was destroyed by a volcano, a popular way to get rid of unwanted continents in those days.[20]

No matter how silly it sounded, something about Blavatsky's work struck a chord in the late Victorian world. One of her followers, William Stead, explained the hold she had on his imagination:

> She made it possible for some of the most cultivated and skeptical men and women of this generation to believe—believe ardently, to an extent that made them proof against ridicule and disdainful of persecution—that not only does the invisible world that encompasses us contain Intelligences vastly superior to our own in knowledge of the Truth, but that it is possible for man to enter into communion with these hidden and silent ones, and to be taught of them the Divine mysteries of Time and of Eternity.[21]

Though I cannot quite understand the appeal of Blavatsky's theories, clearly her work continued to have an impact throughout the twentieth century. Even after skeptics debunked her *Book of Dzyan* as a fraud, her followers continued to assert its reality. One modern author wrote as late as 1970 that *The Book of Dzyan* was filled "with its sacred symbolic signs. No one in the world knows its real age. . . . For thousands of years this esoteric doctrine was guarded as top secret in Tibetan crypts."[22] Even if the lost continent of Lemuria was disproved, the *Secret Doctrine* lived on. H. P. Lovecraft held pseudoscience in disdain, but he was happy to use Theosophy as a prop if it would help make his fiction deeper and more meaningful. That the society embraced the concept of a lost sunken continent could only bolster interest in Lovecraft's own sunken world.

Atlantis and Lemuria went on to become popular subjects for a whole series of lost-continent books, notably W. Scott-Eliot's 1896 *The Story of Atlantis and Lost Lemuria*. Of course, two lost continents vying for the title Cradle of Humanity would not be the only lost continents in the ocean. Sure enough, not long after the battle royal between Atlantis and Lemuria for popular attention, a third lost continent reared its waterlogged head: Mu.

In the late 1800s, working from existing Theosophical ideas about Mu, Col. James Churchward began to compose a series of books advancing his theory of a lost continent, this time in the Pacific Ocean. Called "Mu, the Motherland of Man," the Pacific island continent was the home of ten races, ruled (of course) by the Aryan (white) race. Churchward said that the continent was the origin of all civilization, spreading its culture to Atlantis and then out to Egypt, Mesoamerica, and the rest of the ancient world. Mu was destroyed, as all lost continents seem to be, by volcanic eruptions and other natural cataclysms. Churchward claimed that the last traces of Mu were the standing stones that dot the islands of the Pacific (actually

Polynesian ruins), the final remains of the vanished buildings of the greatest civilization the world had ever known.

The book *The Lost Continent of Mu* first saw publication in 1926, the same year that H. P. Lovecraft wrote "The Call of Cthulhu," where the standing stones of the Pacific served as a reminder of the sunken continent of his alien gods. Churchward's claims were immediately met with ridicule but also garnered a few ardent believers. He told his readers that monks in a Hindu temple in the Himalayas had shown him the history of Mu on tablets written in the lost and unknown language of Nacaal. The tablets, he explained, helpfully translated themselves while he looked at them, allowing him to learn all about Mu.[23]

From these three stories of pseudoscience—Atlantis, Lemuria, and Mu—all the main arguments later used by the authors of the ancient-astronaut hypothesis were born. Owing more than they care to admit to Donnelly's far-fetched and flawed *Atlantis: The Antediluvian World*, the alternative archaeologists carved out an early niche in opposition to the standard archaeological line. If real scientists wanted to argue that various unrelated cultures around the world produced the great monuments and that the myths of the ancient world were independent developments, then this movement would stand against that. This movement would hold that cultures were descended from a common ancestor, that there was only one Original Truth, and that the greatest days of humanity were in the past, not the future. Caught between a glorious past and golden future, the Victorian mind was torn in an age of rapid transition. If Progress were the goal of Victorian science, a return to the Golden Age would be the hallmark of Victorian pseudoscience.

Of course, pseudoscience wasn't limited just to ancient history. Genuine scientists got mixed up in false theories and mistakes. Most famously, the astronomer Percival Lowell caused a frenzy with his 1908 declaration that the canals on the surface of Mars, first seen from Italy in 1877, actually indicated the presence of an advanced civilization on another world. Even though the canals turned out to be nothing more than an optical illusion caused by the low power of the telescopes of the day, this sensational idea would help to move H. G. Wells's *War of the Worlds* from fiction to fact. For the first time, extraterrestrials became the serious subject of scientific thought.

In the run-up to the First World War, all sorts of spiritualism, psychic phenomena, and ghostly apparitions found a willing audience in a population numbed by industrialism, mechanization, and unchecked capitalism. In the books of Charles Fort, for example, entire catalogues of the strange and bizarre were presented uncritically as evidence that science did not know all the answers. In works like 1919's *The Book of the Damned*, Fort wrote about every anomalous event he could uncover, from evidence of lost civilizations to frogs raining from the sky. In *Damned*, Fort suggested that humanity may belong to a higher power, though Martian or otherwise he could not say:

> If other worlds have ever in the past had relations with this earth, they were attempted positivizations: to extend themselves, by colonies, upon this earth; to convert, or assimilate, indigenous inhabitants of this earth.[24]

But Fort was an uncertain author, and his words were hard to take seriously. Sandwiched in between an incoherent discussion of puritan sexual morality and a confused questioning of burned-out Scottish forts, this early germ of the ancient-astronaut theory awaited the elaboration and refinement that only H. P. Lovecraft could give it. When he read the book after its release, Lovecraft said it was wonderful for the creation of weird fiction, but as fact he called it nonsense.[25]

Desperate for an escape from a world that was quickly becoming too complex, too mechanical, and too impersonal, millions had found escape in the romantic fantasies of pseudo-science. For those who were unable to believe in the impossible, another cultural development ran parallel to the flourishing of pseudoscience: the appearance of the first science fiction.

3

SCIENCE FICTION AND HORROR BEFORE LOVECRAFT

Now that H. P. Lovecraft had the material he needed to compose "The Call of Cthulhu," there remained the question of what literary style to use to bring his vision to paper. It was imperative that he find just the right tone to effectively convey the literary concept of alien gods to the world. Though he did not know it, this would be his greatest legacy. In the years before "Cthulhu," Lovecraft had written stories in two different genres: horror and fantasy. Lovecraft's trifles like "The White Ship" or "Celephais" recalled the gentle fantasy of the Irish author Lord Dunsany, while his darker tales like "The Tomb" or "The Rats in the Walls" recalled the dark mind of Edgar Allan Poe. In composing "Cthulhu," Lovecraft instead drew on yet another genre, science fiction, and merged the three into a nearly seamless whole.

In the 1920s, science fiction was still something of the new kid on the block in fantastic literature, but the literature of fantastic was nothing with which Lovecraft was unfamiliar. The weird tale was his favorite form of literature and it was also the subject of a recently completed essay, *Supernatural Horror in Literature*, for which he had digested nearly every work on the subject then published. The role of fantastic literature was quite clear in his mind when, already an established author, he penned "Cthulhu."

If pseudoscience was a romantic escape from reality and the harsh rule of reason to a glorious past, science fiction was its literary opposite: a reasoned attempt to predict a romantic future of scientific advance. In this view, the Golden Age of humanity's greatest days lay not in the mythic past but in the promised future. Tales of technological progress and advancement promised novel thrills that no appeal to a musty, familiar past could match. No one could expect Lovecraft to fuse these stories of wonder with pseudoscience to create a modern myth, but then this was the Age of Progress when all superstitions and prejudices would die away in a technological millennium. No writer captured this mood better than the French author Jules Verne, whose writings about mechanical marvels helped to usher in the first golden age of science fiction.

Jules Verne was first inspired to write science fiction from reading the works of Edgar Allan Poe. Along with his familiar horror stories like "The Masque of the Red Death," Poe wrote fantasies about lunar expeditions, strange balloon journeys, and all manner of mysterious adventures. Often these stories were meant to be humorous and were patently outrageous. Occasionally they were believed true and even used as hoaxes, but they were always entertaining and usually great fun. When translated to French after his 1849 death, Poe's works became an instant hit in the Second Republic, and they found a devoted fan in Jules Verne. Taking many of Poe's stories as models, Verne attempted to fuse the science fancy of Poe's tales with a realistic depiction of the technology that could bring them to life.

In his novels like *Five Weeks in a Balloon* (1863), *Journey to the Center of the Earth* (1864), and *From the Earth to the Moon* (1865), Verne described a plausible yet fanciful near-future when great technological advances would usher in an era of unparalleled progress, perfection, and development. One of his best-known works, *Around the World in Eighty Days* (1872), hinted at a time to come when the great power and prowess of the Victorian world could take a person anywhere on the face of the earth in a relatively short time. Journalist Nellie Bly tried to duplicate Phileas Fogg's great feat seventeen years later to show the world how small it had become. She beat the eighty-day mark by one week, leaving New York on November 14, 1889, and returning on January 25, 1890. Never had science fiction so closely described the rapidly congealing world of tomorrow, and her feat gave Verne's science fiction the air of an oracle. During this, the height of the machine age, anything seemed possible and science fiction seemed to imply that those possibilities would come to pass. Science triumphant would create a new world freed from mystery, magic, and superstition. Like archaeology's attempts to explain away the romantic mystery of the past, science fiction would explain away the romantic and the Gothic in literature in favor of a doctrine of scientific, progressive, and technological wonder.

But even during the height of the Age of Progress, science fiction concealed a quiet undercurrent of horror, often disguised under the name "fantastic literature," or later, "the weird tale." After all, even Verne's mechanical dream world found its inspiration in Edgar Allan Poe, the most macabre of early American authors. It was this morbid undercurrent that would directly carry the romantic pseudoscience of the nineteenth century into the twentieth century, when it would find a willing audience once more. It was the soot on the shining citadel of Progress.

On the other side of the English Channel from Verne, British author H. G. Wells composed his "scientific romances," stories of science fiction written in the romantic vein. Unlike Verne, Wells did not believe that his science fiction creations had to necessarily follow plausible developments. Instead, they should follow the needs of the plot and the story, not the rules of science. In his novels like *The Time Machine* (1895), *The Island of Dr. Moreau* (1896), and *The War of the Worlds* (1898), Wells took his readers to the edge of imagination, incorporating a slightly sad and morbid undertone to his tales of progress and science. In *The Time Machine*, unguided evolution created dark horrors, and the vivisection labs of *Dr. Moreau* showed the march of science, creating blasphemous parodies of good, wholesome virtues. *The War of the Worlds* brought to mass audiences the first major story of malevolent extraterrestrials invading the earth, and in the eventual defeat of the Martians, Wells hinted that the British Empire and the Western world might also end in tragedy. While, like any good Victorian novel, the evil dark is always banished by the enlightened values of Victorian society triumphant, the undercurrent of horror makes Wells's fiction much more emotionally resonant than Verne's comparatively sterile worlds of wonder.

However, for me, *The Island of Dr. Moreau* has always been Wells's most powerful tale. In the story, Dr. Moreau runs an island where he makes himself a god by using animals to create sentient creatures in his own image. He goes too far, transgressing on God's territory, and the results destroy him and his world. Recently author and scholar Noel Carroll proposed that the basic story of the transgressive scientist in *Dr. Moreau*, like that of Mary Shelley's *Frankenstein* (1818), is one of a handful of basic plots of the horror story. Calling it the "Overreacher Plot," Carroll laid out its fundamental structure: The protagonist seeks out forbidden knowledge, releases its power, and must deal with the consequences. The warning is clear: do not go beyond accepted boundaries.[1] Among the other major plots he identifies, Carroll says that the other major plotline related to the Overreacher is its opposite. In the "Discovery Plot," the protagonists discover the existence of something that defies common knowledge and must expend their energy both vanquishing the horror and proving to others that the horror existed: "Such a plot celebrates the existence of things beyond the common knowledge."[2] Unlike Overreacher's, the Discovery Plot's horrors are not within man but beyond his ken. In stories like Bram Stoker's *Dracula* or Algernon Blackwood's "The Willows" (a Lovecraft favorite), the existence of the unknown provides the catalyst for horror and fear. These two themes, so bound to the tradition of horror, would see their full flowering in Lovecraft.

But perhaps these plots are not entirely opposites. Both are overly concerned with knowledge as the first and most awful source of horror, and both seem to reflect the same ambivalent attitude toward the power of science that permeates modern thought. It seems that the core issue at stake in the horror story, like that in the debate over Atlantis and the other lost continents, is the issue of science versus scientism. The former is a way of learning through experimentation, theorization, and testing. The latter is a dogmatic acceptance that what is known is all that can be known, and the accepted way of knowing is the only way to know. In a philosophical sense, horror tales seem to face a very postmodern struggle: the battle between positivism (scientism) and pure science. The authorities are powerless against the unseen forces because they cannot open their minds to investigate the possibility that the unseen can be real. As a result, institutional authority makes impotent pronouncements of impossibility instead of attempting to apply the methods of science to investigate. Like the heroes of *Dracula*, only those with open minds can take in all the evidence to supercede the ignorance of institutional science and vanquish the supernatural foe. True science, not scientism, wins the day but at the cost of admitting that there are other Things of which our philosophies cannot dream. Thus are the believers shown to be the true scientists, an appellation that the pseudoscientists of Atlantean or Lemurian persuasions very much wished to have for themselves.

The modern historian Jacques Barzun recognized scientism as a major theme, and major flaw, in Western civilization, and he provided the clearest explanation of why it produced a profound disappointment and backlash like the one evident in horror tales:

> The clue to the fallacy of scientism is this: geometry (in all senses of the word) is an abstraction from experience; it could not live without the work of the human mind on what it encounters in the world. Hence the realm of abstraction, useful and far from unreal, is thin and bare and poorer than the world it is drawn from. It is therefore an idle dream to think of someday getting along without direct dealings with what the abstraction leaves untouched.[3]

The ultimate result is a profound disconnect in modern life, a feeling that humanity is disconnected from the world and from the path to true knowledge. Mechanization and abstraction had divorced the mind from the natural world, and horror fiction demonstrated that the natural world in its full splendor would fight back. This, in essence, is the origin of Carroll's idea of knowledge as the predominant theme of horror.

H. P. Lovecraft recognized the importance of this vein of literature, especially its impact on him and his creations. When he set about writing "The Call of Cthulhu," the first work to specifically link the gods to extraterrestrial beings (whose high priest is the alien named Cthulhu), he drew on a rich tradition of weird and fantastic literature. Around the same time he was preparing to write "Cthulhu," Lovecraft received an offer from his friend, the amateur journalist W. Paul Cook, to write an article for an amateur magazine describing the developments in weird fiction down to his day. The result, *Supernatural Horror in Literature* (1927), became one of the finest descriptions of the weird vein ever published. Lovecraft thus provided the student of his work with the very footsteps by which he traced the path of the weird.

"The oldest and strongest emotion of mankind is fear," Lovecraft began his essay, "and the oldest and strongest kind of fear is fear of the unknown."[4] Lovecraft marked the start of the modern supernatural tale with the rise of the Gothic novel in the late eighteenth century. Developing out of the Enlightenment as a literary reaction to pure reason, Gothic novels prefigured the Romantic movement. They relied on supernatural phenomena, on ancient curses returning to haunt later generations, and above all on the moldering ruins of a blasted castle. Using emotive, emotional symbolism, these tales provided a rich contrast to the dry world of reason and logic. Such novels as Horace Walpole's *Castle of Otranto* (1764), Ann Radcliffe's *The Mysteries of Udolpho* (1794), and Charles Maturin's *Melmoth the Wanderer* (1820) brought the Gothic tale to its most perfect form, or as Lovecraft said, "to altitudes of sheer spiritual fright which it had never known before."[5] In these tales, the dark secrets of the past yield supernatural horrors that plague later generations invested with the stain of their fathers. In 1818 the Gothic tradition spawned its most famous tale, Mary Shelley's *Frankenstein*, which crystalized the theme that some knowledge should not be had by mankind, and science does not have all the answers. Typical of the Gothic style, *Frankenstein* was the product of a dream and held subconscious resonance. In the famous anecdote, Shelley was involved in a contest with famous Romantic figures: her husband, Percy; John Polidori; and Lord Byron. Their task was to write the best horror story. Shelley had a nightmare and dreamed of *Frankenstein*, the story of a doctor who creates life from dead body parts and unleashes terror. Thus was born the story of "the modern Prometheus."[6]

More important for the development of horror was Lovecraft's literary hero, Edgar Allan Poe. Born in 1809 to a pair of traveling actors, Poe was taken in by a Virginia merchant named John Allan (who never adopted the boy) after Poe's father vanished. Schooled in England and at the University of Virginia,

Poe's gambling debts forced him out of school before he took his degree. Something of a literary prodigy, Poe published his first volume of verse at eighteen, and after a dismissal six months into a stint in the army, he was publishing short fiction. In all, he wrote seventy-two short stories, fifty poems, and one novel. After much drinking and the 1847 death of his wife (a cousin he married when she was thirteen), Poe's life spiraled out of control. He was found disheveled and sick on the streets of Baltimore on October 3, 1849. He died four days later at the age of forty.[7]

Today, virtually everyone has read one of Poe's classic stories, the terrifying "Pit and the Pendulum," the horrifying "Tell-Tale Heart," or the outlandish "Fall of the House of Usher." Most also know his dark poetry, especially his most famous poem, "The Raven." Fewer know that Poe invented the modern detective story. Only specialists and serious fans remember Poe as an accomplished literary critic or as a humorist (though I can't say his humor spans the centuries well). Of course, Poe will forever be identified with horror.

In his horror stories, written in the Gothic style, his narrators were frequently insane or unreliable, and the stories they told were often the figments of a haunted imagination. In chilling tales like "The Black Cat" or "Ligeia," the narrator's diseased mental state is in fact the plot. In Poe's world, the human mind held terrors infinitely greater than the outside. In his landscapes, death, decay, and corruption became the supreme embodiments of the human condition. This is perhaps most beautifully embodied in the last lines of my favorite Poe poem, "Annabel Lee," about a young love cut short by death:

> For the moon never beams without bringing me dreams
>   Of the beautiful ANNABEL LEE;
> And the stars never rise, but I feel the bright eyes
>   Of the beautiful ANNABEL LEE;
> And so, all the night-tide, I lie down by the side

Of my darling—my darling—my life and my bride,
In the sepulchre there by the sea,
In her tomb by the sounding sea.[8]

In his only novel, *The Narrative of A. Gordon Pym*, Poe captures in prose the idea that things on earth are not today as they always were. During a voyage to the South Pole, A. Gordon Pym discovers vast rocky ravines in the form of Egyptian hieroglyphs on the supposedly empty southern continent. They hint that the horrors he finds in the Antarctic are very ancient indeed. In other stories, like "Merzetgerstein," the evil of one generation is visited upon its descendents, again reinforcing the idea that horrors of the past have direct consequences today. In "The Fall of the House of Usher," the entire weight of the familial sin is embodied both in the Ushers and their ancient seat. It would be left to Lovecraft to take this template sketched by Poe and infuse it with the scientific trappings of the modern age.

Meanwhile, the tradition of the weird tale continued after Poe. His contemporary Nathaniel Hawthorne produced notable weird tales in the Gothic tradition, including *The House of the Seven Gables*. Fitz-James O'Brien wrote the horror tale "What Was It?" giving the world an invisible horror, and by century's end, Ambrose Bierce was producing volumes of exquisitely wrought works of horror. When H. P. Lovecraft was born in 1890, tales of the uncanny and the bizarre held their own against a landscape populated with the giants of English-language literature. Even famous authors like Mark Twain and Rudyard Kipling took their turn at tales of the supernatural, and the creator of Sherlock Holmes, Sir Arthur Conan Doyle, came to like writing them better than tales of detection. Ironically, both veins of Doyle's fiction, detective stories and horror stories, owed their forms to Poe. That Doyle also came to embrace pseudoscience and spiritualism, writing credulous works on the existence of fairies and ghosts in the first decades of the twentieth century, only reinforced the thin line separating fact from fiction in the fin de siècle.

Also in this fertile period, Bram Stoker first issued the vampire novel *Dracula* and Henry James wrote the ghost tale *Turn of the Screw*. Interesting for the study of horror literature and its relationship to science, Robert Louis Stevenson produced *The Strange Case of Dr. Jekyll and Mr. Hyde*, which laid bare the underlying principles of Victorian horror fiction. Everyone knows the story of how, in the name of seeking absolute knowledge of the self, Dr. Jekyll creates a potion to release his inner, unconscious, animal self and then loses control of his newfound freedom. But beneath that is a darker layer.

Jekyll represents not the true pursuit of knowledge as much as the attempt of the believer in scientism to push the boundaries of science into those areas where it has no right to be. The human mind, Stevenson seems to argue, is no place for science to probe its instruments and potions. In Jekyll's theorizing at the story's end, there are multiple areas in the human mind. We see the origins of modern theories that hold that the human mind as creator of the laws of science can never successfully employ them to explore itself. This contrasts directly with Sigmund Freud, who was actively and simultaneously developing psychoanalysis in far-off Vienna. Jekyll confesses that he does not know how many parts man truly is; in this he presages the postmodernists, who hold that knowledge is personal and fragmentary, that there is no one knowledge but many, and that science is but one method among many.

That Jekyll dies for his knowledge in the end shows yet another facet of the Western mind: science as self-negation. Susan Navarette argues that death and self-negation are the ultimate result of knowledge in Victorian horror fiction, just as pure impersonal objectivity is the stated goal of pure science.[9] By removing the human element, the horror story says, we

remove the human stain but also the human genius. This literature feared the mechanized, technological world and sought
refuge in the past, in romance, and in mystery. Thus for Lovecraft, the stories of the age taught him that oblivion was the
end result of the unwholesome pursuit of knowledge, a theme
he would employ again and again.

In his own time, Lovecraft held Arthur Machen and Lord
Dunsany as the contemporary masters of the genre. He read and
enjoyed their tales, and he incorporated some of their methods
and ideas into his own works. From Machen he borrowed the
idea of survival of ancient things. Machen, in his stories like
"The Great God Pan" and the novel *The Three Imposters*, postulated a world where the ancient "little people" of Celtic myth
lived on and where archaeological wonders of the ages represented their supernatural handiwork. They were gone now,
underneath the ground and out of sight, but they were always
ready to return. Lord Dunsany, on the other hand, wrote stories
of fantasy based on a fabulous fictional mythology of gods and
demons interacting with his human protagonists. He created
the mythological land of Pegana and populated it with gentle
fantasies in the style of a pagan *Arabian Nights*.

But by Lovecraft's age, what had made the horror story so
appropriate a vehicle for exploring alternative thought and
outrageous hypotheses was the particular structure it had
evolved. As scholar Allen Grove maintains, horror stories
evolved a narrative structure that relied on a battle between
skeptics and believers: "The narrative energy and terror of these
stories depends upon the tension between the skeptical,
rational character and those forces that defy his reason. Ghost
stories often appear self-conscious of their own skeptical audiences as they dramatize the empiricist's conversion to a
'believer.'"[10] In the famous Victorian ghost story "How Love
Came to Professor Guildea," it is the skeptical priest character
that lets the reader experience his conversion to a believer

when a ghost starts to haunt the title character. In Lovecraft, the narrator is almost always a skeptic who comes into contact with the blasphemous revelations of the alien gods.

The supreme horror, then, was the startling realization that the well-ordered universe was not that well ordered and that something unknown lurked deep in the past, ready to return. It was no coincidence that the stories that gave rise to the belief in ancient astronauts took just this form. Thus were the two branches of Western thought, the rational and the irrational, the Enlightenment and the Romantic, juxtaposed for a final synthesis, ready to be united in the person of H. P. Lovecraft.

But just who was H. P. Lovecraft and what was so amazing about his work?

PART TWO

STORIES OF GODS FROM OUTER SPACE

4

THE PROPHET OF PROVIDENCE

Now that Lovecraft had assembled a quasi-factual background for his horror story and had developed the perfect style in which to tell it, all that remained was to create the perfect horror monster. Like so much else, Lovecraft turned to classic literature, borrowing heavily from Alfred, Lord Tennyson's poem "The Kraken" to develop his own horrific creation, the Cthulhu.[1] In Tennyson, the Kraken is an undersea creature fast asleep in his subaqueous prison:

> Below the thunders of the upper deep;
> Far, far beneath in the abysmal sea,
> His ancient, dreamless, uninvaded sleep
> The Kraken sleepeth: faintest sunlights flee
> About his shadowy sides; above him swell
> Huge sponges of millennial growth and height;
> And far away into the sickly light,
> From many a wondrous grot and secret cell
> Unnumber'd and enormous polypi
> Winnow with giant arms the slumbering green.
> There hath he lain for ages, and will lie
> Battening upon huge seaworms in his sleep,
> Until the latter fire shall heat the deep;
> Then once by man and angels to be seen,
> In roaring he shall rise and on the surface die.

Lovecraft's Cthulhu shared all these familiar traits. He lay asleep in his undersea city, "dead but dreaming" and awaiting the resurrection.[2] But Lovecraft modernized this familiar Victorian poem and brought the medieval mythological monster into the space age, transforming a demon of the past into an ancient alien.

It is probably one of the utmost ironies of H. P. Lovecraft's life that he should have given birth to the ancient-astronaut theory. Sitting at his desk in October 1926, Lovecraft could look back on a life led in pursuit of knowledge and reason. He could think back to his early astronomy newspaper columns debunking astrology and even his short-lived dreams of being a scientist. A lifelong atheist and materialist, Lovecraft all but worshiped science and reason, rejecting outright the fantasies of Donnelly's *Atlantis* and Blavatsky's *Secret Doctrine*. Yet it was he above all others who helped these discredited remnants of the Victorian battle for the soul of science live on into the modern age.

Born in 1890 as the last scion of a formerly aristocratic family, Howard Phillips Lovecraft spent most of his life locked away in his Providence home, hiding from the world. Tall, gaunt, and with a face that resembled nothing so much as the elongated statue heads of Easter Island, Lovecraft affected an old-fashioned air in tune with his love of the Enlightenment. His father died at a mental institution when he was young, and his mother raised him under the guidance of his grandfather, the industrialist Whipple Phillips, who entertained the young boy with weird tales in Gothic style. A precocious youth, Lovecraft read voraciously from his grandfather's eighteenth-century library, devouring volumes on Greek mythology and the popular periodicals of the colonial period. The first book he read was Grimm's *Tales*, and at age five he completed a junior edition of *Arabian Nights*. Early on he learned to love weird and uncanny stories. Thus was born Lovecraft's lifelong love of the bizarre.

"As a boy," biographer S. T. Joshi says, "Lovecraft was somewhat lonely and suffered from frequent illnesses, many of them apparently psychological. His attendance at the Slater Avenue School was sporadic, but Lovecraft was soaking up much information through independent reading."[3] Even so, he never graduated high school, a humiliation that would haunt him to his death.

Nevertheless, his reading bred into him a lifelong materialism. He read about all the different faiths and beliefs in the world and was alternately fascinated and repelled by them. Confronted with a wealth of traditions through his reading, he adopted and cast off Christianity, Islam, and paganism before deciding that there probably was no supernatural truth. After a brief period of dressing up like an Arab and claiming to be a Mohammedan named Abdul Alhazred, he gave up his quest for a religious life. From then on he would be a confirmed atheist. For the rest of his life, Lovecraft would espouse a philosophy of "scientific materialism," which held that the matter was all that existed and there were no higher supernatural authority.

By the age of sixteen, Lovecraft was writing astronomy columns for the local newspaper. Always the debunker of superstition, Lovecraft used his column to expose the fraud of astrology in favor of the science of astronomy. This early success would not last. His family had fallen on financial hard times. After his grandfather's death, his family had to sell the old mansion where he grew up and decamp to more modest quarters a few streets over. Lovecraft quit school and went through a reclusive period under his family's domination. By 1917, and in his late twenties, he stepped out of his family's shadow. He had begun writing fiction, producing two stories—"The Tomb" and "Dagon"—that year. He had also taken up amateur journalism and published a journal called *The Conservative*.

Politically, Lovecraft began life as a right-wing reactionary but moderated over the course of his life. His often-miserable financial situation made him suspicious of outsiders, and he developed a pronounced racist streak, once commenting, "To be a member of a pure-blooded race ought to be the greatest achievement in life."[4] He wrote an essay for his amateur journal advocating racial purity. In this opinion, he was not terribly far from the mainstream of early twentieth-century society, which was dominated by old hierarchies and still tinged by colonial-era racial categories. By the standards of the day, racism was on the eclipse but was far from a fringe belief. The inferiority of some races was accepted as proven scientific fact, a fact that the newly created IQ test was designed to confirm. Thanks to D. W. Griffth's epic film *Birth of a Nation*, the Ku Klux Klan was again in vogue, and marches for segregation and white pride were not uncommon. Lovecraft, however, never manifested his theoretical racism in any kind of direct way. He hated people in the abstract.

Though he recanted his racist positions late in life, they had already found their way into his stories, either explicitly or implicitly. In "The Call of Cthulhu," the members of the ancient cult who conspire to raise the alien from its tomb beneath the waves are described as "very low, mixed blooded, and mentally aberrant . . . negroes and mulattoes."[5] Apparently, he held that since they were of lower blood they were evolutionarily closer to the beginning and thus closer to the Things from the past. The dark side of science tinged the dark side of Lovecraft's writing.

He also held that civilization was cyclical, that great cultures came and went through periods of florescence and decay. This pattern is most apparent in his fictional works, like *At the Mountains of Madness*, where Antarctic explorers discover the million-year-old ruins of an alien civilization called "The Old Ones" who had descended to Earth and made life as an experiment in the then-popular theory of eugenics:

When the star-headed Old Ones on this planet had synthesised their simple food forms and bred a good supply of shoggoths, they allowed other cell-groups to develop into other forms of animal and vegetable life for sundry purposes; extirpating any whose presence became troublesome.[6]

But this civilization inevitably decayed into a mockery of itself, letting upstarts rule where once the pure blood had ruled before. Because Lovecraft's childhood wealth slowly gave way to poverty, decline, and the deaths of his grandfather and mother, for him modern civilization invariably had to follow the path of the Old Ones toward chaos, confusion, and dissolution. There was simply no choice about the matter, and one had to do his best to muddle through and keep the decline from coming too fast.

In apparent contradiction to his rule against mixing races, Lovecraft married Sonia Greene, a Russian Jew seven years older than he, in 1924. They seemed happy at first, though Greene said her husband was only "an adequately excellent lover." After more financial trouble and a lengthy separation they divorced in 1929.

During his marriage, he lived with Greene in New York, and "he became increasingly depressed by his isolation and the masses of 'foreigners' in the city," Joshi says.[7] The polyglot and multiethnic hordes violated Lovecraft's aesthetic sense, and he resented feeling like a foreigner in his own country. Lovecraft then wrote some of his most racist and xenophobic fiction, including "The Horror at Red Hook," set in the seedy mixed-ethnicity neighborhood where Lovecraft lived after separating from his wife: "Red Hook is a maze of hybrid squalor. . . . The population is a hopeless tangle, an enigma; Syrian, Spanish, Italian, and negro elements impinging upon one another. . . . It is a babel of sound and filth."[8] While he had little good to say about the area's minorities, the "The Horror at Red Hook" was a good horror yarn in the traditional satanic cult vein.

The popular L. Sprague de Camp biography of Lovecraft

dwells too heavily on his racism, but it does note that prejudice was a surface affectation and that in his life Lovecraft was never anything but polite to people of other ethnicities. He hated foreign groups in the abstract but liked the individuals within them just fine.

Lovecraft returned to his hometown of Providence in 1926, the same year he wrote "Call of the Cthulhu." He moved into an apartment building with his aunt and experienced a period of high productivity that lasted through his death. During this time he wrote his greatest stories, including the short novels *At the Mountains of Madness*, *The Dream-Quest of Unknown Kadath*, and *The Case of Charles Dexter Ward*, as well as the short stories "The Colour Out of Space" and "The Shadow Out of Time." In these stories, Lovecraft presented startlingly original weird literature and laid the foundations for a reputation that would later lead him to be ranked with his hero Edgar Allan Poe among the foremost authors of horror.

As the economy worsened following the stock market crash of 1929, Lovecraft found money increasingly tight, and his earnings from story writing and ghostwriting barely paid his meager expenses. Around this period "he became concerned with political and economic issues," Joshi says, "as the Great Depression led him to support Roosevelt and become a moderate socialist; and he continued absorbing knowledge on a wide array of subjects, from philosophy to literature to history to architecture."[9] The one-time reactionary had done a complete turnabout and was now a socialist. However, he stuck by his scientific materialism, even as he spun his last tales of supernatural horror.

Lovecraft never had many close friends that he saw on any regular basis, but he tried to make up for it through the written word. During his life he maintained a prodigious circle of correspondents to whom he wrote lengthy and often daily letters. In this way, he kept up friendships with people he often never met in person. His collected letters now fill several volumes, and his biographers hold that they are an even greater legacy than his fiction. Taken together, they form a day-to-day account of Lovecraft's life and thought process; so much more is known about him, his sources, and his intellectual development than for most authors.

In the mid-1930s he began to complain of stomach problems, but his poverty and his aversion to doctors prevented him from seeking treatment. H. P. Lovecraft died of intestinal cancer in March 1937 without ever publishing a book. Instead his writings were housed in the pages of popular pulp magazines like *Weird Tales* and *Astounding Stories*, and many were never published at all and existed only in manuscripts circulating among his circle of correspondents. He died believing himself a failure.

But because some thought that Lovecraft's writing deserved better, his friends formed Arkham House publishers to issue a hardcover volume of Lovecraft's writings. The book, *The Outsider and Others*, appeared in 1939. It did not sell well.

Lovecraft's fiction is what sets him apart from the vast majority of struggling writers whose careers lead them to poverty and early death. Lovecraft's stories probed new vistas of horror and set the stage for the ancient-alien theories of today.

As we have seen, Lovecraft was thoroughly familiar with the pseudoscience of the day as well as the Gothic tradition in literature. A lifelong fan of Edgar Allan Poe, Lovecraft started his career writing stories in imitation of his literary antecedent. Much of his early work bears the same literary eccentricities as Poe: too many adjectives, wordy style, and overuse of typographical emphases like italics and boldface. After he encountered Lord Dunsany's fantasies set in the land of Pegana, he imitated these in his own works set in what he called "The Dreamlands." For a time, he wrote pretty fantasies, but even those were tinged with Poe's morbid horrors. But when Love-craft read Arthur Machen's best work, his "Great God Pan" and *Three Imposters*, he encountered an author whose thoughts closely matched his own. The two men shared a love of the past and desire to escape the modern world back to a simpler time. Machen had written about the continuing presence of the little people of ancient Celtic lore in the hidden places of the earth. From Machen, Lovecraft would adopt the idea that strange Things had survived from man's earliest days.

In his first stories, Lovecraft followed Poe's outlines and infused them with Machen's idea that something from the past continued to haunt the present. In the 1919 story "Dagon," Lovecraft first explored the concept of a deity from the past reemerging. For this story, he adapted the legend of the Philis-tine fish-god Dagon, familiar from the Bible.[10] The action takes place on an island in the middle of the Pacific Ocean during the Great War. A German ship sinks the narrator's craft, and he winds up on a murky island. There he encounters a fabulous sight, a large standing stone:

> Across the chasm, the wavelets washed the base of the Cyclo-pean monolith, on whose surface I could now trace both inscriptions and crude sculptures. The writing was unlike anything I had ever seen in books, consisting for the most part of conventionalised aquatic symbols such as fishes, eels, octopi, crustaceans, molluscs, whales, and the like.[11]

The cryptic inscriptions shock our hero, who is privy to a glimpse "into a past beyond the conception of the most daring anthropologist."[12] He sees strange fish-creatures who lived on Earth eons before man and who raised this stone. Then one of them comes back. . . .

In this small story, we have the first version of what would become the ancient alien legend. Lovecraft for the first time gathered together the key elements that would come to define the myth: the archaeological wonders, the past beyond our knowledge, the opposition to conventional thinking. "The Kraken" had met the *Secret Doctrine*. However, he had not yet made the connection between the fabulous creatures and outer space. Instead, "Dagon" is a more conventional fictionalization of the lost continents of popular archaeology with a dose of Madame Blavatsky's primitive reptile races.

The next year he composed "The Temple," a tale of a German submarine commander who ends up lost off the Yucatán peninsula in Mexico. The submariner discovers the remnants of the lost continent of Atlantis, formerly regarded as a myth. The descriptions of the vast city and its amazing architecture were heavily influenced by Ignatius Donnelly's descriptions from *Atlantis: The Antediluvian World*. From it, Lovecraft borrowed the idea that Atlantis spawned later civilizations, making his German sea-captain remark that Atlantis "imparts an impression of terrible antiquity, as though it were the remotest rather than the immediate ancestor of Greek art."[13] But Atlantis is not dead, and lights in the main temple show that *something* has survived. . . .

Now that Lovecraft has brought Donnelly's Atlantis into his expanding universe, it was not hard to add other archaeological mysteries in order to lend ever-greater atmosphere to his tales. By using the tools of pseudoscience for fictional effect, Lovecraft hoped to make the perfect fictional atmosphere because for him the atmosphere of pure horror was more important than characterization or even plot. It was effect through aesthetics. When gathered together, these aesthetic atmospherics would form a core that would make Lovecraft's stories distinctive.

In "The Nameless City," Lovecraft introduced the first concepts of what would later become known as Lovecraftian fiction or "The Cthulhu Mythos," after its most famous creation, the alien god Cthulhu. Written in 1921, "Nameless City" follows its hero to a ruined city in the Arabian desert. The ruin is Irem, city of pillars, borrowed from Muslim mythology. There, the narrator discovers that the haunted city is not the creation of man but is in fact the remains of a fabulous city built by a race of reptiles whose civilization reeked of "an ancientness so vast that measurement is feeble" and whose "astounding maps in the frescoes shewed oceans and continents that man has forgotten."[14] This was foretold by a couplet sung by the mad Arab Abdul Alhazred, of whom more will be said:

> That is not dead which can eternal lie
> And with strange aeons even death may die.[15]

Written in the days before plate tectonics revealed the existence of the vanished worlds of Pangaea and Gondwanaland, the reptiles' lost continents could only have been Atlantis, Lemuria, and their ilk. The reptiles seem to recall Blavatsky's rubbery primitive races. Of course, it wouldn't be a horror story if the reptile people hadn't survived. . . .

By now Lovecraft had essentially reproduced Arthur Machen's idea of primal mysteries surviving into the modern age. In the coming years it was up to Lovecraft to add the final twist that would separate his vision from what had come before. In 1922's "The Hound," the protagonists make mention of an ancient tome that contains the legends of things from outside, the *Necronomicon* of Abdul Alhazred, the same name he used in his childhood flirtation with Islam. This fictional book became a major element in Lovecraft's fiction and was such an effective device for giving his stories a mythic past that many would come to believe that the book was real. Lovecraft increased the prestige of the fictional tome by mentioning it in the same breath with very real books like W. Scott-Eliot's *The Story of Atlantis and Lost Lemuria*, Margaret Alice Murray's *The*

Witch-Cult in Western Europe, James Sprenger and Heinrich Kramer's *Malleus Maleficarum,* and Joseph Glanvil's *Sadducismus Triumphatus.*

In 1923, Lovecraft composed "The Festival" and "The Rats in the Walls," both stories about ancient secrets revealed. "Festival" makes use of the *Necronomicon* as a prop for its story of a bizarre Yuletide ceremony. "Rats" reveals devolution as a titanic horror threatening to peel back the veneer of civilization, since the "rats" are not rats at all, and the caves beneath an old castle speak of gruesome activity that lays bare the inhuman nature of the human mind. "Rats" is probably Lovecraft's most-anthologized story and the one most familiar to casual readers, though its rather traditional horrors bear little relation to what would follow.

In the following years, *Weird Tales* began to run these and other Lovecraft tales while Lovecraft composed *Supernatural Horror in Literature* and began to contemplate what would become his first masterpiece, 1926's "The Call of Cthulhu." Not long earlier, Einstein had inaugurated a new era in physics with his theory of relativity, and as the scientific establishment grappled with the idea that its Newtonian worldview was collapsing, Lovecraft mentally combined the paradigm collapse with the wholesale cultural collapse that everywhere was manifest in the cultural rot that set in following the First World War. The tattered remains of Europe were still convulsing from revolution and the devastation of war. Even if the United States experienced a roaring '20s, the upheavals in Bolshevik Russia and Weimar Germany and the fractured remnants of the defunct Austro-Hungarian monarchy were enough to give pause to anyone too willing to claim a cultural revival. The tenor of the times was expressed in the title of Oswald Spengler's 1922 best-seller, *Decline of the West.* This idea of civilization on the edge, rotting from the inside out, helped to animate the horrors of "The Call of Cthulhu."

In that story Lovecraft first introduced his signature concept, that the Things from the past were in fact cosmic beings from other worlds that came to Earth in primal times and may still be visiting Earth today. Building on an idea found in embryo in Charles Fort's *Book of the Damned*, which Lovecraft often mined for inspiration, here for the first time the great pseudoscientific traditions and the science fiction and fantasy veins came together in one tale, a tale that would later transform alternative archaeology into an extraterrestrial affair.

"Cthulhu" tells the story of Francis Wayland Thurston, who slowly begins to piece together the shocking history of an ancient cult. Thurston tells readers that Helena Blavatsky's "Theosophists have guessed at the awesome grandeur of the cosmic cycle wherein our world and human race form transient incidents. They have hinted at strange survivals in terms which would freeze the blood if not masked by a bland optimism."[16] He says that if humanity knew what he knew it would seek the comfort of a renewed Dark Age. Here the cosmic fantasies of Theosophy became an important prop on which Lovecraft's story rested, the pseudoscience used as a nonfiction touchstone linking "Cthulhu" to reality.

Thurston describes how his granduncle, an eminent professor, was struck down by a sinister fellow, leaving to Thurston a packet of papers describing his research into some singular events that hinted at a strange survival. The professor was investigating the strange dreams of an artist who had sculpted from clay a cosmic horror in an unknown art style belonging to a period likely so ancient only the modern styles futurism and cubism began to approximate it. The bas-relief showed an octopus-headed humanoid monster standing within the twisted backdrop of an ancient city. During the time the artist composed his relief, other people around the world had begun having strange dreams of the octopus-man and his horrible home.

Also included in the packet was the narrative of a police

inspector who was investigating a quasi-religious group in Louisiana. It became known as the Cthulhu Cult after the entity that they said they worshiped, the octopus-headed man. Inspector Legrasse had raided a cult sacrifice, and one of the cultists, a fellow named Castro, spoke of the cult's dark beliefs:

> They worshipped, so they said, the Great Old Ones who lived ages before there were any men, and who came to the young world out of the sky. These Old Ones were gone now, inside the earth and under the sea; but their dead bodies had told their secrets in dreams to the first man, who formed a cult which had never died.[17]

Also present was a carven idol, fashioned by the Old Ones themselves and belonging to no known style. It depicted Great Cthulhu, the high priest of the Old Ones, an octopus-headed being who had come from the stars. It was so utterly alien that archaeologists could not classify it or the nonterrestrial stone or metal of which it was made. They could only fall back on the words of the cultists themselves who chanted rhythmically, "In his house at R'lyeh, dead Cthulhu waits dreaming," though they spoke those words in no earthly tongue.

The cultists confirmed that the star-born Cthulhu was trapped now under the sea biding his time. Cthulhu's prison in the city of R'lyeh was believed to rise from the sea "when the stars were right," ready for resurrection:

> The time would be easy to know, for then mankind would have become as the Great Old Ones; free and wild and beyond good and evil, with laws and morals thrown aside and all men shouting and killing and revelling in joy. Then the liberated Old Ones would teach them new ways to shout and kill and revel and enjoy themselves, and all the earth would flame with a holocaust of ecstasy and freedom.[18]

This was the promise of Cthulhu and the Old Ones, the same promise that the democracies of the West made to their citizens in the hellfires of the First World War: in the twilight of civilization, the old order will vanish, all restrictions would be thrown aside, and the freedom embodied in democracy will be the freedom of the individual. As we shall see, this promise would be fulfilled in the twenty-first century in strange ways.

When Cthulhu's home in R'lyeh sank eons ago, the only trace it left, like Churchward's Mu, was the stones standing on Pacific islands near Nan Madol. Needless to say, the cult's story is not purely legend. Thurston discovers that a Norwegian sailor has indeed found lost R'lyeh, a city of "non-Euclidean geometry" and strange angles. In a scene highly reminiscent of "Dagon," the Norwegian encounters the alien god at the heart of R'lyeh. Like Thurston's granduncle, the sailor, too, was assassinated. Fearing the Cthulhu cult will come for him, Thurston seals away his evidence so the world can continue in blissful ignorance. . . .

The story was a milestone, both for ancient astronauts and for Lovecraft himself. Finally, Lovecraft had brought together the disparate threads of science fiction, horror, and alternative archaeology into one transcendent idea: Ancient societies mistook visitors from the stars for gods, an idea that not even Charles Fort had proposed in his mad ravings. Anomalous pieces of ancient art and architecture were really the work of these visitors. And, of course, the visitors promised to return. To add a spiritualist touch, they even communicated via telepathy ("in dreams"). No tale before or since has communicated so eloquently the idea that visitors from the stars had inspired the first religions. As L. Sprague de Camp noted:

> Like other Ancient Ones and Elder Gods, Cthulhu is called a "god," but the term does not mean what it does in traditional religions. Lovecraft's "gods" are not, like Zeus or Yahveh [sic], concerned with the morals and manners of human beings.

They do not undertake to reward the good or punish the wicked. Their powers, though vast, are ruled by natural law. They are absorbed in their own affairs and are no more interested in the petty concerns of men than men are with those of mice, and they have no more compunction about destroying men who get in the way than men have about slaying mice.[19]

In fact, they are utterly indifferent to man because they are aliens to humanity in every sense of the word. This was Lovecraft's philosophy of "cosmic indifference." Based on his materialist beliefs, Lovecraft could conceive of no other attitude for visitors from outer space to take than that of uninterested, self-centered creatures. After all, in a physical universe defined by the new theory of relativity, what other stance could an intelligent inhabitant of the cosmos take?

In the years that followed "Cthulhu," Lovecraft continued to add to his fictitious mythology, introducing new aliens and still stranger beings that were transdimensional. He developed something of a hierarchy, but one that was never codified in Lovecraft's lifetime. His stories were fragmentary and impressionistic, so they often contradicted one another in the fine details. Nevertheless, the basic outlines were clear: the cosmos were a mindless, mechanical whole populated by an infinity of strange beings of great power but subject to natural law. Some of these appeared to humans more like gods, the less powerful more like monsters. All, however, were extraterrestrial beings tied to the material creation and subject to its rules, even if humanity did not yet know all the rules. Magic, then, was only an illusion and human knowledge could not grasp the more esoteric areas of cosmic physics.

At the center of the cosmos he placed Azathoth, the "demon sultan" and "nuclear chaos" whose very existence, Lovecraft said, was only a mythological mask for the pulsing of the material, godless universe that even the cultists could not contemplate. The mindless, random pulsings of the nuclear center gave birth to universes and continua of time and space. In this way, he came close to predicting the big bang theory, a massive explosion of energy that became the universe. Surrounding this Lord of All were the Old Ones, the mindless, colossal beings who dance madly and mindlessly and represent the quantum forces at the core of creation. Their soul and messenger was the Crawling Chaos Nyarlathotep, a sometimes-humanoid creature with a thousand faces. Connecting all the multiple universes together was Yog-Sothoth, the All-In-One and One-In-All, a kind of Lovecraftian Holy Ghost by way of quantum physics.

In "The Dunwich Horror," the *Necronomicon* held the secret by which Yog-Sothoth could enter the mortal plane, and an ancient stone circle was the gate through which he could enter. In other words, archaeology linked the ancients to the aliens from Outside. Here, as in the stories "Dreams in the Witch-House" and *The Case of Charles Dexter Ward*, the alchemical and magical incantations of the distant past are revealed to be true descriptions of high-level physics. Magic and alchemy, in other words, were also ruled by natural law and were the hidden revelations of the cosmic physics of the alien beings like Yog-Sothoth.

Beneath these quasi-divine beings in the hierarchy were the various races of aliens who visited and lived on the earth. The Mi-Go, or Fungi from Yuggoth, lived on the ninth planet from the sun (Lovecraft was proud of having predicted with Yuggoth the existence of Pluto, discovered only in 1930) and came to Earth to steal human brains for journeys back to their planet. This they accomplished through the use of metal cylinders that can preserve a brain intact. They stalk across "The Whisperer in Darkness," haunting the backwoods and spawning legends of unwholesome survivals in the forest primeval. They are briefly overheard, recorded on a phonograph, worshiping Nyarlathotep and Shub-Niggurath, the black goat of the woods with a thousand young.

The Ancient Ones were winged aliens with many tentacles that flew to Earth in the remote past and created life as we know it.[20] As we learn in *At the Mountains of Madness*, the Ancient Ones created the first cells as food for themselves when they lived in Antarctica millions of years ago. They then let evolution take its course, guiding it when necessary. Eventually their creations gave rise to the shape-shifting shoggoths and even to humanity itself. Though this contradicts some of what Lovecraft wrote in "Cthulhu" about the alien-human connection, it was no matter. Lovecraft was writing for impression, not consistency, and inconsistency only made his writings seem more like genuine memories of an authentic tradition, warped and muddled through time. This was rather like real legends, where Norse myths and King Arthur stories had many different versions, reflecting the time and place of their telling. There was something of a postmodern authenticity in contradiction, even if postmodernism had to wait first for the invention of modernism.

In Lovecraft's last major story, "The Shadow Out of Time," an archaeologist uncovers in the Australian Outback the remains of a city hewn by the Great Race in the hoary depths of time. These conical creatures sent their minds into the past and the future, possessing the bodies of other species to learn everything that was and will be. Here the theme from "Cthulhu" is explicit: archaeological remains are the work of alien beings.

Lovecraft's universe, therefore, is one of ancient horror leading to ultimate revelations about the material nature of the universe. This, then, is the greatest difference between Lovecraft and Ignatius Donnelly or Madame Blavatsky: Lovecraft's worldview would not allow for a spiritual core of goodness at the world's center. Significantly and solely, Lovecraft stripped the ancient past of its spiritual overtones. The mysteries and anomalies of the past find themselves in Lovecraft's fiction digested and spat out as the expected result of a material universe churning through a thousand cycles of endless creation: "For Lovecraft," author Erik Davis says, "it is not the sleep of reason that breeds monsters, but reason with its eyes agog. By fusing cutting-edge science with archaic material, Lovecraft creates a twisted materialism in which scientific 'progress' returns us to the atavistic abyss, and hard-nosed research revives the factual basis of forgotten and discarded myths."[21] In other words, in Lovecraft, the strains of Western thought found their synthesis, and reason and unreason, fact and fiction, science and faith could find their common ground. That this should occur in the years following the Great War, the great trauma and crisis of the Western world, only helped to make Lovecraft's ideas all the more resonant and all the more powerful.

Often criticized as purple and overly filled with adjectives, Lovecraft's stories created an atmosphere of fear that transcended their often-predictable plots. His cryptic references to extraterrestrial gods and strange survivals, his dark hints at forbidden knowledge contained in ancient tomes like the *Necronomicon*, *De Vermis Mysteriis*, or *Unaussprechlichen Kulten* gave an air of grisly authenticity to his writing.

Lovecraft persuaded his friends like California poet and author Clark Ashton Smith or Conan the Cimmerian creator Robert Howard to reference some of his creations in their horror stories, and he reciprocated by including their creations (*De Vermis Mysteriis* and *Unaussprechlichen Kulten* being just two) in his own stories.

"It rather amuses the different writers," Lovecraft wrote in a 1934 letter, "to use one another's synthetic demons & imaginary books in their stories—so that Clark Ashton Smith often speaks of my *Necronomicon* while I refer to his *Book of Eibon* . . . & so on. This pooling of resources tends to build up quite a pseudo-convincing background of dark mythology, legendry, & bibiliography—though of course, none of us has the least wish to actually mislead readers." It was, he said, "sheer fun."[22]

Readers, however, enjoyed being misled, and despite Lovecraft's fervent denials, like the one quoted above, letters continued to come demanding to know Lovecraft's source for occult knowledge. He patiently explained that it was nothing but a figment of his own overwrought imagination, but such denials did no good. The *Necronomicon* took on a life of its own, and many readers became convinced that the grimoire was real and went in search of the text. At one time both the University of California at Berkeley's and Yale University's libraries featured card catalog entries for the book, placed there by practical jokers. By the 1970s, several hoax editions of the *Necronomicon* were on the market, and the practitioners of black magic, the "Magickal" community, had embraced the book as a legitimate entry in their canon. Diabolists, too, embraced the *Necronomicon*'s hints of devilish doings beyond the visible world and they used the hoax editions in satanic rites and ceremonies. So convinced were they that it was real that by the turn of the millennium, the Church of Satan had to issue a statement refuting the existence of the book because so many of its adherents had believed it real.

Lovecraft believed that to be effective horror stories had to be put together with the same skill and attention to detail as a hoax, though unlike a hoax no one was supposed to believe fiction real. He incorporated the widely held beliefs in alternative archaeology and spiritualism in order to bring verisimilitude to his tales, but he did his job too well. Lovecraft was a man of science, an atheist and a materialist, so it is not without irony that he should become the father of an antiscientific, irrationalist tradition. While a hoax is fiction disguised as fact, many readers came to believe that Lovecraft's stories were fact disguised as fiction. Some actually came to believe that Lovecraft was drawing on legitimate ancient traditions and disguising them as fiction to communicate them in secret. This confusion would have deep consequences by midcentury, when some sought to *prove* that fiction was fact.

While this affliction never affected Lovecraft's circle of close friends, they chose to carry on what he called his "Yog-Sothothery" and spread the word about Cthulhu and his alien minions. Soon the whole world would know of the Old Ones and the cosmic fiction of Lovecraft, but, unfortunately, it did not work out exactly according to plan.

5

THE SPREAD OF THE LOVECRAFT CIRCLE

The Lovecraftian theme of aliens lurking in the distant past became a popular theme in the pulp literature of the 1920s, '30s, and '40s. Countless stories sprang up, seemingly from nowhere, with descriptions of the same set of dark legends of fantastic beings. Such diverse names as Clark Ashton Smith, Robert E. Howard, Hazel Heald, and Adolphe de Castro all seemed to be echoing this same and singular idea. In many of their stories, characters encountered the same monsters, the same dark books, and the same idea of extraterrestrials lurking in the distant past. Though to the untrained reader this seemed like a veritable florescence of this primitive version of the ancient-astronaut hypothesis in the minds of many distinct authors, the spread of the ancient-alien idea through fiction was the result of a very specific and premeditated attempt, an open conspiracy of sorts, to impregnate horror stories with a vision of cosmic horror. As with so many coincidences catalogued in this book, it all began in one of H. P. Lovecraft's flights of fancy.

H. P. Lovecraft was often poor and throughout his life had to scrimp to manage the lifestyle he thought that a gentleman of his social class deserved. The money he made from selling his stories barely covered his meager living expenses, even if he was perversely proud of subsisting on only fifteen cents a day during the Great Depression. As a consequence, Lovecraft was forced to take on additional work, and since he had a congenital hatred of paid labor, he took up the genteel art of ghostwriting, often for other aspiring writers of short horror fiction. Fortunately for Lovecraft, the height of the Great Depression also coincided with the florescence of the pulp fiction magazines. These provided Lovecraft with a steady, if not always ample, supply of work when he could bring himself to take it.

The years between the two world wars saw a rapid growth in cheap, mass-appeal magazines. Known as "the pulps" from the cheap paper they employed, these magazines promised worlds of adventure, romance, and horror, all on a price that even the out-of-work denizens of the Depression could enjoy. Beneath their lurid covers of scantily clad women, muscular men, and vague references to sadomasochistic sex, these magazines offered worlds of escape, even if the stories never quite met the covers' implicit promises.

Of course, their writing was often juvenile, but there were gems amid the trash. The most popular author of the early days, Seabury Quinn, was somewhere nearer the trashy end but defined the pulp style: competent but formulaic. Successors to the dime novels, like the comic books that would replace them, pulp magazines featured the full range of sensational stories that would become the bread-and-butter of modern American storytelling: heroes, damsels in distress, detectives, monsters, and above all else adventure. In their pages Edgar Rice Burroughs (of *Tarzan* fame) explored the outposts of Mars, and Robert Howard's Conan the Cimmerian stalked the Hyperborean landscapes. L. Ron Hubbard (later of Scientology) told grand space operas, and the prolific Quinn churned out volumes of strange tales. Titles like *Astounding Stories* and *Detective Tales* brought their readers new and exciting adventures each month.

The first and greatest of the pulp horror magazines was *Weird Tales*. Founded by J. C. Henneberger in 1923, *Weird Tales* offered its readers stories of horror, terror, and the bizarre during its thirty-year history.[1] It was this magazine that formed Lovecraft's primary creative outlet, housing most of what Lovecraft published in his lifetime. Lovecraft was once offered its editorship, though he turned it down, reportedly because it would have meant a move to Chicago. This was a move Lovecraft could not contemplate because the city did not have any buildings old enough to please his antiquarian tastes. Nevertheless, he continued to supply *Weird Tales* with stories throughout his life, and Lovecraft was paid the highest possible rate for his work, one and a half cents per word.[2]

Despite its cult status, *Weird Tales* was not immediately successful. For a time the magazine published irregularly, and its owners contemplated selling or closing it more than once. It was by accident that H. P. Lovecraft saved the magazine's sinking ship. Often near bankruptcy, *Weird Tales* earned a new lease on life when controversy struck one of Lovecraft's revisions. Called "The Loved Dead," the story appeared under the byline of C. M. Eddy and featured a gruesome and (for the time) explicit tale of necrophilia. Telling of a reclusive young man who develops an unnatural obsession with funerals and death, "The Loved Dead" shocked more conservative readers with its disturbing language. Describing his nights in Mr. Gresham's funeral home, the narrator explains what his love of the dead made him do:

> During long nights when I clung to the shelter of my sanctuary, I was prompted by the mausolean silence to devise new and unspeakable ways of lavishing my affection upon the dead that I loved—the dead that gave me life! One morning Mr. Gresham came much earlier than usual—came to find me stretched out on a cold slab deep in ghoulish

slumber, my arms wrapped about the stark, stiff, naked body of a foetid corpse![3]

Outraged readers demanded that this affront to the social mores be destroyed. The issue was ripped from newsstands in some locations, and an effort was made to ban the magazine. However, like many such attempts at prohibition of vice, this effort was a miserable failure and only made people want to read the offending material with greater zeal than had it been ignored. The resulting notoriety made *Weird Tales* popular (and profitable) once more. Sales went up, and Lovecraft gained a larger audience. Some of that audience decided that it wanted in on the action.

In the years before television, reading was still considered a form of popular entertainment, and the pulps appealed to a mass audience. Though they were hardly great literature, they carried on the tradition of the "penny-dreadfuls" and other mass-marketed writing. Written in a direct, entertaining style, their stories were designed to provide escape from the hard world of everyday life, not a highbrow literary experience. As a result, the pulps had a much broader audience than the contemporary literary fiction of F. Scott Fitzgerald or Virginia Woolf. For many in the middle class, writing had become a hobby, and publishing a sensational story in *Weird Tales* was something of a parlor game. It impressed society friends and showed that the writer was a true published author. Getting into the pulps was easy enough, and it gave aspiring authors a place to send their compositions.

Unfortunately, not all of these would-be authors could write, and when they couldn't many went to H. P. Lovecraft. His ghostwriting career, like so much in his life, came about partly as a deus ex machina. As early as 1924, *Weird Tales* had Lovecraft ghostwriting for Harry Houdini, the magician famous both for his escape act as well as his relentless exposure of fake psychic mediums and all forms of fraud conducted by the Spiritualist movement. Spiritualism had become immensely popular in the maddening years following the disaster of 1914 and the deaths of so many millions. With the end of a belief in Progress and progressivism, Spiritualism had satisfied the primitive urge during times of stress to seek solace and meaning in the irrational and supernatural. Houdini bravely opposed this trend and sought to expose the trickery and fakery the Spiritualists used to deceive the bereaved into believing that the dead could talk to the living. Ironically, despite Houdini's efforts, belief in psychic mediums as conduits to the deceased continued into the twenty-first century unabated.[4] However, more as a result of his magic tricks than his debunking, Harry Houdini had become a household name.

Houdini had contracted with *Weird Tales* to write a monthly column, "Ask Houdini," but it appeared only once. However, in a strange confusion of fact and fiction, the debunker Houdini had an idea for a supposedly true ghost tale, and he came up with the basic outline for a horror story to run under his byline. *Weird Tales* editor J. C. Henneberger knew Houdini knew nothing about writing, so he suggested that Houdini "collaborate" with Lovecraft.[5] Taking on the story without consulting the famous magician, Lovecraft turned in a manuscript. In the resulting story, "Imprisoned with the Pharaohs,"[6] Houdini investigates an evil survival of the ancient Egyptian faith in the catacombs beneath the pyramids. There he uncovers a carnival of horrors, including the weird half-human, half-animal gods of the Egyptians. Of course, something survived . . .

Lovecraft had written the whole thing with no input from Houdini beyond the initial outline and molded it to fit his own imagination.

Clearly, Lovecraft was not shy about incorporating his own themes into his ghostwriting, both for Houdini and for the many other authors who went to him for help. As a result, many of the resulting revisions appearing under others' bylines bore strong traces of Lovecraft's cosmic themes and traces of his Cthulhu mythology. He said he did this for "sheer fun" and enjoyed leaving a distinctive mark on the work he touched. Yet the Cthulhu, Nyarlathotep, and their kin did not appear under their own names in these stories. Lovecraft was uncomfortable using his own creations in stories not appearing under his name, so he modified his creations and offered a parallel or distorted vision of them for the ghostwritten tales. This both protected Lovecraft's own fiction from dilution and added another layer of reality to his mythology. Just like real myths, this affectation of Lovecraft's produced variants that enriched his fictional tradition. Adding to the realism, these variants were usually mentioned only briefly and in passing, as though they referenced something real and familiar that needed no explanation.

In the story "Winged Death," appearing under Hazel Heald's byline, explorer Thomas Slauenwite is lost in the jungle with only guides of the Galla tribe to assist him when he encounters rumors of the Old Ones:

> In one spot we came upon a trace of Cyclopean ruins which made even the Gallas run past in a wide circle. They say these megaliths are older than man, and that they used to be a haunt or outpost of "The Fishers from Outside"—whatever that means—and of the evil gods Tsadogwa and Clulu.[7]

Here, Lovecraft altered the names of the evil deities Cthulhu and Tsathoggua for this revision. The Cthulhu is here referred to as "Clulu," and "Tsadogwa" was a respelling of Clark Ashton Smith's creation, the alien toad entity Tsathoggua.

This accomplished two things: first, it separated these stories from Lovecraft's own because he considered revision work to be hack work and his own stories to be his true art. Second, it added another level of verisimilitude to his rapidly expanding pantheon of deities. If other stories referred to slightly different versions of a legend, then it seems more realistic than if each version were the same. Much the way the chief Norse god went by either Woden or Odin, or the Mexican savior as Quetzalcoatl or Kukulkán, Cthulhu acquired variants. Just as true myths and legends had alternate versions, now stories appearing under other names would contain different versions of Lovecraft's fictitious legend of alien visitors. The stories "The Horror in the Museum," "The Man of Stone," and "Out of the Aeons" appeared under Heald's byline and contained other altered traces of the Cthulhu Mythos. "The Mound" and "The Curse of Yig" under Zelia Bishop's name furthered this concept. Other revision work for C. M. Eddy and Adolphe de Castro contained hints of Cthulhu themes, though often only as minor color with little relevance to the plot. Of note, "Out of the Aeons" tells the story of a mummy and its relationship to both the lost continent of Mu and the planet of Yuggoth, the lately discovered Pluto. Lovecraft enjoyed incorporating real science to back up his fictional conceit. By the last years of his life, Lovecraft had stopped describing the backdrop of his mythology and simply stated it explicitly, assuming readers were casually familiar with the idea.

In the 1935 William Lumley–H. P. Lovecraft tale "The Diary of Alonzo Typer," a personal favorite, the title character encounters the *Necronomicon* and the other Lovecraftian grimoires in an old house. To add verisimilitude to the tale, Lovecraft employs Helena Blavatsky's *Book of Dzyan*, "whose first six chapters antedate man, and which was old when the lords of Venus came through space in their ships to civilize our planet."[8] Could the ancient-astronaut theory have been stated any more bluntly, or its relationship to the pseudoscience that preceded it?

By the time Lovecraft died in 1937, he had added his distinctive touch to more than two dozen stories by other authors, though the exact number may never be known because Lovecraft allowed all the revisions to appear under the original authors' names, and some may never be identified. Arkham House later collected the stories as *The Horror in the Museum and Other Revisions*.

But revisions weren't the only place where Lovecraft's ideas blossomed. Other authors were taken by the Cthulhu and his cousins. While Lovecraft was never proud of the revisions he produced and considered most of them substandard hackwork unworthy of his mythological creatures, he always encouraged his friends to utilize concepts he created in their own stories, and he would use some of their creations in his own. They were producing art after all. This group of correspondents, fans and fellow authors both, became known as the Lovecraft Circle in later years, and they continued producing fiction with elements borrowed from Lovecraft long after his death. As we saw in the last chapter, this borrowing led many to conclude that such Lovecraftian creations as the *Necronomicon* were real since so many seemingly independent authors seemed to refer to it. Despite fervent denials, this acceptance never abated. Ominously, this first wave of belief despite Lovecraft's protests would foreshadow the later rise of the ancient-astronaut theory.

But for now, the Lovecraft Circle sent one another manuscripts of new stories. A prolific letter-writer, Lovecraft wrote something on the order of one hundred thousand letters to his correspondents,[9] and he used many of these letters to flesh out his mythos and share it with aspiring authors, collaborators, and friends. These correspondents became some of the most famous and best-loved authors of the pulp era, and many are still household names today. Clark Ashton Smith, Robert E. Howard, Frank Belknap Long, Robert Bloch, and August Derleth all were part of the Lovecraft Circle, and all played an important role in transmitting Lovecraft's vision from the pulp era to today. If not for them, Lovecraft's stories would never have found their way into the hands of those who would use them to create the ancient-astronaut theory.

An early correspondent, Clark Ashton Smith was among the first to adopt Lovecraftian imagery into his own work. Smith was a poet who lived in Auburn, California, and fancied himself an artist, though his paintings were never as good as his literary endeavors. Like Lovecraft, Smith was a self-educated autodidact. Much of his poetry touched on the same cosmic weirdness that Lovecraft evoked, and occasionally Smith would put the same magic into prose. However, Smith disliked prose and insisted that he wrote it only to earn the money necessary to subsidize his poetry and his painting. He first made contact with Lovecraft when Lovecraft wrote him a fan letter in 1922 after seeing some of his poetry. They wrote to each other until Lovecraft's death in 1937, sharing nearly every aspect of their lives with one another. As a sign of warm familiarity, Lovecraft called Smith "Klarkash-Ton," joking that in a past life Smith was an Atlantean high priest. He would later incorporate the name into his fictional universe. Lovecraft was "Ech-Pi-El," an Atlantean version of his initials, HPL. It was Lovecraft who suggested Smith try writing prose.[10]

Composed by a gifted writer, Clark's prose reads like literary poetry. His stories sparkle with the music of the spheres, and he used language in a way that transports the reader body and soul to another, more fantastic realm. Unlike Lovecraft, who grounded his stories in a stylized version of decadent New England, Smith unabashedly set many of his stories in fantasy realms, including ancient Hyperborea, the land beyond the Arctic, where the ancients held that a great civilization once existed; Averoigne, a medieval French province ruled by powers not of this earth; and Zothique, the final continent remaining in the last days before the destruction of the earth, somewhere in the distant future. In this way, Smith very much followed the form of fantasy, but he occasionally strayed into Lovecraft's territory. And in nearly all of his weird fiction, he utilized the Lovecraftian mythology as a backdrop to his own tales. Now and again he wrote truly Lovecraftian tales set in the present.

One of his few stories set on the modern earth, Smith's "Return of the Sorcerer" appeared in *Strange Tales* in September 1931. By then, Smith and Lovecraft had been corresponding regularly for nine years, and Smith's stories had begun to show Lovecraft's unmistakable fingerprints. In "Sorcerer," his first story to use Lovecraftian imagery, a man named Ogden arrives to become secretary for John Carnby, whom he does not yet know is a sorcerer. In Carnby's home, he discovers the *Necronomicon*: "I had heard of this rare, well-nigh fabulous volume, but had never seen it. The book was supposed to contain the ultimate secrets of evil and forbidden knowledge; and moreover, the original text, written by the mad Arab, Abdul Alhazred, was said to be unprocurable."[11]

The sorcerer details the book's history, and Smith makes use of the details of the *Necronomicon*, which Lovecraft set down for other authors to use in a 1927 essay, usually published as "A History and Chronology of the *Necronomicon*." Not published until 1938, Lovecraft circulated it to friends for consistency in referencing the book in their stories. By his reckoning, the *Necronomicon* was the product of the mad Arab, who wrote the book in the early Dark Ages. The Church suppressed the many medieval translations in Greek and Latin, and only a handful of copies yet remain locked away in libraries.

In "Return of the Sorcerer," Ogden and Carnby engage in some disturbing behavior involving a dismembered corpse. Like Lovecraft's own heroes, Smith's Ogden becomes scared beyond measure and flees into the night. Though the story is not overtly connected to the Cthulhu Mythos save through the *Necronomicon*, "Return of the Sorcerer" became one of only a handful of Lovecraftian stories that Rod Serling included in *The Night Gallery*. That episode, starring Vincent Price, aired on September 24, 1972.[12]

In November 1931, Smith published "The Tale of Satampra Zeiros," which introduced one of his two most important contributions to the growing body of Cthulhu fiction: Tsathoggua, the toad god. The story describes the journey of a Paleolithic priest to an old temple where the toad god was worshiped:

> I had never seen an image of Tsathoggua before, but I recognized him without difficulty from the descriptions I had heard. He was very squat and pot-bellied, his head was more like that of a monstrous toad than a deity, and his whole body was covered with an imitation of short fur, giving somehow a vague suggestion of both the bat and the sloth.[13]

Appearing in nine Smith stories under various spellings (like Lovecraft, Smith liked the idea of variants), Tsathoggua became one of the most recognizable alien entities. Lovecraft borrowed him for inclusion in some of his own stories. One suspects that unlike the unpronounceable Cthulhu or the juvenile-sounding Yog-Sothoth, the *sound* of the name *Tsathoggua*, with its juxtaposed sibilant and guttural syllables, contributed much to his (her?) success. The name certainly sounds like a monster.

Smith's other major addition to Lovecraft's mythology was the *Book of Eibon*, also called the *Liber Ivonis*, as his own counterpart to the *Necronomicon*. Like that book, Smith's volume was another grimoire and compendium of elder mysteries. Containing primal secrets, the *Book of Eibon* was said to have descended only in translation upon translation from the original written in the long-ago land of Hyperborea. Introduced in July 1933's edition of *Weird Tales* in a story called "Ubbo-Sathla," the *Book of Eibon* acts as a conduit through which the character Paul Tregardis is able to unlock the secret of a strange object recently uncovered in Greenland. Tregardis merges into a Hyperborean magician and degenerates into the primal void. In this tale, the Lovecraftian conventions are all present: there is a mysterious archaeological find, cryptic references in ancient texts, and, of course, a squishy, formless monster. After the publication of "Ubbo-Sathla," Smith would use the *Book of Eibon* just twice more, but taking its place alongside Lovecraft's own grimoire, the *Book of Eibon* entered into Lovecraft's works and the works of others in the Lovecraft circle who would reference it in ways Smith never imagined in his most fevered dreams of cosmic horror.

A prolific author, Clark Ashton Smith had published fifty-two stories borrowing themes from the Cthulhu Mythos by the time Lovecraft died. By his own death in 1961, Smith had produced more than sixty-five Mythos stories. Fellow author Lin Carter completed nine of Smith's unfinished tales for posthumous publication.[14] Among these stories are many that covered all of Smith's leitmotifs: Hyperborea, Averoigne, and Zothique. Among these tales, there are several that stand out. If not his best tales, "The Mandrakes" and "The Maze of Maal Dweb" are certainly among his most entertaining Cthulhu-themed tales.

Another of Lovecraft's correspondents was the creator of Conan the Cimmerian, Robert Ervin Howard. Born in 1906, Howard's brief career produced some of the pulp era's best-loved tales, notably his Conan cycle, made (in)famous by Arnold Schwarzenegger's campy cinematic version. Conan, of course, was the barbarian king of Hyperborea, fighting epic battles in the deep mythic past of twelve thousand years ago. This Hyperborea was very different than Clark Ashton Smith's version, for it is less civilized and more adventurous. Neither version, though, had much to do with the Greco-Roman Hyperborea, the warm land beyond the north wind where the people lived in endless peace and bliss. Conan would not recognize that land, nor would Smith's worshipers of Tsathoggua.

His most famous work, Conan came to dominate Howard's literary legacy. Author L. Sprague de Camp noted that nearly any of Howard's tales could be rewritten as a Conan story, since they nearly all featured the same themes and a nearly identical main character. This was clear to all who knew Howard, since it was clear that all the characters were idealized versions of Howard himself.[15] A prolific writer, his fiction seemed to serve as therapeutic wish fulfillment for the young man longing for adventures that he could never have.

Howard favored masculine heroes who embodied the noble virtues of the manly ideal. In the style of Friedrich Nietzsche, he looked for the Aryan Superman as the ultimate ideal of human existence. This was a man's world heavily influenced by the rough-and-ready ethos of the Texas that Howard called home. He almost never left the dusty town of Cross Plains, Texas, but his mind was never confined by small-town provincialism. Like H. P. Lovecraft and Clark Ashton Smith, Howard was an autodidact, teaching himself history and writing. Unlike Lovecraft and Smith, Howard was also an athlete and sports fanatic. Where Lovecraft and Smith were gaunt aesthetes, Howard was a burly boxer. In between bouts of exercise, Howard found time to write more than two hundred short stories in nearly every available genre. Significantly, he was one of the few early Cthulhu writers to make any real money writing fiction.

Lovecraft began correspondence with Robert Howard in August 1930, after Howard heard some surprising news about a story he had published the previous winter. Called "Skull-Face," the oriental mystery borrowed heavily from Sax Rhomer's classic 1913 novel *The Insidious Dr. Fu-Manchu* and its sequels. In it, the protagonists face off against the evil criminal mastermind Skull-Face, whose real name is given as Kathulos. Howard's Aryan superhero, Stephen Costigan, battles the "yellow peril," and makes the world safe for white civilization to flourish once more. The "yellow peril" genre was popular in the first part of the twentieth century, when the British Empire feared the rise of Asian nations, whose large numbers could theoretically overrun the white man's colonies in Asia. By the time Howard wrote his take on the genre, Imperial Japan was starting to stir, and within a few years the prophecies of Rhomer and Howard would prove prescient.

Howard was surprised to read in the letters section of *Weird Tales*, called "The Eyrie," that his Kathulos was surprisingly similar to another author's creation, a certain "Cthulhu" from some years earlier. Not only were the names similar, but so were the mythological underpinnings. Lovecraft described in "The Call of Cthulhu" the sad predicament of the Old Ones and their high priest, the alien Cthulhu. The Cthulhu cultists chanted, "In his house at R'lyeh, dead Cthulhu waits dreaming." Their belief was simple:

> When the stars were right, They could plunge from world to world through the sky; but when the stars were wrong, They could not live. But although They no longer lived, They would never really die. They all lay in stone houses in Their great city of R'lyeh, preserved by the spells of mighty Cthulhu for the glorious resurrection when the stars and the earth might once more be ready for them. . . . They could only lie awake in the dark and think whilst uncounted millions of years rolled by. . . . The great stone city of R'lyeh, with its monoliths and sepulchers, had sunk beneath the waves. . . . But memory never died, and high priests said that the city would rise again when the stars were right.[16]

Almost beyond belief, Howard independently created an identical myth for the primal powers whom the archvillain Kathulos served:

> Under the green seas they lie, the ancient masters, in their lacquered cases, dead as men reckon death, but only sleeping.

Sleeping through the long days as hours, awaiting the day of awakening! The old masters, the wise men, who foresaw the day when the sea would gulp the land, and who made ready. Made ready that they might rise again in the barbaric days to come. . . . Sleeping they lie, ancient kings and grim wizards, who died as men die before Atlantis sank. Who, sleeping, sank with her, but who shall rise again![17]

The similarities were striking, so it was easy to see how by mistake a casual reader would conclude that both authors were drawing on the same source material. Howard was at a loss to explain how such similarities could arise by coincidence; nevertheless, he felt compelled to offer some type of explanation. Howard wrote to Cthulhu's creator to explain the situation:

I have noted in your stories you refer to Cthulhu, Yog-Sothoth, R'lyeh, Yuggoth, etc. . . . A writer in "The Eyrie," a Mr. O'Neail, I believe, wondered if I did not use some myth regarding this Cthulhu in "Skull-Face." The name Kathulos might suggest that, but in reality I merely manufactured the name at random, not being aware at the time of any legendary character named Cthulhu—if indeed there is.[18]

Even at this early date, just four years after the publication of "The Call of Cthulhu," we can see that the line between fact and fiction had begun to blur. Clearly, this Mr. O'Neail bought into the Cthulhu myth and believed it real, ready to give credence both to Lovecraft's monster and Howard's criminal as genuine survivals of an ancient myth. The scope of the coincidental similarity made this mistake excusable. Even Howard was at first unsure whether the Cthulhu was entirely a fictional creation, an ominous sign for the years and decades to come.

However, Lovecraft quickly set the young author straight, and the two became fast friends, though they never met in person. On August 14, 1930, he wrote Howard to say, "It would be rather amusing to identify your Kathulos with my Cthulhu —indeed, I may so adopt him in some future black allusion."[19] Both authors went on to identify Kathulos as a Greek transliteration of Cthulhu's unpronounceable name, and the term appeared in both men's stories. Atlantis, by extension, served either as an outpost of the Old Ones or a convenient cover for darker allusions to primal R'lyeh.

Lovecraft called Howard "Two-Gun Bob" in his letters, making light of both Howard's Texas roots and his fiery personality, since the two often argued over whether Lovecraft's beloved English or Howard's Irish were the superior race.[20] Howard kept up his correspondence with Lovecraft through the 1930s, a time when Howard grew increasingly depressed and paranoid. Though he seemed in his letters to be in generally good spirits, there were ominous hints that went unnoticed. Deeply devoted to his mother, Howard committed suicide on June 11, 1936, after his cancer-stricken mother slipped into a terminal coma. He was only thirty years old.[21]

In the six years of his friendship with Lovecraft, Robert Howard produced a number of stories expanding on the fictional Cthulhu mythology. Despite his posthumous legacy as a pulp fiction icon, Howard was never able to master the truly trashy side of pulp fiction. Unlike his contemporaries, he had a hard time churning out hack work. As the critic and admirer of all things Cthuhhu, Robert M. Price observed, "Howard could write epic masterpieces . . . but he couldn't quite stoop to a good potboiler."[22] Fortunately for posterity, this meant his surviving stories are of a much greater literary quality than the vast majority of the pulps' usual output.

One of his first and probably his best was "The Black Stone," published in *Weird Tales* in November 1931. The story tells of a man's excursion to the Black Stone of Hungary, an ancient monolith covered in unreadable hieroglyphs older than even archaeology can recognize. The horror of the tale comes when the narrator realizes that the archaeological mystery is not all that lies buried in Hungary's soil and that the monolith is only a part of a larger horror . . .

In "The Black Stone" and its predecessor, "The Children of the Night," Howard introduced a new tome to parallel Lovecraft's *Necronomicon* and Smith's *Book of Eibon*. Since it was something of the rage to have one's own grimoire, Howard created *Nameless Cults* by Friedrich Wilhelm von Junzt, though it was Lovecraft who supplied von Junzt's Christian names and another writer, August Derleth, who gave *Nameless Cults* its "original" German name, *Unaussprechlichen Kulten*. Supposedly written by the mad German von Junzt, *Nameless Cults* was rumored to contain dark secrets of hidden things. The original versions were lost in centuries past, and only a recent, though expurgated translation was currently available. In its made-up bibliography, *Cults* creates a convincing false reality akin to the *Necronomicon* itself. While making for great literature, this convincing background only helped to perpetuate the illusion that the *Weird Tales* authors were drawing on genuine ancient myths and legends.

Together, H. P. Lovecraft, Clark Ashton Smith, and Robert E. Howard became known as the "Three Musketeers of *Weird Tales*," and their writing propelled the magazine through the 1930s, spearheading the burgeoning pulp industry.[23] Eventually, their stories surpassed in popularity those of Seabury Quinn, then the reigning pulp writer for *Weird Tales*. As the years went on, Lovecraft attracted more correspondents, fans, and admirers. Many of these joined the "Lovecraft Circle" and began to incorporate Lovecraftian themes into their own stories.

Frank Belknap Long was born in 1901 and became a correspondent when Lovecraft read one of Long's stories in 1921. Lovecraft thought Long a new Poe and recommended him to the editor of *Weird Tales*, who bought most of what Long produced from the magazine's founding in 1923 until Lovecraft's death in 1937. Thereafter, Long continued to publish in science fiction magazines and went on to write more than three hundred stories and thirty novels, mostly science fiction, before his death in 1994.[24]

During his early phase he wrote horror in the Lovecraftian vein. His first Lovecraftian story, "The Space-Eaters," featured aliens that ate human brains. In the story, published in the July 1928 *Weird Tales*, Long mistakenly attributes authorship of Alhazred's *Necronomicon* to Dr. John Dee, court astrologer to Elizabeth I. Lovecraft later had to make Dee the English translator of the book to keep his mythology on track. The *Weird Tales* for March 1929 carried Long's most important Mythos horror story, "The Hounds of Tindalos." In that story, a researcher uses consciousness-enhancing drugs to plumb the depths of the universe, only to discover that the powers from Outside have ways to protect themselves. Long was among the first of Lovecraft's friends to drastically depart from the fantasy/horror mode, carving out a new style that would become modern science fiction, though a science fiction largely free of Cthulhu and his kin. One of Long's editors, John W. Campbell of *Astounding Stories*, published some of Lovecraft's longer fiction as serials after Lovecraft's death, and he based one of his stories on *At the Mountains of Madness*. As we shall see, that novella would lead to a veritable wave of alien-themed science fiction–horror movies in the 1950s.

While Long and Lovecraft had corresponded for almost fifteen years, in the last years of his life Lovecraft made new friends. One of these was a young Milwaukee author named Robert Bloch, born in 1917, who was still a teenager when he first wrote to Lovecraft in 1933. Under Lovecraft's guidance, Bloch began writing weird fiction, first seeing publication in 1934.[25] Bloch wrote relatively little in the Cthulhu style. His story of weird goings-on in a church, "The Shambler from the Stars," was part of a playful literary tit-for-tat with Lovecraft, who wrote "The Haunter of the Dark" in response. Each author killed off the other's literary alter-ego in a gruesome way, invoking the aliens from Outside. Bloch returned to Lovecraftian themes in the 1950s, just before he found success with his best-known novel, *Psycho*, which he adapted for the screen for director Alfred Hitchcock. Bloch departed from traditional supernatural horror and pioneered a new form of horror based on abnormal, but very human, psychology. *Psycho*'s Norman Bates may be scary, but he was no extraterrestrial monster.

One of Lovecraft's other young correspondents played a far more vital role in perpetuating his legacy after 1937, though a role that Bloch and many others considered highly controversial.

A Wisconsinite like Bloch, August W. Derleth was born to a Catholic family in 1909 in Sauk City, later moving to Madison. By the mid-1920s he had begun corresponding with Lovecraft about weird fiction following publication of his first professional short story in 1926. In 1930, Derleth took his bachelor's degree in English on the strength of a thesis cribbed from Lovecraft's *Supernatural Horror in Literature*.[26] By the mid-1930s, Derleth had begun writing many pulp stories in various genres, and he published the first of his three thousand works. Notable during this period was the early story "The Thing That Walked on the Wind," which introduced the Native American legend of the wendigo, or wind walker, to the Mythos canon. However, during Lovecraft's lifetime, Derleth was more content to bask in Lovecraft's reflected glory rather than write much of importance in the Lovecraftian style. Derleth offered to type Lovecraft's manuscripts, a task Lovecraft loathed, and he constantly encouraged a recalcitrant Lovecraft to revise rejected stories for publication. Ironically, it was Derleth who would have more influence over Lovecraft's legacy than any of his other friends.

Something of a pompous man with a wide face and burly body, Derleth tried to maintain a mask of literary respectability over the more tawdry pulp stories that he considered trashy entertainment. Writing in his autobiography, Derleth proudly related his literary heroes: "My literary influences, apart from Thoreau, were Thomas Hardy, Edgar Lee Masters, and Robert Frost, and, in work written purely [for] entertainment, H. P. Lovecraft and Sir Arthur Conan Doyle."[27] Derleth piously forgot to mention that his first serious income came from the sale of stories written in imitation of Doyle, the so-called Solar Pons mysteries, and his first success came in appropriating the legacy of Lovecraft. That he placed them so far down on his list only demonstrated how badly he wanted to fit in with a mainstream that had not yet discovered Lovecraft.

At his death, Lovecraft named Robert Barlow as his literary executor, but since the office had no legal standing, Lovecraft's literary property reverted to his heir: his aunt, Annie Gamwell. Lovecraft had granted to August Derleth the right to publish previously unpublished stories for a proposed anthology, and Derleth began compiling his mentor's stories with fellow Lovecraft correspondent Donald Wandrei, with whom Lovecraft had written a short story. The two first submitted their anthology to Charles Scribner's Sons, Derleth's own publisher, but the firm rejected the idea. Next they tried Simon & Schuster, whose editor suggested that the two publish the book themselves.[28] They decided after deliberation that the editor's suggestion was the only way to bring Lovecraft to the world.

The two formed a new firm to publish the book, and they named it Arkham House after the fictional Massachusetts town appearing in many of Lovecraft's tales. In 1939 Arkham House made its debut with *The Outsider and Others*, a collection of thirty-six Lovecraft tales and the essay *Supernatural Horror in Literature*. It did not sell very well, nor did its sequel, *Beyond the Wall of Sleep*. However, Arkham House soldiered on, publishing other weird fiction by other pulp authors (Smith and Howard included) and some classic authors like Algernon Blackwood.

After Annie Gamwell's death in 1941, Derleth claimed Lovecraft's literary legacy as his own property and enforced his control through lawsuits. The company made a modest profit and began to attract new authors who had begun writing in the Cthulhu Mythos framework. Eventually, Arkham House became a clearinghouse for Mythos fiction in particular and weird fiction in general, publishing several anthologies of Mythos tales and putting in print all of Lovecraft's fiction as well as selections from his voluminous letters. Later Arkham House editions of Lovecraft's fiction sold better than their overlong first editions, and Derleth's anthologies helped to secure Lovecraft's posthumous recognition as one of America's foremost horror authors. As Robert Bloch noted, "[O]ne single fact remains all important—he championed the revival of interest in Lovecraft's work. Derleth continued to keep the stories in print, reissuing portions of the collections under other titles."[29]

But Derleth's efforts to bolster Lovecraft's legacy were often controversial. In 1945, Derleth published a novel called *The Lurker at the Threshold*, which he claimed was a "posthumous collaboration" between himself and the long-dead Lovecraft. Writing in a pastiche of Lovecraft's style, Derleth wove together a few leftover ideas from Lovecraft's notebooks and a few unfinished text fragments into a novel, almost entirely written by Derleth. He then published several additional short stories under the title of "posthumous collaborations" with increasingly little contribution from Lovecraft's remaining notebooks. Some critics of Derleth consider these "collaborations" a type of literary fraud that sullies Lovecraft's name.[30]

Derleth also changed the way Lovecraft's creatures were depicted. Whereas Lovecraft had no set system for his entities and saw them as extraterrestrial (or transdimensional) beings living their own lives without consideration for humanity, Derleth saw in them the Aristotelian elements: earth, water, air, and fire. He divided them according to their elements. He rather fairly placed Shub-Niggurath, the Black Goat of the Woods, as an earth elemental. But he assigned Cthulhu to the water, despite the clear indication in Lovecraft's original story that Cthulhu is trapped by the water "through which not even thought can pass," a pretty tough life for a water elemental whose "mode of speech was transmitted thought."[31] When he could find no Lovecraftian monsters for the air or fire, he created them from nothing, inventing Ithaqua the Wind-Walker and Cthugha the fire elemental.

Worse, Derleth attempted to force Lovecraft's creations into his own theological framework. Derleth was born and raised Catholic and continued to hold strong Christian beliefs his whole life. When he began to think about Lovecraft's amoral and material cosmic vision, he started to see patterns that were never there. Where Lovecraft had created material entities that represented self-interested extraterrestrial powers, Derleth instead saw a very Christian world of Good versus Evil.

Writing in his autobiography, Derleth disclaimed any influence of Catholicism on his writing: "I have never thought of myself as a Catholic author, but rather only as a writer who is Catholic, and, apart from a novel in progress . . . have made little attempt at Catholic writing."[32] Nevertheless, Derleth imposed the Christian duality of good and evil onto the Lovecraft framework, for which he coined the term "The Cthulhu Mythos," a term that stuck and now describes the body of work by Lovecraft and his emulators.

He divided Lovecraft's nebulous concept of the Old Ones/Ancient Ones/Elder Gods into a set of binary opposites: the Old Ones and the Elder Gods. The Old Ones were the Lovecraftian monsters like Cthulhu, Nyarlathotep, Azathoth, and the other transdimensional horrors of Lovecraft's fiction. No longer indifferent to mankind, Derleth made them evil. From a slight hint from Lovecraft that some primal entities, like the Celtic god Nodens, stood apart from the Old Ones, Derleth created from whole cloth a group of Elder Gods who were on the side of cosmic good. Thus recast, the Great Cthulhu's imprisonment in R'lyeh under the waves was no longer a random act of a changing planet but instead was the "true" origin of the myth of Satan. In this version, the Elder Gods set their seal on Cthulhu and imprisoned him in R'lyeh for defying their will (or sometimes given as conspiring to overthrow the Elder Ones) instead of Lovecraft's vision of Cthulhu protecting the Old Ones from a changing relationship between earth and stars.

This quixotic interpretation unintentionally set a strange precedent: if religious stories could be explained (even fictionally) as alien interventions, perhaps it would follow that religious history was the history of aliens on Earth. Derleth, however, did not explore this concept. That was for others to pick up. Derleth was too concerned with the battle of Good versus Evil for control of the earth.

After *The Lurker at the Threshold*, Derleth published additional "collaborations" with Lovecraft through the 1950s, stories like "The Lamp of Alhazred" and "The Shadow Out of Space." When he ran out of Lovecraft fragments and notes to build upon, he wrote in his own name, eventually publishing several Cthulhu-themed novels, including 1958's *The Mask of Cthulhu* and 1962's *The Trail of Cthulhu*. These were not terribly good stories or books, but they were competent and entertaining in the style of the bygone days of pulp fiction. But as Robert Bloch noted of his fellow author, "his attempts to convey the essence of Lovecraft's style didn't come off; he sounded the notes but lost the music."[33] August Derleth died in 1961, still claiming control over the Lovecraft legacy, a legacy that he shaped and in so doing helped to shape the ancient-astronaut theory still to come.

Derleth's largest contribution to the ancient-astronaut theory came by accident only a few years after he founded his publishing house, when he attempted to do his patriotic duty and help the American war effort as well as buy some free publicity for Arkham House. With the advent of World War II, American troops spread across the globe, and they took their reading material with them. Cut off from their usual forms of recreation by war, weather, and unfamiliarity with foreign languages, soldiers began to read. Even those who had rarely picked up a book quickly became habitual readers as a way to pass the time and find entertainment and escape.[34] The War Department's Army Special Services Division put out a series of Armed Services Edition books starting in 1943 to occupy troops during wartime. Fantasy, horror, and science fiction titles were among the most popular reads, though the number of such titles was small at first compared with the output of Westerns and mysteries.[35] In all, 123 million paperbound books were distributed to America's overseas forces until the program was discontinued in 1947.

Since thrilling stories and collections of recent short stories were in the highest demand overseas, it was a natural fit for Lovecraft to find his place alongside *Dracula, Frankenstein,* and *The War of the Worlds.* Derleth created a paperback anthology of Lovecraft for an Armed Services Edition in 1945 called *The Dunwich Horror and Other Weird Tales.* It garnered tremendous popularity wherever it was distributed and encouraged the publication of Lovecraft's stories in the foreign press, especially in France.[36] There a pair of Frenchmen would encounter Lovecraft for the first time. Their discovery of the "Gentleman from Providence" would lead directly to the formation of the ancient-astronaut theory. But that still lay in the future. In the meantime, a new postwar phenomenon had taken over the skies of 1947.

6

THE UFO CRAZE
IN FACT AND FICTION

The year the Army discontinued its Armed Services Editions the world saw the rise of a new phenomenon: the unidentified flying object. Long in the making, the UFO craze of the summer of 1947 owed its genesis to a unique intersection of fact and fiction stretching back into the nineteenth century. Parallel developments in science and the arts conspired to create a modern mythology to fill the void that the retreat of religious belief left behind. Seemingly factual events dovetailed into developments in cinema, radio, and literature, and from this nexus was born the modern belief in UFOs. It served as a prototype for the acceptance that a related but equally extraordinary belief, ancient astronauts, would receive two decades later.

In the spring of 1947 came the first reports of unidentified flying discs hovering over America. An Idaho businessman named Kenneth Arnold was flying a Callair airplane near Mount Ranier, Washington, on June 24, 1947, in search of a downed plane and a big reward when he saw something unusual in the skies. He saw a bright flash; then, looking out his plane's cockpit windows, Arnold saw what he said were nine arc-shaped craft in the sky. They glided in a column for a time and then shot off at incomprehensible speeds, which he estimated at 1,200 miles per hour. Their method of flight, he said, "was like a saucer would if you skipped it across water." Building on Arnold's report, a journalist covering the story minted a new term for these strange objects, the "flying saucer."[1] This sensational story was the first reported sighting of an unidentified flying object to receive wide press coverage in the modern era. Of course, it would not be the last.

The public was instantly taken by this amazing new technological apotheosis. Much the way the ancients saw visions of Apollo or fairies, modern people began to see mechanical angels over their own heads. Following the Arnold sighting, others began reporting similar sightings, all claiming to see the same flying saucers on or about the same time Arnold saw his. On June 25, saucer sightings had spread across the western United States. Within days, Canada, New Zealand, and Australia all reported their own sightings of flying discs traveling in formation. Sightings continued into July amid a fury of intense newspaper coverage of this new phenomenon.[2]

Just after the Fourth of July weekend, the residents of Roswell, New Mexico, allegedly were witness to the first documented crash of one of these extraterrestrial spacecraft. Though like any folklore there are varying versions of the story, it is generally said that at least one alien spacecraft crash-landed just outside of Roswell on July 7. The United States Army was dispatched to recover the wreckage as well as the bodies of the small, thin creatures that were inside. The material and the bodies were taken to the military base in Roswell, the same base that was home to the *Enola Gay*, the plane that had dropped the first nuclear bomb used in war on Hiroshima just two years earlier.

Many eventually speculated that the aliens were attracted to Roswell because of the nuclear connection, and the same people speculated that the Roswell wreckage was taken either to Wright-Patterson Air Force Base in Dayton, Ohio, or to the mysterious Area 51 in Nevada, where scientists reverse-engineered its technology to give the United States an advantage in the cold war. But much of this speculation arose in the 1970s, long after memories of the event had become confused and distorted by time. In 1947, all that was known to the general public was that one of the flying saucers had crashed.

The local newspaper in Roswell printed a banner headline the next day proclaiming the capture of a "flying disc." The following day the military announced that the wreckage was in fact a weather balloon.[3] Many refused to believe the military version of events, but the continuing story caused only a minor stir outside of New Mexico after most of the public accepted the weather balloon story. As the years went by, conspiracy theorists and UFO enthusiasts would build on the legend of Roswell, but for now, the story was over. It was only in 1997 that the military finally admitted that the "Roswell Incident," as it had become known, was neither weather balloon nor alien spacecraft but a series of top-secret military programs conflated by residents' confused memories of years past. The bodies, the military said, were 1950s-era crash dummies, the "disc" an advanced anti-Soviet spy balloon.

Nevertheless, in the summer of 1947, the UFO hypothesis was still alive and well, and the Roswell Incident helped to confirm in the public mind Arnold's claims of flying discs not because the Roswell story was true but because the media were willing to take seriously the phenomenon and thus give credence to the stories. It did not take long before seeing UFOs had become a national craze, and the wave of sightings continued at a steady clip thereafter. Aliens had become a firmly entrenched part of popular culture, and with the advent of extraterrestrials in popular media, Lovecraftian tales of aliens in man's past began to seem less fantastic and possibly even reasonable. As the 1940s gave way to the 1950s, aliens went mainstream.

It had not started out that way, of course. People had been seeing strange things in the night skies for as long as anyone could remember, but it was only in the nineteenth and twentieth centuries that these visions became technological rather than religious experiences.

Among the most famous of these early encounters was the Great Airship Mystery. Coming in the years when Jules Verne's and H. G. Wells's science fiction had made technological marvels like space flight seem possible, it was not surprising when people began to report sightings of a Vernelike flying contraption. Beginning in November 1896, blimplike, propeller-driven airships were sighted throughout the United States, often in more than one state at the same time. On April 19, 1897, the *Dallas Morning News* reported that one of the cigar-shaped airships had crashed and its pilot died.[4]

Certainly, it was no coincidence that at the same time that the presence of canals on Mars was a major scientific controversy and the establishment first began to contemplate seriously the existence of extraterrestrial civilizations that some began to identify the pilots of these propeller-driven Victorian UFOs as "Martians." Significantly, however, the "Martian" pilots were described as virtually no different than human beings. While researchers were later able to identify the folkloric influences that went into this mass delusion, some in the 1940s had begun to look back on the airship mystery as the first wave of UFO sightings. It only went to prove a point: if an idea is sufficiently popular, people will believe in it no matter how tenuously it is related to the truth.

The year of the Great Airship Mystery, science fiction author H. G. Wells released his masterpiece, *The War of the Worlds*, serialized in the *Strand* and published in novel form the next year. Read and admired by Lovecraft, Wells's novel fused the theory of evolution with the concept of alien invaders, influencing Lovecraft's depiction of his ancient extraterrestrials. Wells speculated that Martians would have evolved differently than earthlings, and he describes how their bodies had atrophied as their brains grew ever larger. Lacking a proper digestive system, they instead fed on the blood of lower animals. In the end it is only their vulnerability to Earth's bacteria that keeps the Martian menace from completely wiping out humanity. The important lesson of *War of the Worlds* was that the extraterrestrial creatures were the products of the same evolutionary forces that produced humanity. The aliens were limited by natural law and were not manifestations of the supernatural. The horror of the aliens was a *scientific* horror.

With the advent of cinema, science fiction creators obtained a new medium in which to showcase extraterrestrial creatures. In Georges Méliès's classic 1902 silent version of Jules Verne's *From the Earth to the Moon, A Trip to the Moon* (*Le voyage dans la lune*), the first astronauts uncover a moon teeming with life. The film marked one of the earliest cinematic visions of aliens, though the humanoid creatures bore little resemblance to later ideas of aliens. It set an early example of the power of film to convey the imaginary worlds of science fiction and fantasy. However, no one could be fooled into thinking that the creatures on the screen were really out in space. Despite some erroneous reports that early filmgoers thought everything they saw was real, Victorian and Edwardian audiences knew that what they saw was only a movie.[5] It was for the radio actor Orson Welles to convince America for the first time that aliens could not only be real but could be here now.

In his classic 1938 Mercury Theater radio production of Wells's *The War of the Worlds*, Orson Welles broadcast fictional news reports about the landing of the Martians in New Jersey and the battle that developed between Earth and Mars. Because radio used only sound, listeners' imaginations filled in the details of the alien invasion. Without pictures, the audio worked its magic, and the reports were nearly impossible to distinguish from actual news reports. For those who missed the disclaimer at the outset that the broadcast was merely a play, the interruption of a chamber music program for a "news" flash seemed frighteningly like a real bulletin. CBS listeners across the United States fell for the hoax, and there was a nationwide panic on that Halloween eve. While by the end of the broadcast America had realized that war was only a radio play, the incident demonstrated that Americans were prepared for the first time to accept the idea that extraterrestrials were not just theoretically possible but could actually arrive on Earth at any time.

It should have been surprising that a significant proportion of Americans could believe aliens were here. For centuries, the remnants of the medieval geocentric model of the universe had fixed in the Western mind the idea that humanity was the center of the universe and that there could be no other beings (save those in heaven or hell) in a universe created by God for humanity's benefit. If society could now accept, even if only in its nightmares, that there could be beings on other worlds, then the mental framework on which the old theories rested must have been permanently broken.

The medieval cast that had defined the Western mind since the birth of its civilization seemed no longer to be functioning properly. If readers of pulp fiction could believe that Cthulhu was real and listeners of radio could think Martians were invading, what did it say about the psychology of America? Perhaps it implied that the old myths and legends were no longer satisfying, and perhaps it meant that a growing disenchantment with traditional religion had begun to replace the supernatural creatures of old with fairies and angels in modern mechanical clothes.

These themes had only begun to emerge in the cinema, literature, and media of the Depression when the epic battle of the Second World War launched a terrible sequel to the 1914–1918 war that had torn asunder the very fabric of the

West. The old world of empires and clergy, of chivalry and dynasty, was blown away in the guns of August and in the interwar years continued on as a ghostly shadow of its former vitality. The new war would deal the old civilization its death-blow and replace the Western civilization the world had known with a technocratic civilization for which UFOs and aliens were the mechanical versions of the old world's saints and angels. The battle for Europe destroyed that continent and sent the United States and Soviet Union to positions of ultimate power.

During World War II, pilots claimed that strange balls of glowing light had danced and darted around their airplanes during missions. Though many times smaller than the flying discs seen after the war, the pilots often reported that the balls of light—which they called "foo fighters"—seemed to be guided by intelligence, as though they were interested in the airplanes.[6] After the war, the "foo fighters" were replaced in the public mind with Kenneth Arnold's flying saucers and Roswell's alien visitors. The modern age of UFOs had begun.

The end of World War II also saw the beginning of the Cold War, and the growing tension between the United States and the Soviet Union produced feelings of paranoia that found expression through the metaphor of aliens. If the public could not fully absorb the Berlin Airlift, the Korean War, and the domino theory, extraterrestrials could serve as a filter through which to express the sublimated feelings of despair that the years of wars both hot and cold had produced.

Later, the United States government would find UFO sightings a convenient way to disguise top-secret testing of new weapons and aircraft. The CIA helped to make the official government investigations into UFOs ridiculous so that the credulous would continue to believe, buying the government time in the race to outgun the Soviets. Since government agents knew that scientists and elite opinion makers would not believe in flying saucers, the government encouraged the growth of UFO sightings to distract people from its testing and to provide cover for its activities.

But even during this period of heightened interest in the possibility of extraterrestrials, the topic had become cliché. The subject of Saturday afternoon matinee features and children's serials, aliens even found their way into Bugs Bunny cartoons, which mocked the topic in 1949 with the creation of a Martian character whom Bugs Bunny foiled in his attempt to blow up the earth from a base on the moon.[7] Other media had also explored alien themes. Comic books had grown up out of the pulp tradition, and now in their golden age, they had explored virtually every permutation on the visitors-from-another-world theme. Superman was merely the first, originating in 1939, but in his flight from the dying planet Krypton and his compulsion to save humanity from itself, he embodied much of what became the growing myth of the extraterrestrial. Later aliens would also hail from dying planets and come to Earth to offer salvation.

While the mainstream culture had firmly decided that the aliens were the fevered workings of delusional dreams, a sizeable minority embraced the concept and began to have more intimate relations with these strange dream visitors. Almost exactly like the way Greeks and Romans claimed to have met with Apollo or Zeus, some began to claim they had met the aliens, and like the Greek gods, the aliens were very human.

Throughout the 1950s, the alien drumbeat continued to grow louder. In November 1952, a man named George Adamski said he met visitors from the planet Venus in the hot California desert. The most famous visitation from a supposed otherworldly being to date, Adamski related to a rapt audience of readers that the Venusians were tall, blond, humanlike creatures. They wore glittering one-piece uniforms and looked very much like a Buck Rogers or Flash Gordon version of space creatures. Like Superman, these superaliens had a compulsion to save the earth from its manifold problems.

Adamski claimed that he had not just met the Venusians but had traveled the universe with them. In his books *Flying Saucers Have Landed* and *Inside the Space Ships*, he told all about what he had seen in space and what the aliens prophesied for the world. He explained that the aliens had been coming to Earth throughout human history. Taken by Adamski's claims, men like Desmond Leslie and occultist George Hunt Williamson expanded on Adamski's ideas in their own books, providing some of the first nonfiction claims that extraterrestrials visited Earth in the distant past and were responsible for early human civilization. While some of these claims built organically on Adamski, some were likely pulp fiction masquerading as fact. Either way, these books did not reach a level of acceptance or influence as their fortunes rose and fell with Adamski's outlandish claims.

Adamski also provided another piece of evidence that would become a staple of the new study of flying saucers ("ufology"): the UFO photograph. Supposedly, Adamski had captured on film incontrovertible proof that the spaceships were real. In reality, they were crude fakes. Though it was obvious upon examination that the "ships" were made from bottle coolers and chicken feeders, many early UFO enthusiasts accepted Adamski's photographs as legitimate.[8] In the following years, innumerable numbers of photographs emerged that supposedly depicted flying saucers. To date, none has conclusively been shown to depict a real flying saucer.

Others, too, claimed the Venusians had come to them. In fact, seeing people from Venus turned into something of a pastime during the 1950s. Samuel Thompson saw nude leprechaun-like Venusians in 1950. Howard Menger claimed that the Venusians had been visiting him in his New Jersey home since he was ten and further that they were beautiful females and vegetarians to boot. London taxi driver George King founded an entire organization, the Aetherius Society, in

1954 to promote his belief that he met with seven-foot-tall blond Venusians who needed only to breathe to obtain food. King claimed to be the earthly representative of the Saturn-based Interplanetary Parliament where the denizens of the universe's various bodies met to discuss major issues, a galactic United Nations.[9] Through the 1950s, Venusians were aliens to beat. The Venusian craze, however, faded as quickly as it came when the first space probes revealed that the planet Venus was too hot and too stormy to support life. Claims of an interplanetary parliament on Saturn were also hard to swallow when it was learned that Saturn was nothing but a ball of gas. True believers tried to find new ways of believing, unconvincingly interpreting the Venusians as transdimensional or time-traveling beings who lied about their origins in order to protect us from the truth. Presumably even though they were now confessed liars we were still supposed to trust them because they were from another world. Somehow, one would think their moral credibility would be harmed. However, the real damage was done. In the popular consciousness of the 1950s, aliens were now not just in our skies, they were also our friends.

Yet at the movies, aliens were not as warm and cuddly as the people who claimed to have actually met them made it seem. While the aliens from Venus were warm, nurturing, and friendly, their Martian counterparts were on a warlike rampage in the cinema. It was H. G. Wells's fault that Mars was to play the part of cosmic villain, but why Venus should be the celestial planet of good feelings it is impossible to say. Perhaps in the public mind there was still a lingering association between the planets' respective namesake gods of war and love. If so, these qualities would implicate a social construct as responsible for these fantasies about alien life.

Nevertheless, the Martians from Wells to Bugs Bunny were universally the villains of the piece, never more so than during the heyday of extraterrestrial cinema in the 1950s. In 1951, *The*

Thing from Another World became the prototype for a wave of alien-invasion films. In that movie, researchers in an arctic ice station find the crashed remnants of a flying saucer and a frozen Thing that is not quite dead. When they bring it inside, it thaws out and (naturally) goes on a rampage. Echoing Lovecraft's theme, the movie hints that the saucer is not a recent arrival but may have been on Earth for a very long time, twenty million years. The movie was based on the 1938 John W. Campbell novella "Who Goes There," which was, in turn, derived from H. P. Lovecraft's *At the Mountains of Madness*, another tale of ancient aliens in a polar region (the Antarctic this time), which Campbell had just published in his magazine *Astounding Stories* in the spring of 1936. With the success of this low-budget film, Hollywood prepared an onslaught of new invasion films about men from Mars, and by default provided the context for authors like Yonah ibn Aharon, M. K. Jessup, and Brinsley LePoer Trench to write about the possibility of ancient astronauts throughout the 1950s and into the 1960s. Ancient astronauts were now a cultural current, but one that lay submerged, like Cthulhu in R'lyeh, beneath the more popular tales of contemporary invaders. By far, the biggest year for the Martian menace was 1953.

That year *The War of the Worlds* made a return engagement, this time as a big-screen production. Directed by George Pal, the classic film retold the famous story using then-high-tech special effects. The Martians in the film destroy Los Angeles, and a good time was had by all. Also that year *Invaders from Mars* showcased evil Martians zapping ordinary citizens with electrodes to make them obey Martian commands. Another film, *Killers from Space*, played on the same theme. This time, Martians abduct a jet pilot, operate on him, and turn him into their agent. They show him images of their dying planet and inform him that they will emerge from their hiding places underground to take over the earth.[10] In most of these films, the Martians served as a metaphor for the Soviet communists (Red Planet = Red Army), and the tales of alien invasion masked cold war paranoia about the Soviet threat.

This paranoia slipped even into cartoons. As noted, Bugs Bunny took on the Martian menace, but it was Daffy Duck who put this melodramatic cold war cinema into one concise and perfect satire. In "Duck Dodgers in the 24½th Century," a parody of Buck Rogers, Daffy Duck is charged with obtaining the last shaving-cream mine, located on Planet X, for the earth. Unbeknownst to him, the red planet Mars also covets Planet X. Daffy arrives and claims the planet in the name of the earth, but he is knocked over as the Martian rocket arrives and a Martian claims the planet for Mars. ("Isn't that lovely?" the Martian asks.) Daffy faces off against his Martian adversary for the unclaimed territory in an ever-escalating battle until the two, in their zeal to destroy each other, blow up Planet X in mutually assured destruction. Presiding over the rubble, Daffy Duck exclaims, "I claim this planet in the name of the earth!" Hanging on precariously by a root, his cadet, Porky Pig, adds, "Big deal."[11]

Here the anticommunist themes are clear. The Martian represents communism, and Daffy Duck represents liberal democracy. That Daffy is to some degree incompetent and propped up by the help of Porky Pig shows how Western democracies leagued together against the totalitarian menace of monolithic international socialism. That the two ideologies ultimately clash and destroy the very objects over which they quarreled displays the fundamental fear of nuclear war and mutual annihilation. Or perhaps I am reading too much into a cartoon.

Yet there was another side to Mars and the aliens. Like the kindly Venusians on bookstore shelves, occasionally the aliens played the part of the good guy. Also in theaters was a film from 1952, *Red Planet Mars*, in which former Nazi scientists working for Satan with communist money develop a radio capable of establishing contact with Mars. When America uses the invention and makes contact with Mars, the world learns of a Martian civilization superior to our own. The Soviets seem ready to take over the world in the wake of the panic this causes until the Americans learn that Mars is a Christian planet, too, and this causes a religious revival that saves Earth from the godless communists. In this film, Mars is a symbol of what America could be, a better world free from addiction to fossil fuels and living the Christian ideal. No film, it has been said, better captured the paranoia of 1950s Hollywood.[12]

Similarly, *The Day the Earth Stood Still* presented benevolent aliens offering to save humanity from trouble in exchange for large-scale disarmament. The religious undertones were obvious, and such overt religiosity helped to define America in its opposition to the officially atheist Soviet Union. It is little wonder that this decade also saw the addition of "under God" to the Pledge of Allegiance, "In God We Trust" to paper money, and Derleth's recasting of Lovecraft's Cthulhu Mythos in specifically Christian terms. The atheists in Moscow had to be opposed at all costs.

While cinema was using aliens as tools of anticommunist propaganda, science fiction aliens served many and more varied purposes in the burgeoning pulp science fiction magazines. In the mold of *Weird Tales*, new magazines began popping up in the 1930s and reached their peak in the postwar years. Among the earliest was *Astounding Stories*, edited by the legendary John W. Campbell. *Astounding Stories* published several of Lovecraft's longer works after his death, including "The Shadow Out of Time" and *At the Mountains of Madness*, stories rejected by *Weird Tales*. As we saw, Campbell later rewrote *Mountains* as his own "Who Goes There," sparking alien-themed movies from *The Thing from Another World* to *Alien*.

Astounding spawned competitors with names like *Galaxy* and *Fantasy and Science Fiction*.[13] With stories like Stanley Weinbaum's "A Martian Odyssey" and A. E. van Vogt's "The Monster," the science fiction magazines became a home for alien tales of all stripes through the 1950s. Though by the end of the decade tales of robots and automata had largely displaced aliens as the main antagonists (perhaps in anticipation of the social upheavals of the 1960s), the science fiction magazines carried on the pulp tradition. This period became known as science fiction's "golden age" and saw the publication of most of what would become "classic" in the genre. Though largely outside the scope of this book, much of the science fiction literature of this period began to impact society, reinforcing and reflecting ideas about aliens and UFOs and contributing to the continuing rash of UFO sightings.

Several of these classic stories of the 1930s, 1940s, and early 1950s found their way into a new medium: television. The postwar economic boom had made it possible for television to enter nearly every American's living room, and the national radio networks like NBC and CBS lost little time in developing parallel television networks. While many successful science fiction programs had begun airing on radio in the years after World War II, few made the transition to television, perhaps because of the expense of outer space sets and the difficulty of making realistic aliens. But Superman made the transition from comic book to television show, starring George Reeves as the all-American hero. Yet he made it to television in the cold war era not because he was science fiction but because he was American. Superman's alien aspects were largely downplayed in favor of his anticommunist credentials, fighting for "truth, justice, and the American way."

The most important early science fiction show was *The Twilight Zone*, created, hosted, and largely written by Rod Serling. At the time, Serling was best known for his work on the CBS series *Playhouse 90*, producing such works as "Requiem for a Heavyweight." By 1959, Serling decided to try his hand at a new anthology series that would showcase dramatizations of both original scripts and popular science fiction stories. The show's famous opening set the tone, with its creepy music and surreal graphics.

On his show, Serling and his team of talented writers made ample use of aliens. Between 1959 and the show's cancellation in 1964, *The Twilight Zone* presented dozens of tales of alien intervention. In the well-known episode "To Serve Man," aliens arrive on Earth and provide the means through which the world can live in peace and harmony. In a gruesome twist on the *Day the Earth Stood Still* theme, the aliens' beneficence does not come without a price. The classic pun in the title said it all. In another tale, "The Monsters on Maple Street," the residents of a small town turn on each other when they believe that aliens are impersonating their neighbors. Exploiting their prejudices and hatreds, the neighborhood descends into chaos. Here again, aliens were the rubric through which social issues could be explored without confronting them head-on.

While Serling liked to use his aliens as metaphors and symbols for important social and political issues, it is debatable exactly how many in the audience were aware of the sociological opinions in *Zone* episodes. What is indisputable is that *The Twilight Zone* helped to bring aliens and science fiction out of the movie theaters and into Americans' living rooms. Each episode provided a moral at the end of the story and presented its plots as departures from the rational, anomalous breaches in the normal flow of life. The very fact that the stories needed a special "zone" to occur locked the bad parts safely away from the shiny façade of 1950s America.

With the success of *The Twilight Zone* on CBS, in the time-honored tradition of competition, NBC made sure it had a nearly identical program to match. *The Outer Limits*, like the *Twilight Zone*, was a science fiction anthology series. With its ominous voiceover warning viewers that "we are now controlling the transmission," the show captured the irrational fears that lurked under the clean and rational surface of the *Twilight Zone.*

Where *Zone* used its scripts to probe human emotions and motivations, *The Outer Limits* instead used extraterrestrials for shock value, fright, and horror. Fear here was not abstract or contained but an important and inescapable part of everyday life. It was not separate from the viewer but a part of him. Where Serling's aliens were usually humanoid, *The Outer Limits* preferred monstrous entities that, like Cthulhu, were masses of tentacles and slime. In the new episode that aired in the second week of February 1964, *The Outer Limits* featured an alien with wraparound eyes, which were extremely rare in the science fiction of the 1950s and early 1960s.[14] Just twelve days after that episode aired, a New Hampshire couple allegedly reported that aliens matching that description had abducted them.

Betty and Barney Hill underwent hypnosis sessions in 1964 to cure anxiety attacks and nightmares, and during regression therapy they revealed that they had been captured by a flying saucer three years earlier. The aliens, who had wraparound eyes and large noses like the comedian Jimmy Durante, performed medical tests on both the Hills, which involved sticking a needle into the navel, before returning them to their car two hours later. Only after regression therapy could the repressed memories be revealed. In 1966, the Hills' therapist, Dr. Benjamin Simon, gave journalist John Fuller permission to read the Hills' files, resulting in a book, *The Interrupted Journey*, in 1966.[15] While in recent years regression therapy has been largely discredited as a scientific tool, largely because the therapist can influence recollection or create false memories, in the 1960s it was still an active area of research. Therefore, the Hills' abduction case had a level of credence at first that subsequent recovered memories would not have. However, the Hills' story told more about the total saturation of aliens in American media culture than it revealed about alien medical practices.

The Hills' story of abduction seemed to be made up out of the science fiction films of the previous decade, especially the films *Invaders from Mars* and *Killers from Space*, where the evil aliens abduct and experiment on hapless humans. From *Invaders*, the Hills may have borrowed the Jimmy Durante noses, the particular details of the medical procedures done to them, and the imagery of the needle in the navel.[16] From *Killers from Space*, the Hills borrowed the motif of aliens wiping clean one's memory of the abduction and parts of the medical experimentations. And as noted, from *The Outer Limits* they borrowed the distinctive wraparound eyes seen just a few days before they "recalled" them. As folklore researcher Thomas Bullard concluded, "'[A]bduction' motifs circulated widely in popular culture years before abduction reports surfaced" and likely were the cause of abduction reports.[17]

The world had reached the saturation point, and people had begun to believe that the aliens were not just real, but here, and not just here but *after us*. A 1975 NBC-TV movie about the Hill abduction not coincidentally spawned a wave of reported abductions, one of which would go on to found a cult that would intersect with the emerging ancient-astronaut theory with terrible consequences for the future of science. But, like so much of our story, that still lay decades into the future.

Most important, the Hill abduction and the reported UFO sightings brought aliens from fiction to fact. But a philosophical quandary remained for those who came to believe that aliens were real: why now? If the earth were billions of years old, and the universe still billions older, why should the aliens have arrived on Earth only in the few years following the end of the Second World War? Surely, with all those untold billions of years stretching back to the beginning of time, was it not more likely that aliens had visited Earth sometime in the past? After all, the laws of probability would say yes.

Some tried to rationalize this problem. Perhaps, they said,

the aliens had only just learned the secret of interstellar flight. Or maybe they were attracted to Earth by man's discovery of nuclear weapons. Perhaps, some said, their planet was dying and they needed Earth's help to save themselves. Or maybe they had come to save humanity from what they saw as imminent destruction.

Not so, claimed a new breed of authors who would follow the UFO sightings and abduction reports with a fantastic new claim of their own. In fact, the aliens had not just arrived recently—they had always been here and may just have been responsible for the origins of civilization and humanity itself.

Though authors like Jessup, Trench, and Leslie had drawn these conclusions first, the most influential leap of logic would occur not in the United States, hotbed of all things alien, but in postwar France, where the works of H. P. Lovecraft had recently arrived and triggered a chain reaction that would shake the scientific world.

PART THREE
FROM FICTION TO FACT

7

THE FRENCH CONNECTION

The devastation of World War II had left much of France a battered shell. The humiliation of the German capture of Paris and the ignominy of the fascist Vichy government had torn apart the fabric of French civic society, a civil structure that could trace its roots back to the Revolution of 1789 and the very origin of the modern relationship of citizen to state. But like so much of French history, from the bloody Revolution to Napoléon to Sedan, the noble ideals of the French nation did not survive the practices of the French governments: three Republics, two empires, an absolute monarchy, and a constitutional one. When the Allied forces arrived in Normandy in June 1944, they began the liberation of a country that had lost much of what had composed the French identity.

With the war ended and the last Germans expelled from French soil, large numbers of American troops remained in the country during the period of rebuilding under the Marshall Plan. As we have seen, most of these troops were young men who had never before been outside of the United States. Most did not speak any foreign language, and the few who did were not always fluent in French. As a result, soldiers had difficulty relating to the population they had freed, and the population had trouble relating to them. When the joyful cheers of the

French died down and mundane routines resumed as occupation became permanent stationing, many soldiers turned to reading as an escape from the monotony and loneliness of overseas deployment. As we have seen, the soldiers read a lot of science fiction in free Armed Services Editions, and H. P. Lovecraft was one of the authors they read. The Americans' literary taste did not go unnoticed, and a French culture seeking identity in a postwar world rapidly adopted American popular literature as one guidepost toward a new worldview.

With much of the old French civic society smashed beyond repair, postwar France began to rebuild a social order along the classic lines that had defined French society since the Revolution: community, social and civic responsibility, rational progress, morality, and integrity.[1] The renewed French society of the Fourth Republic emphasized youth, since it was the young who rebuilt France's shattered infrastructure and in so doing rebuilt France's shattered society. The French youth, however, rejected their elders' attempts to moralize and control their lives, and they began to resent the older generation's efforts to regulate their lives and enforce their view of traditional French morality. The allure of American popular culture was never stronger than during these years.

American pop culture had begun to invade French media in the 1930s, when such American offerings as Mickey Mouse, Tarzan, and Flash Gordon became best-sellers, easily outpacing their French competitors. During the war, German authorities made American offerings illegal, so with the war's end there was a new rush to American products, the forbidden fruit, and American publishers were eager to find a new market for their backlog of comics, stories, and novels.[2] With the American presence growing ever larger in the postwar years—in the form of occupying troops, NATO diplomats, Marshall Plan advisers, and businessmen—the French elite considered the American presence a threat to French cultural identity. However, the young, who had rejected the old ways that had proved so disastrous to France in the years leading up to war, embraced these new invaders and took in their culture.

The French government began to step in, regulating the content of comic books and pulp periodicals in 1949. After several prosecutions, the government effectively eliminated "morally objectionable" material from magazines and comic books. Their favorite target was Tarzan, whom they considered too savage, too sexual, and too un-French for their children's eyes. In 1958, France began regulating all publications targeted toward youths and adolescents, including romance novels and horror stories. The government held that scary stories in particular were a risk to the mental health of their readers, presumably since they would cause readers to develop morbid obsessions.[3] With the elimination of sex, violence, and fantasy from children's literature, adult magazines and books picked up these attributes and developed them in mature and compelling ways. Perhaps in so doing they imparted a slightly juvenile flavor to French offerings that was not paralleled in the more adult literature of the United States and Britain, whose fantastic literature had descended from adult fiction to kiddie lit in the course of two generations. Classics like *War of the Worlds* ceased to be serious literature for serious-minded adults and were relegated to children's bookshelves, where each dour businessman in a gray flannel suit knew such frivolities belonged. After all, the business of America was business, and there was no time in the postwar world for flights of fancy. In France, the public seemed to think that *la dolce vita* included reading.

By the start of the 1960s, science fiction magazines had become an important part of French popular literature, and the golden age of American science fiction two decades earlier translated into a renewed vital period for French science fiction. Since France had already experienced such an age once before, in the time of Jules Verne and his imitators, this new period became known as the French second science fiction period.[4] However, unlike the original, this period was an Anglo-American phenomenon, and most of the science fiction were translations of English language works.[5] The French seemed to be saying that if America and England had given up on their most original and provocative literary genre, then the French would, as they had so many times in the past, step in to save culture from the uncivilized barbarians.

The most successful of the French science fiction magazines was *Planète*, a journal of philosophy and literature. Founded in the early 1960s, the magazine reached eighty thousand subscribers and had newsstand sales of one hundred thousand.[6] Like many of its competitors, predecessors, and successors, *Planète* reprinted in translation the classic stories of the American 1930s and '40s pulp magazines in between articles on esoteric topics and pure speculation. *Planète's* owners, Louis Pauwles and Jacques Bergier, had read the work of H. P. Lovecraft, whom they greatly admired for his insight, his philosophy, and his creations. They held him as their prophet, and their reprints of his stories helped to popularize him and the Cthulhu Mythos in the French imagination. In *Planète* they republished many of Lovecraft's shorter pieces. Much of Lovecraft's longer fiction had been published in French by Éditions Denoël in a series of books between 1954 and 1961 that were well received by both the French public and the French intelligentsia. Literary criticism abounded, and the philosopher-elites in French culture saw in Lovecraft a new subject to dissect and reinterpret in bizarre and surprising ways. By the 1980s, the French scholar Maurice Lévy examined *Lovecraft: A Study in the Fantastic*, and the French philosophers Gilles Deleuze and Felix Guattari wrote in praise of Lovecraft's use of radical theories in their treatise *A Thousand Plateaus*.[7]

The French have always had a taste for embracing bent genius. Lovecraft's literary hero, Edgar Allan Poe, first found fame and success in France, where intellectuals saw in him the origins of something that could be called an American literature. Translations of his works, especially the Auguste Dupin mysteries, set in France, became much bigger sellers there than they were back home until America was mature enough to recognize in its own authors' literary merit. The film star Jerry Lewis became something of a French national icon following the release of his films there. And Lovecraft, too, slowly came to prominence in France.

Since the 1950s and early 1960s were the fallow years for Lovecraft sales in America, it was surprising that the French elite would come to embrace him. In the United States, Lovecraft's star had ebbed and he had returned to the obscurity in which he had lived. There were few new readers beyond his loyal fans who continued to read him and produce tales in his style. His stories were moody, atmospheric, and Gothic. He wrote of the past and the dark side of the universe. All these thoughts were grossly out of step with the whiz-bang shiny clarity of 1950s science fiction. Progress was the order of the day once more, and Lovecraft was the very opposite, stories where science serves only to return the reader to black depths of the past.

Lovecraft's stories presented a world where ignorance and superstition were welcome respites from unsatisfying truths. Again, this did not resonate with the positivist and modernist traditions of the 1950s and early 1960s. Philosophers had come to believe that science held the key to all learning, and all questions could be answered through appeal to the scientific method. Coming dangerously close to embracing scientism, the positivists projected a "World of Tomorrow" where all problems could be solved and utopia would reign. For the last time in human history, Progress would be the watchword of the day. All around the world, amazing advances in science and technology were propelling the world into a glorious future. Televisions, automobiles, airplanes all spoke to the wonders of the age. Lovecraft's look at a dark past was out of sync with an ascendant America.

But not so in France. By the end of the 1960s, Lovecraft had already become the subject of much literary criticism in the Francophone world. Gérard Klein wrote a lengthy treatise, "Entre le fantastique et la science-fiction, Lovecraft," in the special Lovecraft-themed volume of *Les Cahiers de L'Herne*, where he attempted a Marxist analysis of Lovecraft's fiction, seeing in Lovecraft a definition of the moment when free, autonomous citizens transitioned into slaves of monopoly capitalism.[8] French society at the time was divided among liberal democrats and communists, and Marxism was still considered an effective philosophy for analyzing material. Marx had held that capitalism inevitably moved from free markets to monopolies controlling protected markets, and when this happened, citizens lost their power to the capitalists. In later works, Klein would claim that Lovecraft's fantasy was a creation of bourgeois liberalism in conflict with medieval values and his science fiction a creation of monopoly capitalism, for he saw these genres as opposites, one appealing to the pre-capitalist past, the other to the monopoly capitalist future. Therefore, as Lovecraft transitioned from classic horror (fantasy) stories to science fiction–oriented tales during his career, he represented a transition in capitalism itself from the nineteenth-century free market to twentieth-century monopolies.[9] Lovecraft had in his last years become a socialist in the mold of Franklin D. Roosevelt, but it is doubtful to me that Lovecraft's monsters represented capitalism or that his stories represented the loss of the individual in the face of corporate capitalism. It is interesting speculation but not convincing.

In common with this view of fantasy as a return to the past, the devastation of the war years and the cultural turmoil involved in reconstituting French society created a desire among many to hark back to the glorious days of France's imperial past. As turmoil in her colonies (especially the revolts in Indochina and Algeria) led France to shed her role as a Great Power, many looked back fondly on the years when French power and culture had shaped world events. They could see no more glory in the years when President de Gaulle advocated cutting free France's empire. For this pessimistic streak in French society, Lovecraft's dark stories resonated with a clear and compelling clarion call, providing cold comfort. For the owners of the journal *Planète*, Louis Pauwles and Jacques Bergier, they also sounded a more important note.

Louis Pauwles was a writer of esoterica who was deeply interested in ancient mysteries and the strange questions of humanity's past. An avid reader of books documenting the supposed diffusion of human culture from its "source" in Atlantis or some other incalculably old civilization, Pauwles sought an explanation that would satisfy him more than the tales and legends of Atlantis and its ilk. His partner in *Planète* and coauthor, Jacques Bergier, a Lovecraft fan since the 1930s, was a physicist who brought his scientific training to bear on the question of man's origins and those self-same ancient mysteries. He reportedly angered his professors when in school he wanted to study alchemy, and he believed that alchemical secrets could reveal natural truths.[10] For him, nuclear energy, with its manipulation of atoms to create new substances was no different than the work of alchemists who sought to change lead into gold.

In 1960, the two published their most important work, *Les matin des magiciens*. Translated into English in Britain as *Dawn of Magic* in 1963, the book came to the United States as *Morning of the Magicians* the following year. The book is little remembered now, but it has the distinction of launching a revival of interest in the occult in the 1960s and 1970s that would culminate in the ancient-astronaut craze of the 1970s, Satanism scares, and talking to one's plants to encourage growth.[11] Part philosophical treatise and part catalogue of the outré and anomalous, *Morning of the Magicians* sits in the uneasy position

of straddling many fences. Though it claims to be the birth certificate for a new philosophy, its greatest impact came in what
other authors borrowed from this book, itself a collection of
ideas borrowed and melded together. Pauwles claimed that his
personal intellectual journey to *Morning* took five years for him
to arrive "at a point of view which I believe is rich in its possibilities. This is how the surrealists worked thirty years ago. But
unlike them we were exploring not the regions of sleep and the
subconscious but their very opposites: We call our point of
view *fantastic realism*."[12]

This "fantastic realism" had nothing to do with fantasy,
according to Pauwles. Instead it represented a new way of
looking at the world of the here and now:

> There was no attempt on our part to escape the times in
> which we live. We are not interested in the "outer suburbs" of
> reality: on the contrary we have tried to take up a position at
> its hub. There alone we believe, is the fantastic to be discov-
> ered—and not a fantastic leading to escapism but rather to a
> deeper participation in life.[13]

By seeing with new eyes, he said, a new reality would, in
theory, emerge.

Divided into three parts, *Morning of the Magicians* begins
with an omnibus catalogue of ancient mysteries. With material
drawn heavily from the works of anomalist Charles Fort,
Atlantean speculator Ignatius Donnelly, and other pseudoscientific authors of books about lost civilizations, lost tribes,
and ancient mysteries, Part One focused on vanished civilizations and the mysteries that science could not yet explain. As
his philosophical conceit, Pauwles held that the ancient past is
a mystery to modern people, completely alien in every way.
This position was much like British Prime Minister Neville
Chamberlain's pronouncement in 1938 that part of Czechoslo-
vakia should be handed to Hitler because it was "a far-away

country [with] people of whom we know nothing."[14] Britain was intimately aware of the place, as it had helped create the country from the remains of the Austro-Hungarian Empire less than twenty years before, but now it was a convenient mystery. Pauwles borrows this school of historiography for *Morning*. Since the past was so different, it was therefore unknowable in a scientific sense. Positivism, which was then becoming the dominant philosophy in archaeology, could never provide the answers because the scientific method could not be used to understand the thoughts of past peoples. In so thinking, Pauwles anticipated postmodernism's rejection of the positivist framework. Tellingly, for all postmodernism's power to criticize, reject, and analyze, it is an utter failure in predicting new information or interpreting new data.

Despite this handicap, Pauwles and Bergier attempted an explanation for the past, which they had previously announced was impossible to do. Clearly, only they were capable of truly understanding the past. Archaeology's practitioners around the globe were incapable of this task since their philosophies limited them from accepting true understanding. Utilizing sketchy, ambiguous, or misinterpreted evidence like the sixteenth-century Turkish map of the admiral Piri Reis, which seemed to show along its edge a section of Antarctica mapped from space before it was covered in ice, the authors argued that extraterrestrials had visited the earth in the past and gave rise to humanity's first civilizations.[15] The argument went something like this: If the map showed Earth charted from the air, then advanced technology must have existed to get someone into the air. Consequently, an extraterrestrial civilization must have been necessary to bring that technology to Earth. Other evidence, like Donnelly's claims of cultural diffusion from Atlantis, could then be reworked to replace Atlantis with aliens and thus appropriate lost civilizations as alien outposts.

In the second part of the book, Pauwles and Bergier chronicle the occult fascinations of the Third Reich in an attempt to prove that the past, no matter how recent, is essentially unknowable for those who did not live in the cultural matrix that gave it life. Like modern-day Chamberlains, they sounded the theme again and again. An outsider could never know anything. The third and final part contains ten essays on the future of humanity and its movement toward an "awakened" state in the dawn of a new era. In astrological terms, this would find resonance with hippie radicals hoping for the Age of Aquarius to bring about a new order of peace and harmony.

Essentially an irrationalist, Romantic treatise, *Morning of the Magicians* praised intuition, instinct, and the Romantic values against the ascendant rational, scientific, Enlightenment values in the scientific and philosophical schools of the day. Returning to our theme of modern history as a battle between Classical antiquity and the Middle Ages, between the Enlightenment and the Romantic period, the battle between modernism and the emerging postmodernism, exemplified by *Morning of the Magicians*, is quickly seen as not so modern at all. This was an old battle, but in collecting the previous generation of evidence in a new way, Pauwles and Bergier introduced a new generation of readers to the same ancient mysteries that led Lovecraft to his story ideas decades earlier. Only now, instead of culminating in powerful fiction, this new intersection would yield an endless stream of "nonfiction," whose label, of course, is not synonymous with "fact."

While Pauwles wrote most of the philosophical aspects of the book, Bergier added information about UFOs, extraterrestrials, and the like. Bergier, the scientist, was obsessed with fringe science, and enjoyed digging up information on all aspects of the topic.[16] The book covered everything from pyramidology (the belief that the Egyptian pyramids held ancient secrets) to supposed advanced technology in the ancient world.

Likewise, the authors praised Arthur Machen, the Irish author of horror fiction, about surviving Celtic mythological creatures, and they discussed the genius of H. P. Lovecraft in the same breath as the scientist Albert Einstein and psychoanalyst Carl Jung.[17] From Lovecraft, Bergier and Pauwles borrowed the one thought that would be of more importance than any other in their book. As we have seen, *Morning of the Magicians* speculates that extraterrestrial beings may be responsible for the rise of the human race and the development of its culture, a theme Lovecraft invented.

Since we have seen that both Pauwles and Bergier were fans of Lovecraft, it is impossible to deny that the two were heavily influenced in their assumption of this improbable possibility by the Providence author's fiction. When Pauwles and Bergier founded *Planète* to carry on the dialogue they began in *Morning of the Magicians*, it was H. P. Lovecraft who graced their pages and whom they held as their prophet. Since the extraterrestrial-genesis theory had rarely before been published as nonfiction (dare we call it fact?), it is clearly yet another borrowing from a pair whose philosophy of the future emerged from an explicit collection of borrowings. While chronicler of fringe science R. T. Gault said of *Morning*, "It is also remembered, with ambiguous feelings, for first presenting the germ of the 'extraterrestrial genesis' thesis,"[18] in fact, it is now clear that the germ resided in Lovecraft's fiction, brought to France and embraced by Pauwles and Bergier.

Morning of the Magicians never made much of an impact outside of continental Europe. Few English-language Web sites mention the book, and almost no English-language scientific journals and reference books make mention of it. It is also a difficult volume to track down. It has long been out of print in the United States (though there was a British edition republished in 2001). For all its subsequent influence as the inspiration for a wave of alternative histories, today *Morning of the Magicians* is largely (and deservedly) forgotten.

However, the book was translated into several languages and during its brief heyday was sold in stores around Europe and North America. A German translation came out in 1962 under the title *Aufbruch ins dritte Jahrtausend*, literally "departure in the third millennium," a reference to the book's conclusions about human consciousness and the "awakening." This German edition would find its way into the hands of a Swiss hotelier who, only a few years later, would rock the scientific world with his explosive charge that the ancient gods were in fact aliens. But first, the alien-ancestor theory had to go through one more filter.

With the relative success of *Morning of the Magicians* and *Planète* in France, it was inevitable that others would produce similar volumes expounding on the innumerable facts, theories, and speculations that Louis Pauwles and Jacques Bergier had concocted. After all, every new idea spawns its imitators, from Pepsi following Coca-Cola to Internet Explorer following Netscape, and this idea was no different.

French author Robert Charroux was among the first to expand on the ancient-astronaut theme. In his books like 1967's *Le livre des maitres du monde*, Charroux developed further the Lovecraft-Pauwles-Bergier hypothesis, finding hidden in religious texts from the Bible to the Hindu Vedas allusions to flying discs that he equated with flying saucers. In the colossal carved stone heads of Mexico, believed by archaeologists to represent kings or chiefs of the ancient Olmec culture, Charroux saw helmeted spacemen. The sculptures, recognized around the world as one of the highlights of Pre-Columbian art, stand up to nine feet tall and weigh several tons and date to between 1800 and 1200 BCE.[19] While the heads do wear headdresses that resemble modern helmets, there is no reason to believe that they are helmets, or even if they were, that they were used in space travel. Further, there is no basis to conclude that aliens needed helmets to fly in space, but that was another matter. Nevertheless, as we will see, the Olmec heads would return time and again in ancient-astronaut and alternative-history texts as a lynchpin of several contradictory theories. Charroux went on to explain how nearly every primitive culture around the world has myths of visitors whom he claimed were extraterrestrials.

Charroux's books were not seen in the United States until the 1970s, well after the craze began, and so his impact on the historiography of ancient aliens was minimal at best. Though he was among the first to explore the theory, in America he appeared only as part of the explosion that followed its rise. While he attempted to provide somewhat scholarly reasoning and methodology to back up his dubious historical claims, Charroux, in fact, had much more in common with Victorian antiquarians like Ignatius Donnelly, stringing together unrelated or partial facts to back up a predetermined conclusion. Like much of the ancient mysteries genre, his logic followed post hoc analysis. Post hoc, ergo propter hoc, "after this, therefore because of it," is a logical fallacy whereby an event occurring before another is seen as the cause of it, even if the two are unrelated.[20] Here, aliens are projected as the cause, and all other events are therefore the consequence.

Charroux's works were eventually published in English with titles like *The Gods Unknown* and *The Mysteries of the Andes* in the 1970s after another author borrowed Charroux's ideas and turned them into a worldwide craze.

8

CHARIOTEER OF THE GODS

Two of Charroux's early books, *Historie inconnue des hommes depuis cent mille ans* and *Le livre des secrets trahis*, fell into the hand of a hotel clerk in Switzerland named Erich von Däniken,[1] possibly through the suggestion of a friend who convinced him that the ancient-alien theory held water.[2] Born in 1936, von Däniken married in 1960 and became a father in 1964. At the time he read the books, von Däniken was embezzling money from his hotel to finance trips around the world, for which he would eventually end up sentenced to prison in Churn, Switzerland, for three and half years. He was officially convicted of embezzlement, forgery, and fraud.[3] To help explain his embezzling, von Däniken claimed he used the money to finance the research needed to write a book involving mysterious archaeological sites scattered across the globe. In deriving an idea for that book, he borrowed heavily from Charroux and from the German edition of *Morning of the Magicians*, largely without credit.[4] Almost miraculously, von Däniken had hit upon a gold mine. His argument was simple and uncritical:

> I claim that our forefathers received visits from the universe in the remote past, even though I do not yet know who these

extraterrestrial intelligences were or from which planet they came. I nevertheless proclaim that these "strangers" annihilated part of mankind existing at the time and produced a new, perhaps the first, *homo sapiens*.[5]

The book, which he called *Erinnerungen an die zukunft*, was an instant best-seller, and it easily surpassed the popularity of both its inspirations. Called *Chariots of the Gods?* in English, it would become the best-selling archaeology book of all time. The sheer popularity of the books made Erich von Däniken easily the most important figure in the history of the ancient-astronaut movement and the father of all that was to come. *Chariots of the Gods?* arrived in German bookstores in 1968 from the Econ-Verlag publishers. Since this was also the year of Stanley Kubrick's brilliant *2001: A Space Odyssey*, the block-buster film that speculated that an extraterrestrial technology guided the process of human evolution, there was a willing audience primed to receive such speculation. The next year, an English translation appeared in Great Britain as human beings landed on the moon for the first time, and in December 1970, the tabloid magazine the *National Enquirer* serialized the book in the United States. It became available in American book-stores in February 1971.

Following the broadcast of Rod Serling's 1973 documentary about von Däniken's theories, *In Search of Ancient Astronauts*, *Chariots* was made into a feature film of the same name as the book. It was released in theaters in 1974. With the success of the film, paperback editions of *Chariots* and its sequel, *Gods from Outer Space* (written while in prison), sold 6.5 million copies that year in the United States alone.[6] Virtually no book of history, much less archaeology, ever achieved that level of success. By the early twenty-first century, he had sold 60 million copies of his twenty-six books devoted to the ancient-astronaut theory.[7] Virtually everyone had heard of von

Däniken and his theories in the year following the documentary and film, if not because of the movie, then because of his appearance on *The Tonight Show with Johnny Carson* or his interview in *Playboy* magazine. *Chariots* had moved from intellectual fad to full-fledged phenomenon within months. This despite the fact he told the *National Enquirer* that he had out-of-body experiences that took him to the fourth dimension to learn of the aliens' secrets: "I know that astronauts visited the earth in ancient times," he told the magazine, because "I was there when the astronauts arrived. And I know they'll be back."[8]

Teachers began reporting that their students came to class convinced that extraterrestrials had created humanity, and students were unwilling to listen to "orthodox" explanations of humanity's origins.[9] Scientists rushed to refute von Däniken, but their debunking fell on deaf (or at least unwilling) ears. The ancient-astronaut theory had, virtually overnight, moved from the fringe of French society and the back pages of yellowing pulp magazines to the front pages of every American newspaper. Thanks both to Rod Serling's advocacy (inspired by his producer Alan Landsburg, who wrote his own imitation *Chariots*) and the profound cultural shifts of the 1960s that rejected science in favor of magical thinking, millions became convinced that aliens really were our ancestors.

As a consequence, it is necessary to explore Erich von Däniken's prolific output in great detail to understand exactly what formed the central tenets of the ancient-astronaut faith and what made it just so attractive to so many and for so long.

Von Däniken's first book was *Chariots of the Gods?* and the red, black, and white cover of the American paperback (the edition read by more than four million Americans) shrieked in its large block letters that for just $1.25, you, too, could discover the answers to some of mankind's most vexing questions about the past:

- DID ASTRONAUTS VISIT THE EARTH 40,000 YEARS AGO?
- IS THERE EVIDENCE OF A PREHISTORIC AIRFIELD IN THE ANDES?
- DID EXTRATERRESTRIAL BEINGS HELP SET UP THE GIANT STONE FACES THAT BROOD OVER EASTER ISLAND?
- AND OTHER EARTH MYSTERIES UNANSWERABLE UNTIL OUR OWN SPACE AGE![10]

From the title of the book and the tone of the questions, there could be only one answer to be found within such a work. The answer to all these questions must be an ecstatic yes. Curiously, despite the screaming cover that virtually demands the reader tear open the book and begin devouring the contents, von Däniken begins his tome talking about how much strength it took to bring himself to start such an undertaking:

> It took courage to write this book, and it will take courage to read it. Because its theories and proofs do not fit into the mosaic of traditional archaeology, constructed so laboriously and firmly cemented down, scholars will call it nonsense and put it on the Index of those books which are better left unmentioned. Laymen will withdraw into the snail shell of their familiar world when faced with the probability that finding out about our past will be even more mysterious and adventurous than finding out about the future.[11]

This is a nifty bit of rhetorical sleight of hand, and it sets the tone for everything to follow for the next thirty-five years. Making good use of the persecution complex that unconventional and fringe authors of the twentieth century were so taken with, von Däniken sets up a false tautology to cement in his readers' minds that his theories are prima facie true. If by some miracle his claims were proved true, he wins. If, as was more likely, scientists ridiculed, debunked, or dismissed him, he wins.

By saying off the top that the powers that be will "call it nonsense," von Däniken sets up the expectation that the authorities will reject the book and in so doing prove his prediction and thus his thesis. By mentioning the Index, a reference to the discontinued Catholic practice of banning blasphemous tomes, including books of science that disagreed with the Bible, he means to make himself a martyr for Truth. By saying that average people will flee in terror, he makes his own readers an elite who share the secret revelations. They become a class apart, embarked on the sacred adventure that makes "our" past more exciting than "the" future. Notice that the past is personal and possessive while the miserable future is dismissed as impersonal. Another bit of sleight of hand. If ever a first paragraph did more work toward setting a frame of mind for the reader, I have never seen one.

Von Däniken then launched into his argument, marshalling the first installment of what would become a torrent of "evidence" that he believed supported his argument that aliens founded Earth's cultures. While much of this evidence has since been discredited and his arguments effectively refuted, it is necessary to see what von Däniken said in order to trace the development of his ideas across the decades to their modern form. Of course, the reader will ultimately have to judge how well the ancient-astronaut theory explains the past, and there is ample literature available to contemplate such truths.

It is beyond the scope of this book to establish conclusively the truth or falsity of von Däniken's claims, but the reader will have guessed by now that I do not subscribe to these theories and find his evidence dubious at best. Nevertheless, we will proceed through the yellowing pages of von Däniken's "proof." While this book attempts to refrain from covering the same ground as much more definitive studies of the flaws, mistakes, and errors of the *Chariots* argument, it is impossible to trace the history of the ancient-astronaut movement without to some degree pointing to how the general movement progressed in spite of the demonstrable falsity of its specific claims.

Chariots begins by presenting a rudimentary discussion of the mathematical formulae that purport to show the probability of extraterrestrial life. Essentially, the formula boiled down to a scientific version of the philosophy of infinity: given infinite time and infinite space, all possibilities will eventually happen. Therefore, it was likely that given the size of the universe, there should be at least 180 Earthlike planets supporting extraterrestrial life.[12] Moving from this "revelation," von Däniken tries his hand at science fiction, imagining what would happen if modern humans landed on a primitive planet and gave the savages civilization. This is meant to serve as an analogy to what he said happened to us in the past.

Having thus established that aliens exist and that interstellar travel can yield interstellar cultural diffusion, von Däniken begins his "proof." He begins, like Pauwles and Bergier before him, with the Piri Reis map. Unlike them, von Däniken adds to myth of the map's anomalous sophistication by borrowing the work of Prof. Charles Hapgood, an American professor who believed that he had discovered that ancient people possessed precise maps of the world's coastlines as they appeared before the end of the last Ice Age, around 10,500 BCE, when the melting glaciers raised sea levels and changed the shape of the continents.

Though Hapgood's arguments seemed scholarly, he, in fact, had a massive unrecognized flaw in his research. Using an ex post facto analysis, he proceeds from the conceit that the ancients possessed sophisticated maps to the conclusion that they possessed these maps. It worked like this: Hapgood believed that the ancient maps were accurate and that later copies became increasingly erroneous through copy errors.

Therefore, when he examined the maps he "reconstructed" the original with the idea that they were once accurate. Not surprisingly, he "discovered" these accurate maps following sufficient "adjustments."[13] Quite literally, his book *Maps of the Ancient Sea Kings* (1965) was an argument that begged the question, an exercise in circular reasoning. His other effort, *The Path of the Pole*, claimed that the earth's crust slipped across the surface of the earth every so often, moving the North Pole to the South and vice versa.

An uncritical thinker, von Däniken accepted Hapgood as an authority and used his analysis to conclude that aliens had mapped the world from space before the end of the Ice Age and had given the resulting maps to Earth's first cultures. These space aliens, of course, needed places to land their ships. Since von Däniken's aliens were trapped in the 1960s ideas of flight and, for all their interstellar prowess, had not mastered vertical take-offs or landings, they needed air fields. For von Däniken, the lines of the Nazca plain served as these fields.

Nazca is an area in South America where seventy-seven acres of lines and drawings were etched into the desert landscape by the Nasca people sometime before 500 CE. An astounding mixture of animal shapes, geometric shapes, and lines, the Nazca art spawned innumerable interpretations, from sacred precincts to ritual pathways, to astronomical calendars.[14] So difficult to discern from ground level, they lay in the desert until the age of air travel, when pilots finally saw the huge drawings while flying over them.

From this quirk of circumstance, von Däniken concluded that the lines and pictures were made to be seen from the air, made for aliens. From the vague resemblance of some of the later lines to the shape of a modern airport, he concluded that Nazca was an airfield. He provided no evidence of this but made the assertion anyway. And of the Nasca culture, he said it was unreasonable to attribute the Nazca sites to them for there was no way of knowing that the artifacts found in, on, and around the lines could have anything to do with them.[15] This is roughly equivalent to arguing that we cannot conclude that the Americans built Washington, DC, since they could simply have found an abandoned city and taken up residence. The archaeological community's response to the airfield theory was short and simple. As the Smithsonian's book on South American prehistory notes: "This view received great attention, but no scientific support."[16] Further, the Nazca plain was made of gypsum. If the aliens had landed there, they would have gotten stuck.

Moving on through South America, von Däniken marvels at the size of the blocks used for the Tiwanaku (Tiahuanaco) and Inca cultures' massive constructions. Assuming that the ancient inhabitants of the Americas were too weak, too dumb, or too lazy to build for themselves, von Däniken argues that the precision architecture, which features blocks so well fitted without mortar that razor blades cannot fit between them, implies that aliens built them. Since archaeology records that Nasca flourished around 300 CE, Tiwanaku around 1000 CE, and the Inca around 1400 CE, it would seem difficult for the aliens to have come and built these structures without the Romans, the Chinese, or the medieval scholars taking some note of odd occurrences in the sky. But, since von Däniken had little use for logic or facts, he simply announced that, following the Nazca model, the buildings were incomparably older than anyone could imagine, archaeology be damned.

Wrapping himself in the mantle of iconoclastic scientists like Copernicus and Galileo, who challenged the authority of the Catholic Church on the positions of the earth and the sun in the universe, von Däniken calls "narrow-minded" those who criticized those theories for being found "[n]owhere in the Bible."[17] Claiming that orthodox science was the new religious dogma, he said his theories were equivalent to Copernicus and

Galileo. Ironically, despite his seeming rejection of biblical literalism, it was exactly that type of textual analysis that formed the next section of his book.

Von Däniken examined ancient texts, exhaustively misinterpreting them to support the alien hypothesis. He saw in the Book of Genesis a chronicle of alien interventions. Citing Genesis 1:26, where God says (in the King James version), "Let us make man in our image, after our likeness," von Däniken concludes that the plural pronoun (the "royal we") refers actually to a group of extraterrestrials creating humanity. Later, in Genesis 6:1–2, when "the sons of God saw the daughters of men that they were fair," he saw aliens. In every reference to angels, to God, or to "giants," he saw aliens, aliens, and aliens. Interpreting the Bible literally, in accordance with his extraterrestrial conceit, he found aliens wherever he looked: visiting Ezekiel, causing Noah's flood, and destroying Sodom and Gomorrah. Here, building on the description of the death of Lot's wife when looking back at the destruction, von Däniken "speculates" that the aliens "simply wanted to destroy some dangerous fissionable material and at the same time to make sure of wiping out a human brood they found unpleasant"— that is, a nuclear explosion.[18]

But in an example of von Däniken's intellectual rigor, he tackles the subject of the Ark of the Covenant "[w]ithout actually consulting Exodus. . . . I seem to remember that the Ark was often surrounded by flashing sparks," which meant that aliens had given Moses instructions to make an electric transmitter.[19] Had he consulted Exodus, he would have found that his remembered sparks never occurred. His fantasy, however, is good enough to provide proof for ancient astronauts, no facts needed.

Giving the book its title, our humble author next discovers ancient myths from around the world that describe the descent of the gods in fiery chariots, which he equates with rockets, apparently in deference to the 1960s-era rocket technology used to propel men into outer space. It apparently never occurred to Erich von Däniken that the technology of the 1960s may not be the same as the technology of hypothetical alien visitors. Nevertheless, in his explanations of fiery chariots and the coffin lid of the Mayan king Pacal in Palenque, which he saw not as a typical Mexican funerary scene but as a man in a rocket, he consistently stuffed his alien hypothesis into the material box of 1960s technologies. Perhaps it spoke to a lack of imagination in an author who appeared to have cribbed his thesis from H. P. Lovecraft, and perhaps it spoke to an intellectual laziness in an author who refused to cite sources or think critically about his own ideas.

Moving onward, he next tackled the fabulous Nilotic civilization of ancient Egypt. In the Egyptian pyramids he saw fantastic perfection unmatched and unrivaled in human history, and therefore clearly the work of extraterrestrials. Like many fascinated by the pyramids ("pyramidiots" to archaeologists), von Däniken was overly taken with the process of building the massive structures. The most famous pyramids, those of the Fourth Dynasty pharaohs Khufu, Khafre, and Menkaure at Giza, were built around 2500 BCE and comprised millions of blocks. The largest of the pyramids, that of Khufu, is called the Great Pyramid for a good reason: standing 451 feet high, the "Horizon of Khufu" contains 2.3 million stone blocks weighing an average 2.5 tons, and the pyramid is built so perfectly that it is nearly level and oriented off true north by only three and a half feet.[20] In these measurements (which von Däniken got wrong), he saw the handiwork of aliens. He claims that the Great Pyramid is located at the very center of the earth's land-masses, for it "divides continents and oceans into two equal halves [and] it also lies at the center of gravity of the continents."[21] That this was not true (it works only on a Mercator projection) was beside the point. It "proved" that aliens laid out the Egyptian landscape. "In this connection let us not forget Piri Reis' maps! It cannot all be coincidence or explained away as fairy stories."[22] Fairy stories they may not have been, but they were close. Yet the sheer audacity of the number of assertions had numbed the mind and produced an acceptance in the reader's mind of the rickety edifice he built on shaky foundations. Oh, and of course, Egypt was a space travel center for alien refueling stops.

On Easter Island, a rocky outcropping in the Pacific famous for the hundreds of giant stone heads called *moai* that dot the island landscape, von Däniken proclaimed that aliens had inspired the heads or set them up themselves when stranded their during a shipwreck. Since the island had no trees, von Däniken rightly asked how the natives could have moved the heavy stone statues. He could not have known in 1968 that new research would eventually show that there once were trees, felled in the transport of the statues. This would eventually cause ecological devastation and the collapse of the island's population. Therefore, the aliens were no longer needed to explain the heads.

He also provided an endless list of "mysterious" artifacts, already well known and explained, from the so-called Baghdad battery, an early electrical experiment—which he does not say dates from the first centuries of the common era when scientific experimentation had begun—to the Delhi pillar, made of iron that never rusts. Providing no sources, his assertions are simply presented as true on his word alone. Or, rather, he presents them as questions to which the reader is expected to provide an extraterrestrial answer: "Could this be . . . ?" "Might it not have been . . . ?" That way he never really says anything at all, and when shown wrong on the specifics, he can instead argue that it was a mere question that he did not definitively answer.

He finishes the book with descriptions of UFO sightings, thus raising the possibility that the ancient gods were returning in our own day and age. In his conclusion von Däniken apparently decides that his earlier assertion that the past was more exciting than the future is not true: "Man has a magnificent future ahead of him, a future which will far surpass his magnificent past."[23]

This, for all its inconsistency and contradiction, was the phenomenon that was *Chariots of the Gods?*

But its lack of facts, its anti-intellectual hubris, its contempt of academia and established authority should have torpedoed the very notion of alien ancestors in the water. But something in the zeitgeist of 1970s America embraced all these facets as the ultimate manifestation of the postmodern ideal. The counter-cultural revolution and the social upheavals of the 1960s had smashed the power of old paradigms, old ideologies, and old faiths. Authority figures were no longer afforded the same power they once held, thanks largely to the debacle that was the Vietnam war, that horrible outgrowth of France's failed efforts in Indochina to hold on to the remnants of her empire after the nineteenth-century imperial age had ended. If the authority figures in the world were willing to enter endless ideological quagmires and stalemates, if they were willing to bring the world to the brink of nuclear war, as they had in the Cuban missile crisis, perhaps they did not have all the answers. Perhaps they never did. In a world that was all too frightening and all too coldly mechanical and scientific in its instruments of death, it became easy to understand why so many would try to escape into fantasies and the mysteries of the past as a way out of the all-too-explicit horrors of the present.

As conservative author David Frum noted in a study of the 1970s, "[V]on Daniken's science-fiction fantasies satisfied the needs of an age that hungered for mysteries. In its content, the God is a Spaceman theory may have been scientistic flim-flam; for its adherents, it came to be a substitute faith."[24] In fact, religious belief had been on the decline for decades, the result of a century of scientific progress and the decline of all types of institutional authority. The old faiths represented the old world, the antebellum world before the catastrophe of 1914, and their very structure could no longer jive in a modern new world that increasingly came to define itself in opposition to the earlier age's morality and culture. As a new secular faith, *Chariots* embodied the spirit of the times and as such it found its greatest success.

Chariots had an immediate impact on pulp culture. The *National Enquirer* serialization, the NBC documentary hosted by Rod Serling, and the feature film version of the book had conspired by 1975 to propel Erich von Däniken to the upper echelons of pop culture stardom. His theory was on everyone's lips, and many outside the academic sphere embraced *Chariots'* shocking interpretation of ancient history. To put it quite bluntly, history as taught in schools was (and is) boring, and the history that von Däniken rewrote was so much more exciting that even if it were not true, readers *wanted* it to be true. And since schools had done such a bad job of teaching history anyway, most of von Däniken's readers did not know enough of the academic view of the past to think critically about what they read. Students had come out of school without a working knowledge of the methods of archaeology or history, and so they were especially receptive to pseudoscholars' simplified versions of those disciplines.[25] In the pages of von Däniken one could find an explanation of everything, neat and tidy, without the complications or shades of meaning that had grown so tiresome in modern life.

Von Däniken followed up the success of *Chariots of the Gods?* with a sequel, *Gods from Outer Space*, which he wrote while a guest of the Swiss government at Remand Prison following his conviction on fraud charges. Originally titled *Return to the Stars*, the new book picked up where *Chariots* left off. When he wrote it in 1968, he could not know how big a success *Chariots* was about to become; nevertheless, write it he did. Like his previous effort, this book, too, begins with a shocking first paragraph, though this one was written for him by his publisher: "Erich von Däniken is not a scholar. He is an autodidact, which the dictionary defines as a man who is self-taught."[26] In his introduction, von Däniken wishes to find answers to the questions of "Louis Pauwles, Jacques Bergier, and Robert Charroux."[27]

Gods from Outer Space focuses more heavily on the modern implications of his theory. He argues that current archaeological methods will never uncover the "proof" of the ancient-astronaut hypothesis because the "proof" cannot be found in the ground. Instead, he says, it lies in our very DNA, which the aliens manipulated to create humanity. He discusses space travel at length, as well as the arguments for aliens arriving in metal spheres, the "ideal" shape for space travel.

In this new book, von Däniken was just as careless with his facts. Describing the ancient drawing of a trident carved into a cliffside on the Bay of Pisco in Peru, he says the trident cannot be seen from land and can only be seen from a mile out on shore, therefore making it probable that it was actually meant as a signal to aliens. He was wrong, and the trident is clearly visible from many locations around the bay. He also finds traces of his extraterrestrials in Ice Age cave paintings, descriptions of flying machines in the Indian Vedas, and once more in Easter Island, which he calls the "inexhaustible topic."[28]

Sadly for him, as we have seen, research in subsequent decades would prove him spectacularly wrong. He also quotes extensively from the *Book of Dzyan*, praising its tremendous antediluvian grasp of Earth's primal heritage. He is blissfully unaware that said book, as we have seen, originated in the mind of Helena Blavatsky and is known only from her book, *The Secret Doctrine*. It was possibly one of the inspirations for H. P. Lovecraft's *Necronomicon*.

He finishes *Gods from Outer Space* with more literal interpretations of ancient texts, concluding from mythological descriptions of hybrid animal-humans like the Minotaur (half man, half bull) and centaurs (half man, half horse), that such creatures really existed and that aliens made them. After all, our ancestors were but children compared with smart old us, so they could not have had imagination.[29] They could be only reporters, since they had no intelligence of their own. This theme was to dominate ancient-astronaut and lost-civilization theories for the rest of the twentieth century.

Completing the trifecta of his early 1970s trilogy, von Däniken next released *The Gold of the Gods* in 1972, "illustrated with 100 photographs and color plates" to anticipate the success of the NBC documentary *In Search of Ancient Astronauts*.[30] Aside from covering much of the same ground as his previous outings, *Gold* added chapters on similar "proofs" in China and on the Pacific island ruins of Nan Madol (Ponape), the same stone ruins that H. P. Lovecraft had used as his inspiration for Cthulhu's sunken city of R'lyeh. These were also the same ruins that Col. James Churchward held as proof of the existence of the lost continent of Mu. Nan Madol is a beautiful series of boat-shaped ruins gracing islands irrigated with artificial canals. The ruins were built of basalt "logs" of uniform size and hexagonal shape. Von Däniken rejected the geological explanation that these pillars were natural lava flows mined by the people of Ponape. Unable or unwilling to understand the complex geology involved in forming hexagonal "logs" (the same geological processes as the "Giants' Causeway" in Ireland), he dismisses the geologists' findings as "inane" and instead announced without proof that the stones of Nan Madol were instead "accurately worked."[31] Naturally, such workmanship could only come with extraterrestrial help.

However, these were mere minor filler compared with the most extraordinary claim in *Gold of the Gods*, a claim that von Däniken himself conceded seemed too good to be true: "To me, this is the most incredible, fantastic story of the century. It could easily have come straight from the realms of Science Fiction if I had not seen and photographed the incredible truth in person."[32] What was this magnificent find? It was a set of mysterious caves in Ecuador that proved aliens had visited Earth.

Von Däniken came to the caves with their owner, Juan Moricz of Argentina. "Suddenly, from one step to another, broad daylight changed to pitch darkness. Birds fluttered past our heads. We felt the draught they created and shrank back. We switched on our torches and the lamps on our helmets, and there in front of us was a gaping hole which led down into the depths."[33] A very atmospheric entrance, it was. Once inside, the intrepid von Däniken discovered caves that intersected at perfect right angles, with smooth vertical walls that looked as though they had been sliced from the living rock by super-hot lasers. "Obviously, these passages did not originate from natural causes—they looked more like contemporary air-raid shelters!"[34] Von Däniken exclaimed on seeing the walls, "I'd like to see the archaeologist with the nerve to tell me that this work was done with hand axes!"[35] It seems odd in retrospect that he jumped to the conclusion that the caves were carved and not natural, but given his histrionics, the reader goes along with him at first. He even provided a photograph of the interior of the cave to demonstrate his convictions, though I must confess that the walls never looked to me as vertical or orthogonal as von Däniken described.

Inside the vast galleries of caves, von Däniken discovered tables and chairs, made of what he says was "some kind of plastic."[36] There were statues of animals strewn about the caves, all of them cast in solid gold. Along one wall stood an entire library written on metal plaques, only "millimeters thick" and measuring about three by one and a half feet, and they stood upright without crinkling, made of some unknown material. Sadly, the words on this ancient library were indecipherable, written in a language never before seen, the only example of Pre-Columbian writing in all of South America. "This metal library was created to outlast the ages, to remain legible for eternity."[37]

Also in the cave were pieces of art: an amulet that depicts a man striding a globe centuries before the shape of the earth was known and a plaque that shows a dinosaur, sixty-five million years after they went extinct. Here, too, von Däniken provides photographs of the artworks. Immediately the reader notices that the pictures are crude, almost childlike. The amulet shows a stick figure on a semicircle crisscrossed with lines (latitude and longitude). The plaque shows a child's version of a dinosaur, complete with spikes on the head and the back, rendered in the curvilinear style of one who cannot draw. For a sophisticated civilization making libraries on alloys millimeters thick, their visual arts are decidedly lacking. To remedy this, he proposes that later peoples reused the aliens' laser-built caves, an elite guarding the library's secret.[38]

Shocking von Däniken was a stone sculpture of a skeleton, anatomically correct in bone structure. "Were there anatomists who dissected bodies for the prehistoric sculptor? As we know, Wilhelm Conrad Röntgen did not discover the new kind of rays he called X-rays until 1895!"[39] Apparently, the natural process of decay and the familiarity of the ancients with death never crossed his mind when a technological presupposition would do. Nor, for that matter, did the idea of simply feeling one's ribs by running one's fingers up and down the chest. Again, a photograph accompanies, and the sculpture is notable only for its crudeness.

He also claims that vast amounts of golden artifacts came from the cave, and he reproduces in color plates pictures of this amazing art, art that shows Egyptian-style pyramids, flying serpents (recalling the Mexican god Quetzalcoatl, the "feathered serpent"), and elephants. Also noticeable is that every piece of art emerging from the Ecuadorian cave was clearly inscribed by the same hand. Each piece features the same childlike drawings, the same rounded forms, and the same 1970s-style "smiley faces" on cats, flowers, and the sun. Though von Däniken dates these gold works to 12,000 BCE, he seems in *Gold of the Gods* incapable of coming to any other conclusion than these works represented a school of art inspired by aliens.

Of course, as with any good tale of mystery, the natives won't go near the cave because powerful curses protect it. The 1973 American edition of the book concludes with a back flap announcing (or threatening?) a new von Däniken book to be published the next year, in 1974. That book, *In Search of Ancient Gods: My Pictorial Evidence for the Impossible*, unintentionally provided the answer to the dilemma. Describing the old priest who collects the gold plaques von Däniken finds so amazing, he says, "They [visitors] say he owns nothing but worthless junk made by present day Indians and palmed off on him. It is true that [the priest] is no longer in possession of all his mental powers."[40]

Von Däniken's claims were extraordinary, but this time he seemed, on the surface at least, to have proof. There were photographs and witnesses to the impossible, even if this story did sound amazingly like the H. P. Lovecraft story "The Nameless City," where underground caves yielded alien secrets. Surely, this claim of Ecuadorian caves filled with gold writing would cause a major upheaval in archaeology. Surely, every archaeologist, linguist, and historian would clamor to Ecuador to take part in the deciphering of the greatest discovery in world history. As one archaeologist with twenty-five years' experience in Ecuadorian prehistory told a journalist:

> In all the time I was there I found no basis for any of these claims by von Däniken. There have been legends in Ecuador about gold and so on, but nobody has ever found anything. There really is no evidence that there were books or writings of gold.[41]

The journalist Gavin Souter confronted von Däniken about this and asked where his proof was. Von Däniken pointed to a Spanish-language newspaper article about the cave: "I think it says something about metal plates." It did not.[42]

But this was not evidence that von Däniken was lying. It was only one archaeologist's opinion, after all. So in 1976, Neil Armstrong, the first man to walk on the moon, led an expedition into Ecuador to verify or refute von Däniken's claims. After some fruitless searching, he returned with the conclusion that there was nothing in the Ecuadorian jungles except jungle. Von Däniken replied that Armstrong was clearly confused and had searched the wrong caves, though he would not say where the right caves were. Nevertheless, newspaper headlines proclaimed "Däniken Unmasked!" and "The Charlatan Makes a Fool of Himself."[43]

Finally, a British expedition attempted to provide a definitive answer. Their trip to the caves found no trace of von Däniken's gold library, only some evidence of early, primitive habitation in caves that were utterly ordinary, not laser-hewn perfection. Von Daniken finally admitted that the caves he described were not real, that his evidence was not real, that *Gold of the Gods* was not true. He said in his defense that because he was writing "popular" works for mass consumption, not scientific treatises, he could take "poetic license" with the truth. In short, he admitted to what amounted to fraud.[44] Of course, few of his fans bothered to listen; the idea was more important than the man, and the idea meant everything to them.

Von Däniken would go on to write more books, totaling twenty-seven by 2005, though none would come close to the success he found with his first books. Gradually, the ancient-astronaut craze would slow and fall out of the public consciousness during the no-nonsense 1980s. His 1979 book, *Signs of the Gods*, did not do as well as earlier efforts, though this time he used the recent birth of the first test-tube baby for exploring whether aliens ordered ancient cultures to mummify their dead because they would need to preserve their body cells "to produce beings in your own image."[45] The aliens were now ordering human cloning.

After this, fewer of his books made it to English translation, none of the eleven written between 1983 and 1996. Only with the revival of interest in alternative archaeology in the New Age 1990s did von Däniken's star again ascend. Capitalizing on new theories that claimed Egpyt's iconic statue, the Great Sphinx, predated the end of the Ice Age, which we will discuss in more detail later, von Däniken released a book in 1996 cribbing shamelessly from the new wave of "alternative archaeology" books that were his indirect stepchildren. Borrowing from them, he accused Egyptologists of a vast conspiracy to hide the truth and appropriate the glory for themselves with his usual quiet dignity: "Do spoiled little children ever grow up?"[46] He could have asked it of himself.

The next year his new book proclaimed *The Return of the Gods* and seemed to promise hope that the ancient visitors would return. The last chapter of that book was simply a reproduction of the final chapter from the book released the year before, an economical way to keep churning out books without writing new material.[47] By the twenty-first century he tried his hand at Greek mythology, proposing that ancient Greek myths were, like everything else in the past, the legacy of alien gods.[48]

I tried to get a comment from Erich von Däniken about the genesis of his theories and about how much of them he took from Robert Charroux and Pauwles and Bergier, but I was unsuccessful. His spokesman, Greek-American body-building promoter Giorgio Tsoukalos, had this to say to me:

Just the fact that you so desperately attempt to dismantle our theory *proves* that we *are* on the *right* track. Otherwise you would *not* feel so threatened by our theories! . . . I will certainly not forward your questions to Erich, and his secretary has already been informed about your malevolent intentions.[49]

Defensive posturing is the last refuge of the desperate, and the ancient-astronaut theory had already started to show its desperation. By the first years of the twenty-first century, Erich von Däniken had become a joke, a punch line in archaeological circles. Though once a very popular author, he would never again be taken seriously. His intellectual dishonesty and sloppy research discredited any chance he had at scientific acceptance, small though it was. He eventually tried his hand at television, marketing *Chariots of the Gods?* as a twenty-first century action-adventure, where (not so) hot young coeds uncover mankind's hidden history in spite of an archaeological-military conspiracy to hide traces of alien life. In 2003, von Däniken opened in Switzerland "Mystery Park," a $60 million theme park re-creating Earth's ancient monuments and explaining in a fun, family-friendly atmosphere, that aliens created them. It receives a reported five thousand visitors a day.[50] The best reason to visit, says its Web site, is that the park is "a year-round attraction for young and old that can be visited in any weather."[51]

Though more popular today than in the 1980s, the extra-terrestrial-genesis theory would never again see the popularity it had in the 1970s. The *Chariots* phenomenon had run its course as early as the mid-1970s. It was then that the most important spawn of *Chariots* would launch the sequence of events that would inevitably tick down to the massive explosion of the late 1990s, this spawn of Cthulhu that would change our view of science and morality forever. However, it was over for the hotelier in Zurich. Erich von Däniken had done his job. H. P. Lovecraft's ancient extraterrestrial gods had successfully wormed their way from the pages of fiction to the realm of fact. At least in the popular mind, anyway.

INTERLUDE
THE VIEW FROM 1976

9

THE FORK IN THE ROAD

By an odd turn of events, the year 1976 became the defining time for the ancient-astronaut theory. As we shall see, numerous forces converged in or around that year to solidify and define what was to come. Though the ancient-astronaut theory seemed to be running its course and would retrench during the 1980s, the events of 1976 would solidify the theory's base of support and prepare the theory for the renaissance of the 1990s and the resurgence of occultism in the twenty-first century.

By 1976, Erich von Däniken's theories had reached a massive audience, and he had spawned a wave of similarly themed books. Yet there were troubling signs that the ancient-astronaut theory was running out of steam despite the proliferation of books on the topic. To shore up support, von Däniken had helped found the Ancient Astronaut Society, but the organization devoted to exploring his claims had just two thousand members worldwide when von Däniken was the guest of honor at its annual Congress in 1974, the year *Chariots of the Gods?* became a feature film.[1]

Detractors and debunkers, too, were active in combating extraterrestrial-genesis theory. They offered refutations, including Clifford Wilson's famous *Crash Go the Chariots* (1972)

and Peter White's *The Past Is Human* (1974), both of which dev-
astated nearly every one of von Däniken's major claims.
Inspired in part by these and other attacks on von Däniken, in
1976, Neil Armstrong launched his expedition to Ecuador, discussed in the previous chapter, which all but conclusively
demonstrated that von Däniken's fantastic "proof" in *Gold of
the Gods* was nothing more than literary fantasy. PBS's *Nova*
also rebuked von Däniken in a well-researched, well-explained
special, "The Case of the Ancient Astronauts." From this multimedia assault, a great number of people initially intrigued by
von Däniken came to realize how empty his promise of extraterrestrial salvation was. By all accounts, the theory should
have been dead and buried.

Nevertheless, since the ancient-astronaut theory was less
about facts than about the emotional resonance of extraterrestrial gods, these attacks had little impact on the hard-core
believers. For every person disaffected by the debunkers,
another still held to the *Chariots* faith. As with so many things
in life, the initial mistake got all the press, and the later correc-
tions never made it to the front page. At least four million had
read *Chariots of the Gods?* by 1976, but only a fraction of that
number had read *Crash Go the Chariots*. As a result, millions
were still open to the idea of ancient astronauts.

The success of *Chariots of the Gods?* as both book and
motion picture had propelled the speculation of man's alien
origins into the public consciousness. Erich von Däniken's sensational claims had received a public acclaim that his Victorian
predecessors like Ignatius Donnelly could never have imagined. But Donnelly's Atlantis begat Blavatsky's Lemuria and
Churchward's Mu, so it was only a matter of time before von
Däniken spawned his own imitators. Just as we have seen with
the wave of emulators who followed in the wake of H. P. Lovecraft's bold new idea and Pauwles and Bergier's repackaging of
that idea, so, too, did von Däniken inspire waves of imitators

who wrote endlessly about ancient mysteries. By 1976, store shelves were flooded with reams of ancient alien and UFO-mystery books. Oddly enough, Jacques Bergier, whose speculations inspired von Däniken, was himself one of those imitators, publishing *Extraterrestrial Visitations from Prehistoric Times to the Present* and *Extraterrestrial Intervention* in 1974. Among the other notable entries were some of the most speculative, pseudoscientific, and bizarre books ever brought to market. It is doubtful now exactly how many took their claims seriously, but millions were intrigued enough to buy copies, and presumably these readers believed at least some of what they read.

To capitalize on the *Chariots* phenomenon, many of these new books bore covers designed in imitation of the large block letters appearing on von Däniken's paperbacks. Ralph and Judy Blum received one such design when they published *Beyond Earth: Man's Contact with UFOs* (1974), whose cover pointedly asked, "Are von Däniken's Ancient Astronauts landing in America today?" Trying to connect ancient astronauts to modern UFOs, two modern myths came together not for the last time. Joseph Blumrich built on a suggestion in *Chariots* and produced *The Spaceships of Ezekiel* (1974), arguing that the biblical prophet really witnessed ancient UFOs. Tony Earll brought us *Mu Revealed* (1975) with all that it implied. Robert Charroux returned with several new books pushing the alien angle, and R. L. Dione summed up the ancient-alien craze succinctly in the title of 1975's *God Drives a Flying Saucer*.

The next year was the so-called *Viking* Summer, when NASA's *Viking* space probes reached the surface of Mars and renewed speculation about whether life had existed on the Red Planet. Though chemical tests found no conclusive proof of ancient life, many of the old theories of ancient Martian life sprang to the forefront. Only later would a researcher notice that one of the *Viking* photographs seemed to show a facelike structure on Mars, fuelling decades of speculation about ancient Martian life. However, in the *Viking* Summer, the Mars frenzy helped create demand for books on space, science, and, of course, ancient mysteries.

In 1976 alone, new releases took us in search of the Tunguska Event (the 1908 comet strike in Siberia), Noah's Ark, Bigfoot, UFOs, lost civilizations, standing stones, Frankenstein, and every other mystery imaginable. Quite literally, the catalogue of books, movies, and documentaries on esoteric and occult topics was too long to list, though one recent Web site tried.[2] Most bizarre of all, a novel published in English translation that year, Walter Ernsting's *The Day the Gods Died*, featured Erich von Däniken as its hero, bravely searching out the truth of humanity's alien past.[3]

While von Däniken had crossed over onto the fiction shelves with Ernsting's idol-worshiping novel, H. P. Lovecraft was making his triumphant return to America's book stores, ironically enough, in the nonfiction section. The science fiction author L. Sprague de Camp produced a long biography in 1975 of the author from Providence, abridged in paperback in 1976. In it he documented for the first time Lovecraft's life in an accessible, mass-produced volume. De Camp was justly famous for his science fiction as well as his nonfiction books on ancient mysteries, but this adventure in biography proved to be his most controversial work. It portrayed Lovecraft as a neurotic, sexually repressed mental case and made many strong judgments about Lovecraft's character and actions. De Camp had reduced his life to Freudian neuroses and used the Freudian framework to interpret much of Lovecraft's personal failures and literary successes. A warts-and-all biography, de Camp seems to delight in focusing on Lovecraft's flaws, his xenophobia, racism, and laziness. Yet de Camp's H. P. *Lovecraft: A Biography* remained the only account of Lovecraft's life readily accessible until the S. T. Joshi biography in 1996, which quickly went out of print until 2004. For many amateur Lovecraft fans, de Camp remained the most available source for Lovecraft's life, and if one can discount the Freudian imagery, his recitation of facts is generally accurate (even though it does have several errors) and makes for a good read.

The release of the de Camp biography capped a stunning few years of revival for Lovecraft. After spending most of the 1950s and early 1960s condemned to wherever it is old pulp stories go to die, new American paperback editions of Lovecraft's work came out in the late 1960s and early 1970s following his rediscovery in France and subsequent popularity in America. His dark, brooding stories struck a chord with the disenchanted youth of the counterculture, and, as before, Cthulhu called to those seeking the extraordinary and the bizarre. He was a perfect fit for the new times. Six new editions of Lovecraft (plus a Derleth "collaboration") came out between 1965 and 1976, and no fewer than nineteen anthologies reprinted Lovecraft stories during those years. French attention had saved Lovecraft; now finally America began to give him the recognition he failed to find in life.

Also during this revival, the movies found Lovecraft. Throughout the 1960s Edgar Allan Poe had been a favorite source for horror movie writers, notably in the series of Vincent Price films based on Poe's poems and stories. Now Lovecraft had his turn. Vincent Price tried his hand at Lovecraft in 1963's *The Haunted Palace*, based on the alchemy novel *The Case of Charles Dexter Ward*. However, for marketing purposes, the movie was given a title from Poe since Lovecraft was not yet famous enough to carry a film in his own right. Boris Karloff, well known as the monster in *Frankenstein*, starred in 1965's *Die Monster Die!*, based on Lovecraft's "The Colour Out of Space," and 1968's *The Crimson Cult*, based on "The Dreams in the Witch-House." And Dean Stockwell starred as the spawn of the Old Ones in a campy adaptation of *The Dunwich Horror* (1970), notable more for its psychedelic special effects than for anything else.

All in all, the Lovecraftian cinema left much to be desired. All these films had one thing in common: none of them was terribly faithful to either the spirit or the letter of Lovecraft's stories. They mined out of Lovecraft the rudiments of plot and atmosphere, but they were loath to touch the primal horrors or the philosophical conceits that made Lovecraft's stories better than standard pulp fare. Much more faithful to the Lovecraftian spirit was 1979's *Alien*. Though not based on any Lovecraft story in particular, the tentacled, amorphous alien entity terrorizing the denizens of a lone spaceship was inspired by Lovecraft's monsters. The "biomechanical" alien was designed by the artist and sculptor H. R. Giger, a Lovecraft afficianado, who in 1991 produced a picture-book version of Lovecraft's *Necronomicon*. In the shape and form of the creature, one can see the legacy of Cthulhu and the Old Ones, and in its behavior one can see the essence of Lovecraft's work. The alien is a killing machine, without conscience or mercy, just as the Old Ones. As the ship's science officer remarked in the movie, "I admire its purity, its sense of survival; unclouded by conscience, remorse, or delusions of morality."[4] A clearer statement of Lovecraft's "cosmic indifference" had never been spoken. *Alien* took its inspiration from *The Thing from Another World*, itself derived from John W. Campbell's "Who Goes There," a rewrite of Lovecraft's *At the Mountains of Madness*.

Television, too, tried its hand at Lovecraft. As we have seen, *Twilight Zone* creator Rod Serling returned to the air with the anthology *Night Gallery* in 1968, and he incorporated a few of Lovecraft's lesser tales into his mixture of horror stories before the show's cancellation in August of 1973. The Gothic soap opera *Dark Shadows* featured plots based on the Cthulhu Mythos, the so-called leviathan episodes of 1969–1970. Lovecraft would not come to television again until the *The Real*

Ghostbusters cartoon series did an episode in 1986 titled "The Collect Call of Cthulhu," featuring a tentacled beast stealing a copy of the infamous *Necronomicon.*

That book was quickly taking on a life of its own, one that dovetailed in the 1970s with the rise of magical thinking. By 1976, the *Necronomicon* was a pop culture phenomenon. In the decades before and following Lovecraft's death, his stories began to become increasingly popular as ever-greater numbers of people found his work through reprints in *Weird Tales*, anthologies, and Arkham House books. Soon there were scattered reports that readers actually tried to find copies of the *Necronomicon* at public libraries and old book shops, prompting Lovecraft to say he felt "quite guilty" for all the confusion. A bookseller named Philip Duschnes went so far as to publish a hoax catalog featuring a listing for the *Necronomicon.* As time passed, hoaxers began placing fake entries for the abhorred volume in the card catalogs of university libraries. Both Yale and the University of California at Berkeley once sported listings for the work of the Mad Arab, Abdul Alhazred.

Others began to plant fake references to the book in the bibliographies of legitimate works in the 1970s. Even Michael Crichton, eventual author of *Jurassic Park*, placed the *Necronomicon* in the bibliography for his 1976 novel *Eaters of the Dead*. It was obviously a joke, as he named Lovecraft as the editor. However, spoofs and pranks like that lent a false reality to the book that never existed.

Just a few years previous, in 1973, George Scithers and Lovecraft biographer L. Sprague de Camp had released a volume they claimed was the original Arabic text, under its original title *Al-Azif*. However, the text was nothing but a few pages of meaningless calligraphy repeated over and over again. As de Camp admitted, "Having decided that if the *Necronomicon* did not exist, it should, George Scithers hired an artist to decorate blank pages with a series of squiggles vaguely resembling Arabic and Syriac writing."[5] But this self-described "little hoax" had nothing of the impact of the Simon *Necronomicon*.

Not long after, in 1977, a man known only by the name of Simon released an inexpensive paperback edition of the *Necronomicon*, which he claimed was a genuine translation of the text written by Abdul Alhazred in the wastes of Arabia. The next year George Hay, along with many other authors, including Colin Wilson, released *The Necronomicon: The Book of Dead Names*. Hay, too, claimed that his volume was the genuine book of the mad poet, but Wilson quickly admitted that the book was a pure fake designed for entertainment, not magic. But the Simon *Necronomicon* did not seem to be joking.

New York City, the hub of so many cultural phenomena, was also the hub of occult thought during the first heyday of the New Age in the 1970s. As Daniel Harms and John Wilson Gonce III discovered while researching the *Necronomicon*, "Into this atmosphere walked a supposed Eastern Orthodox bishop known as 'Simon.' He carried a manuscript that, he claimed, two monks of his denomination had taken from a library or private collection as a part of the biggest book heist in recent history." Despite claiming to be a bishop, Simon was not above making money, and he released 666 copies of *Necronomicon* in hardcover, and a full paperback edition appeared in 1980.[6]

The Simon volume purported to be a series of magical rituals for invoking the dread gods of the Lovecraftian pantheon. Though it warned its readers not to attempt any of the rituals, it reprinted previously known instructions for magical rites: "It mostly consists of ritual récipé texts transcribed from various Mesopotamian sources, Sumerian, Akkadian, Babylonian, and Assyrian, with assorted references to Lovecraftian (and Derlethian) deities tossed in at random," said Dan Clore, an author and researcher into the history of weird fiction.[7] The Simon book tells its readers that owning an original copy can produce all manner of harmful side effects, so "as a matter of policy, we cannot honour any requests to see the *Necronomicon* in its original state."[8]

The illustrator of the Simon *Necronomicon*, Khem Caigan, whose work continues to masquerade as genuine ancient mystical symbols, confirmed, though, that the manuscript to the Simon volume was hand typed with sketchy illustrations that did not seem to be genuine copies of eighth-century originals.[9]

Dan Clore noticed that the Simon volume contained another mistake that gave away its hoax nature. While it claimed to be the dread volume of Lovecraft, the Simon volume specifically stated that the entities described therein were in a great cosmic battle: "Lovecraft developed a kind of Christian Myth of the struggle between opposing forces of Light and Darkness," Simon wrote.[10] But this is *not* a concept from Lovecraft. As we have seen, that idea was first introduced by August Derleth after Lovecraft's death. Intriguingly, many of the undisputed inventions of August Derleth, like Ithaqua the Wind-Walker, appear in the supposedly ancient *Necronomicon* of Simon, along with other Derleth creations, like the identification of the Old Ones with the elements.

In 2004, Alan Cabal finally told the true story behind the Simon tome, identifying Peter Levenda as the elusive Simon and explaining that the whole book was cooked up by devotees of Satanist Aleister Crowley's Ordo Templi Orientis by inserting Lovecraftian names into Sumerian and Babylonian myths.[11] However, the Simon *Necronomicon* continues to draw the faithful to its cause, as do many of the other hoaxes. Today there are at least ten different fake *Necronomicon*s available, and there are those who believe that Lovecraft's magic is real.

In response, the Church of Satan set up a Web page devoted to debunking the *Necronomicon* hoax because they say they receive many e-mails asking about the book. Though they admit that the Simon volume, and all other published versions, are fakes, they hedge on whether they can be used as a genuine magical grimoire, especially since many Satanists (including, it was rumored, church founder Anton LaVey) use the book for magical rituals. According to the church, "A careful look at *The Satanic Bible* will tell you that Dr. LaVey encouraged the magician to use any and all elements of fiction, fact and fancy to create his Intellectual Decompression Chamber," a sort of Satanic yoga.[12]

The use of Lovecraft in Satanic cults and magical gatherings in the 1970s prefigured the rise of ancient aliens as a belief system for the UFO cults that began to emerge at the same time. But during the 1970s, these forces remained in embryo. Yet this repeated crossing of Lovecraftian concepts from fiction to fact and back again proved that the power of Lovecraft's ideas continued long after he had died. Lovecraft could not imagine that forty years after his death, Satanists would be using his creations to summon the dark powers, and it would have depressed him greatly.

Nevertheless, thanks to this uncoordinated multimedia campaign of books, movies, and hoaxes, Lovecraft was back, and he would never again go out of print. His books continued to sell steadily through the 1980s and 1990s, when high-quality trade paperbacks repackaged Lovecraft in attractive volumes. In 1985, *Re-Animator* became the first popularly successful film based on a Lovecraft tale, the minor Frankenstein-themed "Herbert West: Re-Animator." A small gaming company started selling a role-playing game named "Call of Cthulhu," bringing Lovecraft to the *Dungeons and Dragons* set. By the 1990s, Lovecraft, like alternative archaeology, was set to explode into the public consciousness. At the same time that the Lovecraft renaissance was beginning, other developments in society paralleled the resurgence of Lovecraftian fiction and the success of the extraterrestrial-genesis theory in many of the same quarters.

The resignation of Richard Nixon in August 1974 served as a capstone to a ten-year period of increasing distrust in American government and authority. Halfway across the world, it was quickly becoming obvious that the Soviet system, founded on the utopian promise of universal socialism, had instead trapped itself in an inevitable quagmire of corruption and decay. The Vietnam War finally ground to an end with an ignoble peace and the realization that American power and resolve no longer meant what they had in decades past. That same year the NBC documentary *In Search of Ancient Astronauts* made the case that the scientific authorities were just as corrupt, entrenched, and wrong as the political powers-that-be. The effects of the cultural revolution of the 1960s continued to be felt, though the revolutionary fervor had given way to a mellower embrace of the occult, the pseudoscientific, and the alternative.

But moreover, the ennui that had begun to set in showed itself in the nomination of peanut farmer Jimmy Carter as the Democratic candidate for president in July 1976. Almost as a concession to the climate of the times, Carter admitted before the election that year that he had seen a shining UFO the size of the moon while governor of Georgia in 1969 and filed a report.[13] Not the towering figure that the pre-Nixon presidents were, Carter and his predecessor, Gerald Ford, represented in their informality (could one imagine Billy McKinley or Johnny Adams?) and lack of stature the feeling of decline that came over America in those years. As Carter himself told the nation in his famous "malaise speech," America was in a crisis:

> It is a crisis of confidence. It is a crisis that strikes at the very heart and soul and spirit of our national will. We can see this crisis in the growing doubt about the meaning of our own lives and in the loss of a unity of purpose for our Nation. The erosion of our confidence in the future is threatening to destroy the social and the political fabric of America.[14]

This loss of purpose could be attributed to many things, but mostly it was simply the culmination of the natural processes that govern the course of civilizations. Western civilization had run its course; its major goals—liberty, equality, fraternity—were largely, if not completely, accomplished with the advent of civil rights laws and women's liberation. The emerging sexual freedom broke the old forms of social control that dated from the Church's rollback of Roman liberties after Constantine's revolution.[15] Liberal democracy was the order of the day, and its rivals, fascism and communism, had largely been destroyed or contained. There was, despite advocacy groups' protestations, nothing major left to do. There was only cleanup. In such a climate it was no wonder mystery and the occult were replacing logic and reason. As a concession to the national embrace of extraterrestrial topics, Carter announced he would open the government's UFO files, but eventually decided against it.[16]

Like Rome before it, the decadent West saw a crisis in faith, when the old gods and old religions no longer held the power they once did. Beginning with the Darwinian revolution, science gradually replaced religion in the minds of intellectual elite, and religious belief reached new lows each year.[17] By the 1960s, the youthful generation had lost its religious faith, and in the 1970s, belief hit rock bottom; secularism was the watchword of the day.[18] But also like Rome, new forms of faith would rise up to fill the void that the decline of traditional religious authorities left behind. As we have seen, the first hoax edition of Lovecraft's *Necronomicon* came out in 1973. That year another dark book would give Satanists another reason to cheer. With the publication of William Peter Blatty's *The Exorcist*, and the 1973 movie of the same name, the rite of exorcism took on a new meaning in America and helped spawn a religious revival and the development of evangelical Christian deliverance ministries to drive out demons (real ones, from hell) that Americans discovered after seeing the film.[19] Everywhere, Americans began to see demons and, through them, a way to touch the supernatural and find faith once more.

For the secular who could not return to religion, no matter how strange its trappings, ancient astronauts and the occult became a type of surrogate faith that allowed believers to have something to cling to and something to advocate and share in secret. It was a secret doctrine that had become a modern myth, for it allowed readers to once more believe in the literal truth of the Bible by replacing the divine with the extraterrestrial. It restored the comfort of authority and the sense of awe and wonder that went missing with the subjugation of the universe to man's laws of science.

Cousin to ancient astronauts, UFOs were also a surrogate for religion, with space aliens playing the role of angels. After the 1975 broadcast of an NBC-TV movie about the abduction of Betty and Barney Hill, suddenly UFO abductions became the cultural equivalent of an apotheosis. In November, Travis Walton and his Arizona logging crew claimed a UFO abducted Walton and held him hostage for five days before dumping him on the highway.[20] Dozens more reports sprang up once this hit the newspapers. Suddenly aliens were stealing people out of their houses, aliens were impregnating women, and aliens were fulfilling all the functions of medieval ghosts, witches, and fairy creatures in what one researcher called "technological supernaturalism."[21] For those who could not touch evil through demonic possession à la *The Exorcist*, UFO abduction allowed for a meeting with the secular version of angels. One of those 1970s abductees was a French journalist and race-car driver named Claude Vorilhon, who in 1973 was allegedly taken by aliens. In 1976 he took the name Raël, and he published his first book proclaiming the Raëlian Revolution, a UFO cult built on the ancient-astronaut theory and flying saucers. We will hear much more from Raël in Part Five, when he tries to create the world's first cloned human being.

All this really showed was that Western society was longing to find a replacement for the religious heritage it had increasingly ceased to believe in. It also showed that people would believe anything they see on television or the movies. Ancient astronauts, UFO abductions, and demonic possessions all saw their modern origins in movies or television shows, and it was only following their popularization in those media that they became full-fledged phenomena.[22]

One puzzled sociologist expressed dismay by the rise of clairvoyants, witchcraft, and devil worship during these years. "Bookstores specializing in occult works of various kinds, frequently found in proximity to college campuses, are flourishing," and the ivory tower universities began offering seminars and courses in everything from "alchemy to Zen Buddhism."[23] And, of course, college campuses, home to the rebellious youth, were the hotbed of occult and supernatural beliefs in the 1970s. A retreat from the rational, belief in the esoteric helped students to separate themselves from the declining society around them and to escape the "empirical practices of science and the depersonalization of the industrial order."[24] It was an embrace of the subjective, the irrational, the Romantic. For every Satanist chanting prayers to Cthulhu and for every ordinary person imagining alien abductions, this was a way to embrace the supernatural and the divine. In its way it was also an individualist movement that held that the mysteries of the world were for the individual to solve and embrace, unlike the group-think of science and the endless committees and conferences of bureaucratized knowledge. Plus, it was simple, easy, and sexy.

Philosophically, it was a reaction to the positivism of the 1950s and early 1960s and a rejection of their values, their culture, and their beliefs. To sociologists studying the phenomenon, the pan-national rebirth of supernaturalism across the Western world could only be seen as "a major sociological happening."[25]

Educators started to pick up on this sea change by the mid-1970s. In 1975, H. E. Legrand and Wayne E. Boese, then assistant professors of history at Virginia Polytechnic Institute and State University, became increasingly concerned that their students were arriving on campus already indoctrinated into anti-scientific ethos. The sheer popularity of bizarre beliefs in flying saucers and ancient aliens had made teaching "orthodox" history difficult. Students did not have familiarity with the methodology of archaeology or history and could not understand where the authors of space fantasies went wrong.[26] The professors decided that they needed to teach a course on alternative theories of the past to provide students with the tools they needed to evaluate the odd ideas they heard in books, magazines, television, and movies. The professors tried to teach students the relationship between evidence and interpretation and show how ideas relate to one another. By the conclusion of the semester, there was a change in student outlook. As one student reported:

> I came into this course fairly open-minded concerning "strange views." However, after studying them, I have become highly skeptical. The evidence presented is interesting and "mysterious," but the conclusions drawn from the evidence are often too far-fetched. Proponents of such views are not scientific, rational, or objective. The evidence is sufficient to question man's orthodox views but not sufficient to conclude that we are the product of visits from outer space.[27]

While the professors present this as a triumph for science education, the shift in attitude they experienced with their students more likely proved that students will accept whatever explanation is favored by the authority figure. One can hope that such courses helped educate a new generation of scientists, but given the subsequent history of alternative archaeology, we know this was not necessarily the case. Nevertheless, the subject was extremely popular and the course was emulated at colleges across the country in the years that followed. Adding a quaint note of caution, the professors reminded their peers, "Popularity of the subject matter alone, however, is not a sufficient justification for a course; otherwise, courses on football, beer-drinking, and sex would be offered at most universities."[28]

In support of this book's thesis on the decline of the West, most universities do now offer such subjects, confusing popularity for importance in the rush to get more students in the door and more cash in the coffers. Academics were increasingly replaced with feel-good courses during the 1980s and 1990s. As author Neal Gabler eloquently explained:

> Having grown up within the bubble of entertainment and having been educated at least in part through the methods of entertainment, more and more university students were arriving on campus with the expectation that their educations would be entertaining as well. And since the universities, in the fallow years after the matriculation of the postwar baby boomers, needed students, they frequently obliged. . . . It was campus as theme park.[29]

Such a decline eventually would create an environment receptive to the return of occult ideas in the 1990s. By the turn of the twenty-first century it became necessary for colleges to once more offer the same course on alternative theories of the past. Some did, but more preferred to avoid critical thinking courses lest they offend students or challenge the beliefs of their paying customers.

But in 1976, the war between science and pseudoscience for the soul of popular archaeology was still in its first battle. That year, the two most important books for the future of alternative archaeology both made their debut: *The Sirius Mystery* by Robert Temple and *The Twelfth Planet* by Zecharia Sitchin. The former book would attempt to provide ethnographic and scientific proof of ancient aliens, inspiring a genre that catalogued a slow descent in its ideas, reducing its conceit from ancient aliens to an all-powerful Atlantis-like lost civilization. The latter book would reinforce von Däniken's worldview, provide a pseudoreligious explanation for man's origins on Earth, and begin a process that would lead to UFO cults as a substitute faith and eventually to human cloning. This division leads us down two different tracks, each of which we will explore and discuss in greater detail in Parts Four and Five. In short, the time around 1976 produced a series of remarkable events:

- Neil Armstrong proves von Däniken lied about Ecuador's alien caves.
- L. Sprague de Camp's biography helps revive interest in Lovecraft.
- Robert Temple publishes *The Sirius Mystery*.
- Zecharia Sitchin publishes *The Twelfth Planet*.
- *Viking* records the so-called face on Mars.
- Claude Vorilhon begins the Raëlian Revolution.

All told, from *The Sirius Mystery* to *The Twelfth Planet*, from the biography of Lovecraft to the Raëlian Revolution, 1976 set the stage for the ultimate consequences of Lovecraft's fevered dreams from the summer of 1926. It is to another summer, fifty years after "Call of Cthulhu," that we once more turn, gazing up toward the brightest star in the night sky and *The Sirius Mystery*.

PART FOUR

FROM SIRIUS TO ORION AND BEYOND

10

THE SIRIUS MYSTERY

On the surface, Robert Temple was not the first person one would expect to embrace the ancient-astronaut hypothesis. A respected American expatriate scholar living in London and accomplished historian of science, Temple served as a member of several important and prestigious organizations: the Royal Astronomical Society, the British School of Archaeology at Athens, the Institute of Classical Studies, the Institute of Historical Research, and many others. The author of numerous books, including *The Genius of China* and an illustrated edition of James Frazer's *Golden Bough*, such a credentialed scholar was one of the last people anyone would expect to announce that frog people from the star Sirius gave civilization to mankind around 5000 BCE.

Yet in January 1976 Temple did just that with the publication of *The Sirius Mystery*, beginning his descent into a nightmare realm where he believed government spy agencies attempted to destroy his life for bravely advocating the existence of frog people from space. His masterwork on Sirius capped a career that skirted the borderline between mainstream and fringe science.

In his youth, Robert Temple was a friend of Charles Hapgood, the professor who erroneously deduced that ancient maps represented advanced cartographic skills from a lost civilization like Atlantis. As we have seen, Hapgood had become convinced that the ancients made perfect maps and later copyists' errors made them less accurate. The assumption of accuracy let him "reconstruct" the original maps and "prove" what he had assumed, that is, their accuracy. During the late 1960s, when Hapgood was in his heyday and the ancient-astronaut hypothesis was beginning to make waves, Temple used to argue with Hapgood. He told the good professor that "I do not interpret them as evidence of 'Atlantis'; I see them as yet more survivals of knowledge left by visiting extraterrestrials, who were able to map the earth from space."[1]

Temple was active in other areas of "alternative archaeology" throughout the 1960s. He began a correspondence with the widow of Arthur Posnansky, the eccentric German mathematician who went to the ancient city of Tiwanaku (formerly spelled Tihuanaco or Tihuanacu) in Bolivia to search for evidence of ancient civilizations. Posnansky, in his 1945 book *Tihuanacu: The Cradle of American Man*, used an early form of archaeoastronomy, the science of using star alignments to date archaeological sites, to conclude that the city of Tiwanaku was fifteen thousand years old. Though archaeologists date the city to 400 BCE to 100 CE, Posnansky had become convinced that the site was older because of his fifty years of mathematical research.

He believed that the city's central precinct was an astronomical calendar over whose gate the sun should rise on the solstices. But when he measured, he found the sun was offset from perfect by eighteen degrees. Calculating when the sun would have aligned perfectly with the stones, he concluded the site was set up fifteen thousand years earlier. Like Hapgood with his maps, Posnansky believed fervently that the ancients laid out their sites with perfect accuracy; therefore, any mistakes must be the fault of the sun, whose position in the sky changes with the cyclical wobbles in the earth's axis of rotation. Taking that into account, he calculated that in 15,000 BCE the sun aligned perfectly with the city, so that was when it was built. Thus, he proved his assumption through circular logic.[2]

Temple believed Posnansky had made an important contribution to research, and in the early 1960s, when archaeoastronomy was still new, there were not yet the tools to technically disprove Posnansky. However, his logical fallacies should have been evident. Apparently, the inability to discern circular logic is a particular weakness to which Temple was particularly susceptible, falling under the spell of two of archaeology's most infamous purveyors of such fallacies.

These were also the years when an open-minded Temple attended the University of Pennsylvania. There, he met Arthur M. Young, author of *Reflexive Universe: The Evolution of Consciousness*, on which Temple worked, and which was published in 1976. A brilliant mathematician and philosopher, Young invented the Bell helicopter in 1946. He then turned his attention to the fringes of science, exploring astrology, extrasensory perception, and psychic powers. He became convinced that there were unexplained mysteries in the human mind and that telepathy was real. He set up the Foundation for the Study of Consciousness in 1952 to explore these mysteries, and in the 1950s some said he was part of a group who claimed to have made contact with the nine creator-gods of Egypt, who claimed to be space aliens from Sirius, though the sources for this are suspect.[3] What is beyond doubt is that Young made a twenty-one-year-old Temple the assistant secretary for his Foundation for the Study of Consciousness in 1966, though Temple would decamp for England before year's end. Only a few months earlier, Young had introduced him to the work of a pair of French anthropologists who had made startling claims about an obscure tribe in the heart of Africa. This would become the "Sirius Mystery."[4]

As Temple recounts, the "eminent anthropologists" Marcel Griaule and Germaine Dieterlen traveled into the depths of

West Africa during the 1930s. There they encountered the Dogon tribe, who told a startling tale:

> The starting point of creation is the star which revolves round Sirius, and is actually named the "*Digitaria* star" [*Digitaria* is a very small grain]; it is regarded by the Dogon as the smallest and heaviest of all the stars; it contains the germs of all things. Its movement on its own axis and around Sirius upholds all creation in space. We shall see that its orbit determines the calendar.[5]

For Temple and Young this was an amazing revelation, for the two knew very well that modern science had confirmed that Sirius, the brightest star in the night sky,[6] was in fact a double star. Located in Canis Major near the famous Orion constellation, the small and heavy white dwarf Sirius B—the smallest type of star—orbits the larger Sirius A, making the Sirius system binary. But what was this knowledge, available only to the modern, industrial West, doing in the hands of a primitive tribe wandering the middle of West Africa? Fascinating though this question was, Temple put it aside for the time being.

Two years later Temple had come to know the science fiction author and scientist Arthur C. Clarke, who wrote the script for *2001: A Space Odyssey*, then just about to open in theaters. A respected scientist, author, thinker, and longtime Lovecraft fan,[7] Clarke had gained worldwide renown for his role in inventing the communications satellite and for his science fiction stories. He had retired to the island of Sri Lanka and pondered in exile the philosophy of science. Though a committed scientist, Clarke took an active interest in ancient mysteries and scientific curiosities, eventually producing documentary series like *Arthur C. Clarke's Mysterious World* for television. Unlike other such presenters, Clarke usually concluded that the "mysteries" of the world were explainable by science, not the supernatural.

Together, he and Temple discussed Erich von Däniken's "exciting" theories (which Temple would discuss with von Däniken beginning in 1976) in the months before *Chariots of the Gods?* came out in English, when the embryonic idea was still a German-language phenomenon. Intrigued by his discussions with Clarke, Temple began preparing a book on ancient mysteries on the lines of von Däniken's compendium of odd "mysteries." Along the way he remembered the interesting enigma of the Dogon, which Young had first shown him two years before. Temple changed course in midstream and began to focus exclusively on one question: How did the out-of-place knowledge of Sirius enter into Dogon mythology?[8]

Now residing in London, Temple raced to the Royal Anthropological Institute, where he discovered that all the relevant literature on the Dogon was written in French (since their homeland was in the French West African colony now called Mali) and that the majority of this literature was written by Marcel Griaule and Germaine Dieterlen, who were apparently the only anthropologists to have professionally studied the Dogon. Their 1950 article "A Sudanese Sirius System" and their 1965 book *Le renard pâle* (*The Pale Fox*) formed one of the only records of this African tribe, and it also contained the only record of their extraordinary knowledge. Temple had their work translated into English, and he sat down to absorb the enormity of their story.

The two anthropologists recorded that the men of the Dogon tribe held secret knowledge that only the most senior initiates could obtain. Since Marcel Griaule had become the most honored man in the tribe, the Dogon entrusted to him the secrets of the senior men. The star Sirius, which they called "sigu tolo" in their language, had an invisible companion that revolved around it, a companion that was small and very heavy. They compared this companion to *Digitaria*, a type of grain whose seeds were the smallest known to the Dogon. Griaule and Dieterlen were confused by the Dogon's strange knowledge, and in a footnote to their 1950 article asked how the Dogon could know about this star with no instruments with which to detect its tiny presence.[9] Quite logically, it followed that the Dogon possessed special knowledge that was obviously out of place in the hands of a subsistence-level tribe of approximately 250,000 scraping out a living in the wilds of French West Africa. The Dogon even drew pictures of the Sirius system that bore a striking resemblance to a modern astronomical chart for the binary star system. Further, they held that the smaller star orbited the larger over a period of fifty years, exactly matching twentieth-century calculations. They even indicated that Sirius might be a triple star, a fact that modern science had suspected but not confirmed in the 1930s. Clearly, something was up.

Griaule and Dieteren also described the Dogon's religious belief system, which indicated that Sirius held a special place in their worldview because it was the home world of the gods. The Dogon apparently believed in a savior god called O Nommo, who through his crucifixion on a tree redeemed the sins of the Dogon. His body provided a sacrificial meal, and his resurrection guaranteed the promise of redemption. He and his companions, the Nommos, arrived on Earth from Sirius in a large ship, and the semi-aquatic amphibious Sirians brought with them the seeds of civilization. Predictably, the Dogon foretell that the Nommos will return again someday.[10] The anthropologists did not claim to know how long the Dogon had known their amazing knowledge, nor did they attempt to understand whence it came. That was where Robert Temple tried to pick up the story.

But Temple had begun to suspect that someone did not want him uncovering this information. Temple claimed that an operative for the Central Intelligence Agency stole his copy of *Le renard pâle* and another intelligence operative later told him that the theft was justified, presumably to protect the world from the mind-blowing truth.[11] Nevertheless, Temple soldiered on and attempted to trace the story of the Dogon back to its roots.

Rounding up an impressive catalogue of anthropological, historical, literary, and mythological sources, Temple tried to demonstrate that the Dogon were in fact the descendants of ancient Egyptians who fled during the tumultuous reign of the heretic pharaoh Akhenaten, or perhaps of the Argonauts (of Jason and the Argonauts fame), privy to the secrets of Egypt. The Egyptians, he believed, possessed advanced knowledge that could be deduced from their amazing accomplishments and their surviving mythology. In turn, he suggested that the Egyptians had obtained their civilization from the Mesopotamians (or, alternately, both cultures learned from the same source). He believed the Mesopotamians, among the oldest known civilizations on Earth, had inherited civilization from still another source. Building on the Sumerian and Babylonian legends of Oannes (Dagon), half fish and half man who was believed to have given civilization to the first people, Temple concluded that the old myths actually recorded an encounter with amphibious creatures. These creatures were Oannes, were Nommo, and were from Sirius. Ironically, H. P. Lovecraft had come to a similar conclusion when he used the myth of Dagon to create a horror story about an amphibious monster from a civilization older than man. Dagon, of course, was the prototype of Great Cthulhu, Lovecraft's primal answer to the more civilized Oannes.

From these speculations, Temple then theorized that the ancient world shared the secret knowledge of amphibious space gods, and he brought together a collection of representations of half-human, half-fish creatures to prove his point. From Isis and Serapis in Roman Egypt to Nereus and Scylla in Greece, to Mesopotamian Oannes and Chinese Fuxi, he collected tales of these hybrid gods. Of course, only some were fish-gods. Others had serpents' tails, prompting Temple to conclude, reasoning in the circular style of Hapgood, that the fish motif was eventually transformed to a serpent motif over the course of centuries.

Further, many myths, from Jason and the Argonauts to the Babylonian Annunaki, were associated with the number fifty (fifty Argonauts, fifty Annunaki). He further concluded that these myths related to Sirius B, the esoteric star whose orbit around its exoteric companion takes fifty years to complete. He amassed a truly impressive catalogue of mythological references to the number fifty and provided a powerful analysis from flawed premises that concluded that the myths housed and transmitted the ancient knowledge of Sirius's true nature. That this reasoning was circular logic once more escaped Temple, unable to see that it was equally likely that he found myths featuring the number fifty not because they were influenced by Sirius but because *he* was—that is, that knowing the Sirius orbit, he sought out explanations for myths to conform to that idea. As we have seen, this is a fallacy to which Temple was especially susceptible. At any rate, the whole thing recalls nothing so much as Douglas Adams's claim in *The Hitchhiker's Guide to the Galaxy* that the answer to everything is forty-two. Only no one knew what the question was. Here, too, fifty is the answer, but it is Temple, not the myths, who provides the question.

Having thus demonstrated the existence of the Sirius cult, Temple went on to speculate on its operation. For him, the ancient world's oracle centers, like the famous Oracle at Delphi, were not centers of drug-fueled hallucinations but were in fact an ancient version of the Internet, using trained birds (!) to send messages across long distances and perpetuate the power of a mystical elite housing the secrets of the gods from outer space. Each oracle center was known as the "navel of the world," which the Greeks represented with the *omphalos* stone, a conical rock wrapped with a net, perhaps indicating a world grid, something like the latitude and longitude lines of the modern globe. Some of this mystical brotherhood retreated into Libya in North Africa, where they took with them the secrets of the Sirius star system. Eventually, some of these people intermarried with the local tribes and their knowledge defused to the Dogon, who were once Greek-Africans who moved farther south and disappeared into the local population.

Important for our further discussion, Temple deduced from all of this that the ancients designed the Mediterranean world to imitate the stars they loved. Since for the Greeks the myth of Jason and the Argonauts was supposed to embody the essence of the Sirius mystery because it was their corrupted version of the *Epic of Gilgamesh*, which somehow encoded the mystery, Temple hypothesized that the oracle centers should mimic the stars important to that story.

The Jason myth (one close to my heart, as he is my namesake) tells the story of a man who was dispossessed of his kingdom by an evil uncle who gives him a challenge: He can have the throne if he can obtain from the Kingdom of Colchis the Golden Fleece, the skin of the divine ram that saved Prixus and Helle from danger in the mythological past. To regain his kingdom, Jason and his fifty anonymous companions (later given names by the poet Apollonius of Rhodes) sail to Colchis on the Black Sea (which Temple believes was an Egyptian colony) aboard the ship *Argo*, which gave the companions of Jason their name. The ship's prow foretells the future, as its wood came from the sacred grove of oaks at the oracle center at Dodona. After many adventures, Jason steals the Golden Fleece with the help of Medea, the witch-princess of Colchis. With his Fleece, Jason completes the task given him, and he triumphantly sails home to his kingdom. In his old age, Jason is killed when the dry-docked *Argo* falls down and crushes him while he sleeps in its shadow.

The *Argo*, therefore, was connected in Temple's mind to the oracle network through its magic prow and to the fifty-year orbit of Sirius B through the fifty men in the boat. The ship could then be seen as a representation of the orbit of Sirius B itself, and the men, each year's travels on its orbit. Therefore, he considered the boat to be an esoteric symbol for the Sirius Mystery. He suggests that the Argonauts' descendents were the same Libyans who eventually migrated and intermarried to become the Dogon's ancestors. Turning to the oracle centers, he tried to tie the Argonauts back to the oracles. Looking at a map of ancient oracle sites, he picked out four from the myriad ancient oracle centers. These four were Siwa, Behdet, and Thebes in Egypt and Dodona in Greece, origin of the *Argo*'s wooden prow. He noted that when viewed from above, these four oracle centers lay across the surface of the earth in the same pattern as the four major stars of the constellation *Argo* in the sky. In other words, it seemed that the ancients had laid out the oracle centers to mimic on the ground the constellation in the sky.[12] He also found the *Argo* redrawn at a ninety-degree angle, this time using Thebes, Behdet, and Mt. Ararat, where Noah's ark was said to have come to rest. There is no fourth site (he says it is "undiscovered") to complete this *Argo*. Temple did not pursue this idea much further, but he laid the groundwork for others to propose that the ancients attempted to draw the heavens on earth.

Temple made ample use of comparative mythology to link ancient religions to one another and thus back to the gods from outer space. In the myth of the *Argo* he saw a corrupt reflection of the divine ark used by the immortal Utnapishtim to ride out the Great Flood, which the gods sent as punishment for mankind's sins in the Sumerian *Epic of Gilgamesh* from millennia before. He also linked *Gilgamesh* to the Greek myth of the Great Flood, where Deucalion and Pyrrha ride out the Flood in a wooden ark, coming to rest on a mountain at the future oracle center of Dodona. Similarly, the Judeo-Christian

Noah was nothing but Utnapishtim in Hebraic clothes, still sailing that same ark in the Bible. Clearly, the gods had a vendetta against people in arks. Nevertheless, if all these tales of floods and arks could be traced back to the *Epic of Gilgamesh*, circular logic would clearly tell us that space frogs from Sirius must have been responsible since that is the assumption Temple made when concluding that the aliens were real.

Ironically, this mythological cross-comparison is an active field of investigation, and many eminent historians have noted and attempted to explain these similarities. Some claimed that *Gilgamesh* showed that the Bible was true because the pagans had copied the Noah story in ages past. Others held that the Bible, being the more recent work, was the product of Jewish exposure to Babylonian (the successor to the Sumerian) mythology during the Jews' sixth-century BCE captivity. Until Temple, no one had suggested that *Gilgamesh* recorded a real visit from Sirian amphibians.

This, then, was the Sirius Mystery.

Though in attempting to expose some of the fallacies in Temple's thinking I have given the impression that the book is silly or reductionist, *The Sirius Mystery* seemed on the surface to be a scholarly, impressive investigation into the origins of the Dogon's secret knowledge. The book's length, its scholarly complexity, its ample footnotes, and its seeming air of academic inquiry combined to produce in the reader the clear impression that Temple had arrived at his conclusions only through the most rigorous process of academic research. After all, in 1976 the heart of the Sirius Mystery remained: the available literature clearly indicated that the Dogon maintained powerful secret knowledge about the Sirius star system that was out of place for a group of subsistence-level tribesman on the outskirts of Timbuktu.

Some troubling questions should have emerged, but—at

least in the popular press—they did not. Scientists and anthropologists knew all along there was no mystery. The Dogon god O Nommo was supposed to have died and was resurrected, fed his body to the tribesmen as meal, and promised to return to usher in an endless period of heaven on earth. The parallels to Christ were unmistakable. Temple did not consider the obvious reason for this, that the Dogon were exposed to Christian beliefs for centuries before Griaule and Dieteren had contacted them, both from missionaries working in French West Africa (the French were notorious missionaries in the eighteenth and nineteenth centuries) and through contact with the Christian and Islamic worlds bordering their homeland.

Instead, he contemplates another theory, that the Dogon, as descendents of Argonauts/Egyptians, shared the same core beliefs that Christianity would later appropriate. His proof? The creator god of the Dogon, Amma, sounds like the high god of Egypt, Ammon (also spelled Amun or Amen).[13] Also, "the 'O' describing this Nommo is remembered from the name of Osiris as its first syllable."[14] Osiris was the Egyptian god of death, who died and was resurrected. Some consider him an early prototype for Christ. Thus, since Temple assumed that the Dogon are descended from the Egyptians (or Argonauts privy to Egyptian secrets), he "proves" his case through linking the Dogon back to Egypt. Yet the connection exists only in his own mind and in the strictures of circular logic.

More troubling should have been the basis on which the whole massive edifice of the *Sirius Mystery* rested. Ultimately, Temple's speculations, as scholarly and academic as they seemed on the surface, rested wholly upon the work of Griaule and Dieteren. If their work contained any errors, then the *Sirius Mystery*'s house of cards would come tumbling down. However, in 1976, the anthropological work of Griaule and Dieteren was still not conclusively refuted, and this scholarly underpinning gave a powerful credibility to Temple's work. As we shall see, this would continue into the 1990s, when others would dispute Griaule and Dieteren's reports.

When the book was published in January of 1976, journalists embraced the *Sirius Mystery* as a respectable alternative to *Chariots of the Gods?* Here, then, was the proof that believers in the ancient-astronaut theory had been waiting for. *Time* magazine gave Temple a glowing review:

> *The Sirius Mystery* argues with some sophistication the likelihood that superior beings from Sirius visited earth between 7,000 and 10,000 years ago. . . . Temple unleashes a torrent of arcane information . . . a swirl of genuine astronomical mysteries, anthropological dates and the tricky cross-currents of comparative mythology.[15]

The journal *Nature* also praised the book, convinced by the academic credibility of Griaule and Dieteren, whose work was the "nugget" from which *The Sirius Mystery* sprang: "A fascinating book because the nugget of mystery Temple has mined and polished is from a pure vein. . . . *The Sirius Mystery* should be taken seriously."[16] Isaac Asimov, the famed science fiction author of *I Robot*, was quoted in promotional material as saying he could find no errors in the book.[17] By Temple's own account, his book was favorably reviewed in nearly every British newspaper and then in newspapers and magazines around the world.[18] The book was most warmly received in Germany, the first country to embrace von Däniken not long before. The press and public, it seemed, were enamored with this convincing proof of the sensational theories about aliens circulating on television and in books. Scholars, however, were not so easily convinced.

Recalling the publication of his book for the revised 1998 edition, Temple remembered the reception *The Sirius Mystery* received among scholars: "A number of British scholars whom I knew used to ridicule the fact that I discussed something as lowbrow as spacemen, and I was clearly therefore not a respectable person."[19] Yet few went on the record to refute Temple's work. The magazine *Skeptical Inquirer*, which investigates claims of the paranormal, attempted to refute Temple in 1978,[20] but without a firm rebuttal to Griaule and Dieteren, could not prove its case definitively. Further, the *Skeptical Inquirer*'s small circulation (less than 60,000) kept such rebuttals limited only to those who already sought them out. In the public sphere there was little opposition, and this seemed a concession that Temple was clearly on to something.

With no firm rebuttal such as von Däniken had received, Temple's work took on the air of a closed case among the developing ancient-astronaut subculture. *The Sirius Mystery* inspired a symphonic poem by Karlheinz Stockhausen, who came to believe he had actually gone to Sirius, and a series of science fiction novels by Doris Lessing.[21] Radical African-American scholars, in the process of revitalizing black culture in America, seized upon Temple's revelations to "prove" that Africans had advanced science in ancient times and gave their knowledge to the rest of the world in an African cultural genesis.[22]

Temple came to believe that he had brought to light one of the most important discoveries in human history, the actual key to unlocking the mystery of extraterrestrial life. He assumed modern governments subscribed to the school of thought that held that final proof of the existence of alien life, even in the remote past, might cause social upheaval. Therefore, the line of thought went, governments feared that their citizens would stop believing in religion, abandon the structures of power, and enter a new age of anarchy. Of course, this thinking was patently ridiculous since so many people had already abandoned traditional religion and had already stopped believing in the old power structures. And nothing about aliens should destroy this faith, even if it existed. As we saw with the film *Red Planet Mars*, some expected that aliens would share a Christian faith. As far back as the early twentieth century, some authors like Mark Twain contemplated whether Christ was the savior of every planet or just our own.[23] Yet Robert Temple came to believe that the American and Soviet governments had entered a conspiracy to suppress *The Sirius Mystery*.

Temple claimed that there was "a pattern of behaviour which has assailed me on many occasions."[24] The British security services, notably MI5, reportedly opened a dossier on *The Sirius Mystery*, which, though Temple found it suspicious, was not unusual for security services. Many individuals eventually get a file due to the paranoia of the security establishment and the prurient interests of powerful officials. Book authors are no exception. Temple claimed that the American CIA took an active interest in him, harassing his friends and coworkers to cut their connections with him. Temple believed that the Soviet Union was using double agents to infiltrate the CIA and directed their members to investigate and neutralize him so that the Soviets could gain the upper hand in paranormal research. He also suspected the Soviets of purposely inflicting brain damage on prominent American paranormal scientists to neutralize them.[25] He got this information from Uri Gellar, the Israeli "psychic" spoon bender who became inexplicably famous in the 1970s. Temple did not question Gellar's claims, nor did he express any skepticism in Gellar's much-ridiculed "psychic" powers.[26]

For fifteen years, this harassment allegedly continued, costing Temple time, money, and promotional opportunities. At one time, NASA allegedly got in on the act, trying to stop the BBC from airing Temple's theories on its *Horizon* program in 1977.[27] Fortunately for Temple, the government bad guys apparently failed. The program, "The Case for Ancient Astronauts," aired as scheduled.

However, the conspiracy seemed to make great gains. Arthur C. Clarke decided that influence from missionaries and nearby peoples was responsible for the Dogon's knowledge, not ancient aliens. Further, Isaac Asimov, whom Temple cited as being unable to find fault or error with *The Sirius Mystery*, vociferously complained that Temple misrepresented him:

> Robert Temple on three different occasions, by mail and phone, attempted to get support from me and I steadfastly refused. He sent me the manuscript which I found unreadable. Finally, he asked me point-blank if I could point out any errors in it and partly out of politeness, partly to get rid of him, and partly because I had been able to read very little of the book so that the answer was true, I said I could not point out any errors. He certainly did not have permission to use that statement as part of the promotion, I'll just have to be even more careful hereafter.[28]

Clearly the conspiracy got to him. It seems something of a shame if the world's intelligence agencies did indeed spend so much time and effort trying to destroy Robert Temple. If it were true, it would represent a gross waste of taxpayer dollars. For, you see, the Sirius mystery simply isn't true.

As early as 1967, right around the time Temple began work on *The Sirius Mystery*, fellow anthropologists began criticizing Marcel Griaule's methodology (Dieterlen was a junior partner) after the appearance of his book *Le renard pâle* in 1965, nine years after Griaule's death. A museum anthropologist with a fascination for religion, Griaule had worked with the stated aim of redeeming African philosophy and thought to show it the equal of Greek and Indian philosophy.[29] He gathered his information on Sirius through formal interviews with only a few key informants, and he did not record the Dogon knowledge or myths as verbatim texts, only as fragments in his interviews and ethnographies.[30] None of this was good anthropological practice, and it cast serious doubts about the authenticity of his research, which contradicted existing research on neighboring peoples.

Entering the field with the stated aim of "redeeming" a culture seems to presuppose what one expects to find. Consequently, it was no surprise that Griaule found what he sought. Worse is the use of limited informants. When an anthropologist tries to record a culture, he or she will often live among the people and become a part of their culture to whatever extent is possible. By talking to many different individuals, the informants, the anthropologist can begin to piece together the fabric of a foreign culture. If the researcher speaks to only one individual (or one set), how would anyone know whether this person was telling the truth? Many myths, legends, and rituals are recorded as they are told or performed, not by asking one person. At very least, after asking, the anthropologist should try to confirm the information. None of this found its way into Griaule's field methods.

Worse still for Griaule, a new generation of scholars had even stronger doubts, fueled by an inherent distrust of Temple's extrapolations from Griaule's Dogon mythology. Walter van Beek, a Belgian anthropologist, spent eleven years living and working with the Dogon. He noticed that while Griaule's early work with the tribe and his descriptions of their material culture were thorough and scientific, beginning in the 1940s, something changed. Griaule uncovered in the Dogon a philosophical system that had gone unnoticed by all other researchers.[31] As we have seen, Griaule's account of Dogon mythology seemed to echo Christian and Egyptian lore.

Through a penetrating analysis, van Beek was able to show that Griaule's ideas about the Dogon changed over the years; his ethnographies produced at least three different views of the Dogon belief system, all mutually exclusive or at least contradictory.[32] To find out which (if any) was correct, van Beek conducted a restudy to try to replicate Griaule's research and findings. While it is not my purpose to go into all the evidence van Beek collected, he was able to demonstrate convincingly in

1991 that Griaule's studies, including and especially *Le renard pâle*, were the products of Griaule's own mind and not the Dogon themselves. He found that Dogon religion is less secretive and less coherent than Griaule made out; the myth of the Nommos has no set form, and in fact religion has little relevance for the Dogon's daily lives.[33] However, some traces of Griaule's mythology do exist in the Dogon culture; they can be shown to come from Christian missionaries and Islamic neighbors.[34] Further, the stars were unimportant to the Dogon: "Most important, no one, even within the circle of Griaule informants, had ever heard or understood that Sirius was a double star (or, according to [*Le renard pâle*], even a triple one . . .)." Further, the idea of Nommo as a Christlike redeemer, dead and resurrected, is also "totally absent."[35]

It seems that Griaule actively helped shape his informants' perceptions, guiding them unconsciously toward telling him what he wanted to hear. They were more than willing to tell him whatever he asked, since he paid them generously for their time. When Griaule showed them star maps, they actively invented stories based on the maps and the fragments of data Griaule let slip about Sirius and its companion stars.[36] Of Griaule's surviving informants, van Beek writes that they are unsure which star was Sirius's companion, some identifying it with Venus, others with an invisible star. "All agree, however, that they learned about the star from Griaule."[37]

This damning report made a compelling case that there was no Sirius mystery. While it is of course possible that the Dogon lied to van Beek, or that the Dogon who knew of the Sirius secrets died before van Beek spoke to them, it is much more likely that Griaule unconsciously created the ethnography he wanted to find. At any rate, by 1991, it was clear that there was no firm foundation for the Sirius mystery. The house of cards should have come crashing down.

Yet by the 1990s, the Sirius myth had become an important

touchstone in alternative history, ancient-astronaut studies, and Afrocentrism (the belief that ancient cultures originated from a high civilization in Africa). Consequently, it was not surprising that those with a vested interest in the profitable mystery were slow to give it up. In 1998, seven years after van Beek published his study, Temple revised and expanded his *Sirius Mystery* with the new subtitle *New Scientific Evidence of Extraterrestrial Contact 5,000 Years Ago*. The new edition trumpeted the recent sightings of a third Sirius star, which seemed to confirm Griaule's account of Dogon Sirius knowledge. Temple did not (and still has not) acknowledged the rebuttal to Griaule. To this day he ignores this information and continues to peddle the Sirius secrets as an authentic ancient revelation.

Though by 1998 Temple should have known better, he cannot be faulted for failing to test Griaule's conclusions in the 1976 edition of his book (though he should have acknowledged the 1960s-era criticisms). He could not have known that his source material would someday be proved wrong. So when an engineer named Robert Bauval picked up a copy of *The Sirius Mystery* at London's Heathrow Airport in 1979, he could not be blamed for accepting what Temple had written as factual and grounded in solid, scientific evidence.

11

THE ORION MYSTERY

Trying to reach his flight at London's Heathrow Airport in 1979, construction engineer Robert Bauval stopped to buy a paperback book at one of the airport's bookshops to take with him to the Sudan. He picked up Robert Temple's *Sirius Mystery* and devoured its contents. Bauval had a long-standing interest in Egypt, having been born in the cosmopolitan city of Alexandria, though he had no formal training in its study, Egyptology. He found Temple's work intriguing.[1] Though Bauval found much of Temple's conjectures on amphibious alien gods "highly speculative," he considered the germ of *The Sirius Mystery* "worthy of further investigation."[2]

He honed in on the work of Marcel Griaule and Germaine Dieteren, on whose authority Temple piled his speculations. He was transfixed by the idea, then still credible, that Griaule had uncovered a genuine ancient tradition of anomalously accurate knowledge of the double-star Sirius among the Dogon tribe of Mali: "Most people today remain ignorant of Sirius B, and not many would even be aware of Sirius A, so how could the Dogon have accurate information about Sirius B in the 1950s?"[3] Specifically, Bauval thought about Egypt. Since Temple had connected the Dogon to Egyptians (or Argonauts), then Egypt was the source of this strange knowledge: "If the Dogon had inherited their knowledge of Sirius B from the Ancient Egyptians, what other knowledge might these ancients have had concerning the stars?"[4]

As much as this fired up Bauval's imagination, he had to set aside his interest in the mystery until he finished his engineering contract in Sudan.

In 1980, the contract expired and he moved on to Saudi Arabia, and during a holiday in 1982, Bauval returned to his native Egypt. There, he visited the three most famous pyramids, those at Giza, which as we saw earlier, Erich von Däniken believed were constructed by aliens, or at least from extraterrestrial plans. The plateau's pyramids were built in the Fourth Dynasty by three related pharaohs around 2500 BCE: Khufu, his son (or brother) Khafre, and grandson Menkaure. During his visit to the Cairo Museum, Bauval studied a map of these pyramids and noticed a peculiar trait. Though the two largest pyramids, those of Khufu and Khafre, are on the same diagonal (one can draw a line connecting their apexes that passes through the corners of the pyramids), the third and smallest pyramid, that of Menkaure, was offset from the other two. It did not line up with those of Menkaure's two predecessors' pyramids. He considered this strange but, unable to explain it, returned to his home base in Riyadh, Saudi Arabia.[5]

There, Bauval tried to find answers to his questions, and he came to reject the standard answers about Menkaure's pyramid. He did not believe Menkaure had fewer resources than Khafre and Khufu to devote to pyramid building, nor did he believe that Menkaure had to hurry to build his pyramid because of bad health. Bauval rejected the latter theory thus: "His statues show him healthy and strong."[6]

Exposing his ignorance of ancient Egyptian artistic conventions, he did not realize that all Egyptian royal portraits presented an idealized king, no matter how paunchy or sickly he was. The royal portraits of the female pharaoh Hatshepsut even depict her as a man. Surely this was not evidence of sex change operations. At any rate, Bauval could not accept any of the standard explanations Egyptologists provided for why Menkaure's pyramid was so small. Similarly, he rejected ideas that the pyramid's placement off the diagonal was dictated by the landscape of Giza and the realities of construction. He reasoned that the Egyptians could have built wherever they chose, not just where was easiest. As a result, he was back at square one.

In November 1983, Bauval and his wife went camping in the Saudi desert, the same desert under whose stars the hero of Lovecraft's "Nameless City" finds the primal horrors of Irem, city of pillars. One night, Bauval awoke at 3 AM, "subconsciously motivated" to scan the stars. From his sleeping bag, Bauval looked up at the Milky Way, the bright band of stars running across the night sky (actually our galaxy). On its shore, he saw the bright star Sirius. Above it, he saw the famous constellation of Orion the Hunter, easily the most recognizable and easiest to find group of stars in the night sky. Orion's three distinctive belt stars, two in a diagonal and a smaller one offset, make it unmistakeable and unmissable. For Bauval, those three stars had another context and another meaning: "The three pyramids at Giza. . . . No, I am quite serious."[7]

Bauval believed that the Milky Way was a heavenly version of the river Nile, and the pyramids were the counterparts of the stars. This made perfect sense since Robert Temple had demonstrated that the ancients had laid out their oracle centers across the earth's surface to reflect the stars of the constellation Argo. It did not take much of a stretch to scale down this practice and equate individual buildings instead of whole cities with the important stars of another constellation: "Throughout antiquity the Milky Way was looked upon as a celestial river analogous to the Nile and in Giza we had, quite literally, Orion's belt on the ground."[8]

Drawing on ambiguous references in the Egyptian *Book of*

the Dead, funerary texts written down in the Fifth Dynasty (about a century after Giza was built) but based on originals of indeterminate antiquity, Bauval concluded that the Egyptians saw Orion as the celestial body of the god Osiris. He, in turn, was the most important diety in the Egyptian pantheon because he alone could guarantee immortality to the human soul.

While many Egyptologists held that Osiris's heavenly manifestation was simply one star near Sirius, Bauval believed that the whole of Orion was Osiris himself. Further, Bauval started to match other pyramids to still more stars, eventually redrawing the map of Fourth and Fifth Dynasty pyramids as a veritable Egyptian national obsession with laying out star maps on the sacred soils of the land they believed was the twin of heaven.

Thus the three Giza pyramids became the three belt stars of Orion. The size of the pyramids, he reasoned, represented the varying brightness (magnitude) of the Orion stars. The smallest pyramid represented Mintaka, the smallest and dimmest of Orion's three belt stars. Khafre's pyramid, second largest, represented the middle star, Alnilam. Khufu's pyramid, the largest, represented Alnitak, the westernmost star on Orion's belt.

Having equated the three pyramids at Giza with Orion's belt and the Nile with the Milky Way, Bauval found still other stars in other pyramids. In the minor (and largely ruined) pyramids at Zawyat-Al-Aryan and Abu Ruwash, Bauval saw two of the four stars that mark Orion's shoulders and feet. (The other two stars are nowhere to be found on the Egyptian ground.) In the city of Letopolis, he found the star Sirius. Even more radically, he expanded his theory outside of Orion to include other pyramids.[9]

The two older pyramids at Dashur, built by the pharaoh Sneferu, were long considered curiosities. The older of the two, the Bent Pyramid, got its name because the pyramid "bends" halfway up its profile, curving in from an approximately fifty-four-degree angle to one closer to forty-five degrees. Archaeologists assumed this was because the steeper angle had become

H. P. Lovecraft (1890–1937). Hailed as the greatest horror writer since Edgar Allan Poe, his signature creation, the so-called Cthulhu Mythos, first gave voice to the idea that aliens were responsible for ancient ruins and civilizations.

The extraterrestrial god Cthulhu rises from his tomb on the lost continent of R'lyeh in this scene from Lovecraft's 1926 story "The Call of Cthulhu."

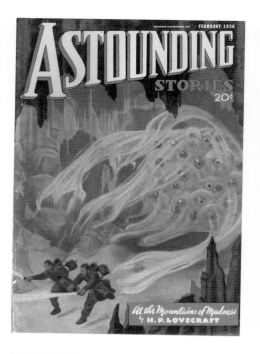

Top left: In life, Lovecraft found his greatest success in the pages of pulp magazines like *Weird Tales* and *Astounding Stories. Astounding* editor Joseph Campbell borrowed from Lovecraft for his own "Who Goes There?" the story that inspired *The Thing from Another World.* (courtesy John W. Anderson)

Top right: After his death, Lovecraft's friends founded Arkham House to publish his work. The first edition of Lovecraft's collected works, *The Outsider and Others* (1939), sold poorly, but later collections garnered more robust sales. (courtesy John W. Anderson)

Bottom: The World War II–era Armed Services edition of Lovecraft's *The Dunwich Horror and Other Weird Tales* gave Americans a taste for Lovecraft, a taste they shared with the Europeans they met in liberated Europe. (courtesy John W. Anderson)

THE LOST CONTINENTS

Above: Lost continents populated both Lovecraftian fiction and alternative-archaeology theories. If all the lost continents were real, there would be no room for all the water in the oceans, but that didn't stop authors from speculating about their reality.

Left: Archaeology's gadfly Erich von Däniken "buzzes" H. P. Lovecraft in this cartoon from *Skeptic* magazine. (courtesy Pat Linse/*Skeptic*)

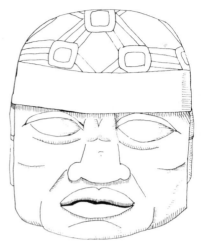

Top left: Erich von Däniken's best-seller *Chariots of the Gods?* was read by millions. His claims about extraterrestrials and ancient civilizations launched the modern ancient-astronaut movement.

Top right: Carved from large blocks of basalt, the Olmec heads are popular evidence for alternative theories. Helmeted spacemen or ocean-faring Africans, alternative historians never consider the obvious, that the Olmec heads, like this example from San Lorenzo (c. 1500 BCE), represent native Olmec chiefs.

Bottom: Complex stonework that fits without mortar, like this Inca example from Sacsahuamán (c. 1450 CE), has led some to believe that only aliens could fashion such structures or move such large stones, some of which weigh many tons. (photo courtesy Jon Bodsworth)

Top: Pyramids are a popular topic in ancient-astronaut literature. Despite differences in style and function, many claim Mayan pyramids, like this one from Chich'en Itza (c. 1000 CE), are related to Egyptian pyramids, which are three thousand five hundred years older. (photo courtesy Jon Bodsworth)

Bottom: The most important structure for alternative archaeologists, Egypt's Great Pyramid (c. 2500 BCE) has spawned legions of bizarre theories, earning their authors the title "pyramidiots." (photo courtesy Jon Bodsworth)

Top: Hard evidence of a lost civilization? Some claim that erosion patterns prove the Sphinx is up to twelve thousand years old and therefore a relic of a lost culture. Egyptologists date the Sphinx to around 2500 BCE and say it represents Pharaoh Khafre. (photo courtesy Jon Bodsworth)

Bottom: The Giza Plateau with its three pyramids. Lovecraft set Harry Houdini's supernatural adventure here, and others found their own paranormal experiences in the shadow of these monuments. (photo courtesy Jon Bodsworth)

Right: Graham Hancock's *Fingerprints of the Gods* proposed that a lost civilization, not aliens, was the answer to ancient mysteries. It became the best-selling alternative-archaeology book of the 1990s and launched the modern fluorescence of "ancient mysteries" books, documentaries, and Web sites.

Bottom Left: Artist's impression of the Giza pyramids as seen from above aligning with the belt stars of the Orion constellation in 10,500 BCE, the time Robert Bauval and Graham Hancock believe Giza commemorates in stone.

Bottom right: The Message Given by Extra-terrestrials gives an overview of Raëlian philosophy as dictated by the extraterrestrials. Note the use of Egypt's Great Pyramid, an influence from the ancient-astronaut movement. (courtesy Raëlian Movement)

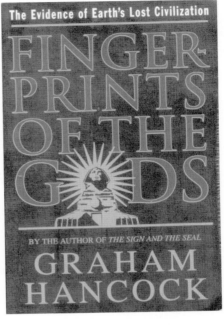

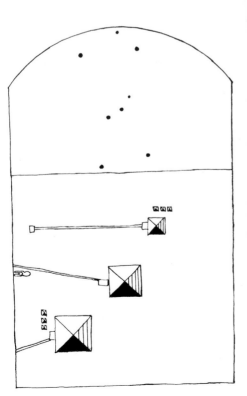

Above: Lovecraft continues to influence pop culture today, from literature, movies, television, and games to Lovecraftian comics like *The Unspeakable Vault of Doom.* Here Cthulhu (*right*) and Nyarlathotep joke about the aftermath of the 2003 Iraq war. (courtesy Frances Laurent/Groomi Studios)

Top right: Raëlian leader Raël (Claude Vorilhon) poses in front of a mock UFO at the group's UFO Land theme park. (photo courtesy Raëlian Movement)

Bottom right: A multitasking alien pauses from abducting humans to leave behind some "alien art" in the form of ancient images some believe represent ancient astronauts.

unstable and the pyramid had to be hastily finished at a shallower angle to keep it from collapsing. The pharaoh, unhappy with this ugly pyramid, then ordered a new one built next to it; this was the Red Pyramid, rising at a slope of about forty-three degrees. Bauval turned this on its head, arguing that Sneferu intended to build two pyramids because they were meant to represent the horns of the heavenly bull, the constellation Taurus. (These stars are also called the Hyades.)[10]

Up until this point, Bauval's theories were within the scientific mainstream. While Egyptologists disliked the idea that the pyramids at Giza represented Orion's Belt, the hypothesis was not unreasonable. It made predictions about the placement of the pyramids that could be tested on the ground. Of course, there were minor problems from the beginning. Orion's brightest stars were Betelgeuse and Rigel, the shoulder and foot of the constellation, yet the pyramids Bauval tried to identify with them were smaller than the Great Pyramid, which theoretically represented a dimmer star. Further, even when restricted to the three Giza pyramids, the structures on the ground did not quite match the stars in the sky. The angle by which Menkaure's pyramid was offset from the Khufu-Khafre diagonal was larger than the angle by which Mintaka was offset from the Alnitak-Alnilam diagonal. Bauval protested that this was irrelevant,[11] but it undermined his claims of ancient Egyptian precision astronomy and construction. Nevertheless, it was true that there was a superficial correlation that deserved a thorough investigation.

Bauval first tried to garner scholarly support for his thesis. T. G. H. James, the Keeper of Egyptian Antiquities at the British Museum, rejected the Orion Correlation Theory, as it was now known, as unsubstantiated by facts.[12] Two other scholars, Egyptologist I. E. S. Edwards and astronomer Jaromir Malek, agreed with Bauval that the stars were important to the Egyptians but did not agree without reservation that the pyramids represented Orion.[13] Bauval took this in stride and aired part of his theory in *Discussions in Egyptology*, a journal of Egyptian studies whose contributors were largely not professional Egyptologists. *Discussions* was also not peer reviewed, a standard procedure in scientific journals where other scientists read submissions to determine before publication whether they meet the requirements of good science. Here Bauval offered only the theory that the Giza pyramids were the belt stars of Orion, not the larger theory encompassing the Nile and other pyramids. Scholarly reaction was tepid at best. One Egyptologist told him to forget his theory and try to be a good engineer instead.[14]

While Bauval researched ancient Egypt, a number of other developments had helped to catapult the Giza plateau back into the public spotlight and renew interest in alternative theories about the pyramids' construction. Much of this interest revolved around another monument on the Giza plateau, the Great Sphinx, the massive statue with the body of a lion and the head of a man that guards the pyramids. Believed to have been built by the pharaoh Khafre and to bear his likeness, the Sphinx has been a source of wonder and mystery nearly all of its five millennia in existence. Everyone who gazed into its eyes, from the Greek historian Herodotus to the French Emperor Napoléon, found a baffling view into the grandeur of the prehistoric world.

In the late 1980s, tour guide John Anthony West had become partially famous for his book *The Serpent in the Sky: The High Wisdom of Ancient Egypt* (1979), which claimed among other things that a lost Atlantis-like civilization had built the Sphinx and given civilization to the ancient Egyptians: "[T]he earliest calculations would place the founding of Egypt around 30,000 BC, the latest around 23,000 BC. . . . 'Atlantis' can no longer be ignored by anyone interested in the pursuit of truth."[15] West borrowed much of his proof from Robert

Temple's *Sirius Mystery* and used the Dogon's "anomalous" knowledge to bolster his case. West, however, rejected the extraterrestrial intervention hypothesis, preferring to see Egpytian civilization as a legacy of a high human civilization lost to time.

For this idea of a cultural legacy, West drew heavily from the works of the early twentieth–century Alsatian researcher René Schwaller de Lubicz, who in his youth had read deeply the works of Madame Helena Blavatsky of Theosophical and Lemurian fame as well as other occult and pseudoscientific authors of the late nineteenth century. These were the same works that had influenced H. P. Lovecraft to create the Cthulhu Mythos, and it was no surprise that they produced a similar effect on Schwaller, who spent fifteen years in Egypt trying to prove that the temples and pyramids reflected an esoteric body of knowledge dating back to a lost civilization equivalent to Atlantis or Lemuria and that Egypt was thousands of years older than Egyptologists assumed.[16] Schwaller was active in France's Theosophical Society, and he wrote primarily as a philosopher whose complicated beliefs predicted the rise of a "new consciousness" in the Age of Aquarius.[17] This was the same "new consciousness" that Louis Pauwles and Jacques Bergier discussed in *Morning of the Magicians*, the book that launched the ancient-astronaut theory into the realm of fact.

John Anthony West considered Schwaller a personal hero. Embracing Schwaller's last book, 1957's *Le temple de l'homme* (*Temple of Man*), he wrote that its conclusions about Egypt and consciousness represented "in my opinion, the single most important work of scholarship of this or any other century. It is a work of pure genius; the more you study it, the more it seems impossible for a single man to have accomplished."[18] Further, building on a passing suggestion from Schwaller, West suggested that the unique undulating pattern of weathering on the body of the Great Sphinx was not the result of being repeatedly inundated with desert sands but was instead the result of water erosion. He first published this theory in *Second Look*, a magazine edited by none other than *Sirius Mystery* author Robert Temple, who found it "interesting."[19] He later repeated his claim in *Serpent in the Sky*. West used this claim to argue that Schwaller was right and a "lost civilization" indeed built the Sphinx, though Temple believed (and continues to believe) that both the Sphinx and Giza pyramids were built by extraterrestrials.[20]

In the early 1990s, West convinced an actual geologist to look into the weathering of the Sphinx and conduct a scientific study. In 1992, geology professor Robert Schoch informed his colleagues that he had concluded that the Great Sphinx was several thousand years older than previously believed. He confirmed that the weathering of the Sphinx was the result of rain, and since the last major rainy period in Egyptian history occurred around 7000 BCE (before Egypt was a desert), then the Sphinx must be at least that old. This proved, ipso facto, that there was a high culture capable of building monuments at that early date. That the assumption of a high culture led to the investigation that "proved" its existence was not discussed. We will have much more to say about the Sphinx and its dating in the next chapter, but it is important to note here that there was at least a veneer of scientific respectability attached to a redating of the Sphinx (and thus Egypt) during the early 1990s.

West seized on this "discovery" and confidently asserted that the Sphinx was twelve thousand years old, despite Schoch's reluctance to entertain a date older than 7000 BCE. The pair aired their views in an NBC documentary special, *The Mystery of the Sphinx*, in 1993, which along with its anti-evolution twin special, *The Mysterious Origins of Man*, brought alternative theories of the origins of Egyptian civilization and mankind to an audience numbering in the millions. *Mystery of the Sphinx* alone attracted 33 million viewers. The same television network that broadcast Rod Serling's *In Search of Ancient Astronauts* two decades earlier again found itself at the forefront of a wave of "alternative" science. Further, thanks to a burgeoning number of cable television channels desperate for programming, these documentaries aired repeatedly for years and still air occasionally today.

I decided that I needed to ask John Anthony West about his evidence for the impossible. I wrote to him while he was traveling in Egypt, and he was kind enough to answer one of my questions about the Sphinx, which we shall discuss in more detail later. To my broader questions about his cosmology and the circuitous path from H. P. Lovecraft to the ancient-astronaut theory, he had this to say:

> Your other questions, by the way, are maladroit attempts to sucker me into saying something that you will be able to use for a work quite obviously designed to trash whoever and whatever does not correspond to your foregone conclusions. Sorry. I won't play.[21]

I felt sorry that West had declined to answer my questions. Though I disagreed with his conclusions, the reader will by now have seen that my conclusions were anything but foregone. Having started life as a firm believer, I knew full well the immense appeal that alternative theories held. I also knew that for better or worse, the purveyors of these ideas were by and large good, honest people who were doing what they believed was right. If I disagree with their theories, it is by no means an indication that I intended to "trash" the men (and they are almost all men) behind them. I respected their enormous courage for daring to challenge the complacent mainstream science, which had often become calcified in dogma. But good science means having the ability to criticize ideas that one knows are erroneous. In 1993, a German researcher challenged the archaeological view of the Great Pyramid's mysterious "air shafts."

In March 1993, a German engineer named Rudolph Gatenbrink received permission to use a new type of robot to explore the so-called air shafts—long, thin masonry tubes stretching at angles from the interior chambers of the Great Pyramid almost to the exterior of the structure. In 1993, these shafts were unexplored and widely considered to be short, unimportant tubes of an uncertain function in the pyramid.

The Great Pyramid has several interior chambers, which archaeologists believe represent several attempts to create an acceptable burial chamber for the pharaoh Khufu. The lowest of these chambers is located underground and is rough and unfinished. In the center of the pyramid is the so-called Queen's Chamber, once erroneously believed to have housed one of Khufu's wives. Neither of these chambers was ever used for the king's burial. They were superceded by the King's Chamber, the largest of the interior chambers, located above the Queen's Chamber. This room was believed to be Khufu's resting place, as it contains the granite sarcophagus in which the king was likely buried. A magnificent Grand Gallery rises at an angle from the pyramid's original entrance to this room.

There are two sets of "air" shafts in the pyramid, two in the King's Chamber and two in the Queen's Chamber. In both rooms, one shaft faces north and the other south. The King's Chamber shafts were cut through the walls into the room, while the Queen's Chamber shafts were sealed behind the chamber's walls. Since they were only a few inches in diameter, no one had been able to explore the full length of these shafts. Gatenbrink proposed to use a small robot equipped with a camera to do this. The robot, named *Upuaut* after the Egyptian deity who "opened the ways," could climb up the shaft and send back pictures. When Gatenbrink's *Upuaut* reached the top of the Queen's Chamber south shaft, he discovered an unexpected surprise: a small sliding door that blocked the shaft sixty meters up.

Immediately, ancient-astronaut authors and alternative historians began to speculate that the door was the gateway to the long-rumored treasure of the pyramid. Erich von Däniken suggested that Egyptologists had entered into a conspiracy to suppress the discovery of the door and that a secret chamber may lay behind it.[22] Excited Egyptologists, supposedly conspiring to prevent amazing secrets from coming to light, instead made plans to open the chamber and make money by selling the rights to the opening to television. In 2002, the "secret chamber" was finally opened on live global television, simulcast in the United States on Fox-TV and the National Geographic Channel. Behind the door, the investigators found . . . nothing. The chamber was empty.

All the while, Bauval kept working on his theory, eventually producing a book on the subject, a book for the general reader, not a scholarly treatise. That book was *The Orion Mystery*, whose title purposely evoked his inspiration, Robert Temple, and the year was 1994. Along the way he acquired a coauthor to help write and publish his work.

His coauthor, Adrian Gilbert, was the owner of a small press that republished out-of-print occult works like the Gnostic *Hermetica*. He eventually became best known as the coauthor of *The Mayan Prophesies* (1995), which claimed that the Maya were scientifically more advanced than modern people and knew that because of sunspots something like the Apocalypse would occur in 2012, the year their complex calendar ended.[23] Gilbert went on to write *Signs in the Sky*, which claimed that the summer of 2000 marked the beginning of the biblical Apocalypse. Relying on biblical literalism, he interpreted the book of Revelations as a description of astronomy and believed that beginning in 2000 humanity would experience a great change, as great as the transition from Cro-Magnon to modern humans.[24] The Age of Aquarius would begin, Jesus Christ would start his countdown to return, and the prophecies of the Virgin Mary at Fátima would come to pass for a Catholic Church triumphant.[25] Gilbert sent this important information to the

Pope, whose representatives dismissed him with a polite note wishing him God's blessing. This was the man Robert Bauval chose to help him bring his "scientific" theory to the world.

While it is unclear exactly how much influence Gilbert had on the developing Orion Correlation Theory, the hallmarks of his speculative, sensational style manifest in the conclusion of *The Orion Mystery*. The first sections detail the more plausible aspects of Bauval's argument, but in the last third of the book, things get a little wild, reflecting West's new revelations about the age of the Sphinx and the radical redating of Egypt that the emerging field of "alternative science" was trying to accomplish. Not content to simply acknowledge the Orion Correlation, Bauval and Gilbert needed to explain it.

To explain it, they had to rely on a strange astrological phenomenon known as the Precession of the Equinoxes. This is a rather esoteric happening in the sky where, due to the slow wobble of the earth's axis, there are two major apparent effects in the sky: the sun seems to rise in a slightly different place along the zodiac each year, and the stars seem to move in the sky over centuries.

Because many ancient cultures measured the year from the spring equinox (March 21), that was a date on which sunrise was often observed and recorded, and it is the date most often used to document precession. The sun always rises against one of the twelve constellations of the zodiac, the imaginary astrological bestiary stretching in a band around the earth. Each of the twelve constellations ("signs") stretches thirty degrees, for a complete circle of 360 degrees. When people believed in a geocentric vision of the universe, they believed the sun traveled along this path, though in our heliocentric age we now know this is merely an apparent motion as the earth orbits the sun. After 71.6 years, the sun seems to rise one degree off where it started, so roughly every 25,776 years, the sun makes a complete circuit of the zodiac. Thus, every 2,148 years there is a new constellation behind the sun at the spring equinox. This zodiacal constellation then gives its name to the astrological "age"; the upcoming age is the Age of Aquarius. Currently we are leaving the Age of Pisces. The whole cycle is known as "precession" because the sun appears to move "backward" along the zodiac, from Aries to Pisces to Aquarius instead of the "normal" astrological view, from Aquarius to Pisces to Aries, and so on.

The other major effect of precession is the slow movement of the stars. As the years go by, the stars shift positions slightly but regularly. The exact amount of movement per star is determined by its exact position in the sky, but many good computer programs have now simplified the task of calculating these positions. As a result, we can reasonably reconstruct the night sky for any given year along the twenty-six-thousand-year cycle of Precession.

That the ancients knew of this in outline is beyond doubt. The ancient Greeks clearly knew the concept, if not the numbers. How far back this knowledge stretches, though, is controversial. In 1969 Giorgio de Santillana and Hertha von Dechend wrote a lengthy, dense, and poorly constructed book called *Hamlet's Mill*, subtitled *An Essay Investigating the Origins of Human Knowledge and Its Transmission through Myth*, where they attempt to demonstrate that global mythology encodes a prehistoric science of the stars. I must confess that I find their comparative mythology fascinating, though I have always had reservations about exactly how much "science" is really there, especially as the authors credit Marcel Griaule for inspiring them, bringing us full circle again. I have always thought that prehistoric people had more than enough time to come up with complex and interesting philosophies, but without the written word, much of this must have been lost. It would not surprise me if ancient sages knew much of the stars, but in no way would that necessarily imply any anomalous skill on their part, only the human brains we all possess.

In *Hamlet's Mill*, the authors argued that mythology around the world, from Greece to India to Mexico, encoded certain numbers generated from the Precession, notably the number 72, an approximation of the 71.6 years needed to make a one-degree shift in the sun's position. Other important numbers included 144 (twice seventy-two), 360 (five times seventy-two), and 432 (six times seventy-two). Thus mythological figures like the 432,000 warriors of Valhalla or the 72 conspirators who killed Osiris are codes for Precession. De Santillana and von Dechend suggest that scientifically knowledgeable ancients purposely encoded this insight in their myths, and that its purpose was to point back to their antediluvian wisdom and power, an initiation into their religio-philosophical worldview. However, they did not draw any conclusions about who these encoders were lest they "fall into the bottomless pit of speculation."[26] These speculations were for Bauval and others to attempt.

Working from this view of ancient life, Bauval drew two conclusions, one logical and defensible, one illogical, both using Precession. His logical conclusion was that by calculating the positions of the stars for the date the pyramids were built, one could check for alignments that had since changed. This was the essence of archaeoastronomy, a legitimate science that we saw misused by Arthur Posnansky at the Bolivian city of Tiwanaku to achieve his dates. Here Bauval used the science properly, analyzing shafts in the King's and Queen's Chambers of the Great Pyramid. Bauval correctly noted that these shafts pointed to stars at the time of the pyramid's construction, around 2500 BCE. He found the King's Chamber shafts pointing to the old North Star, Alpha Draconis (since moved) and to the belt stars of Orion. The Queen's Chamber shafts targeted Sirius and Beta Ursa Major.[27] All of this was, if radical, a solid use of data and worthy of further research and investigation. So far so good.

The illogical conclusion was predicated on the belief from *Hamlet's Mill*, *The Sirius Mystery*, and John Anthony West that the ancients not only knew about Precession but knew it perfectly. He reasoned that the layout of the pyramids in Egypt was aligned to a specific date in time and that Precession could be used to find it. So he plugged the numbers into his trusty computer program, Skyglobe 3.5, to find the date when Orion's belt would have found a perfect mirror in the pyramids on the Giza necropolis. Watching the stars turn round, rotating slowly through the centuries, he finally found his match. At one time and only one time (in the current twenty-six-thousand-year cycle) did Orion hold the same position in the sky as the pyramids on the ground. That year was 10,450 BCE: "The pattern of Orion's Belt seen on the 'west' of the Milky Way matches, with uncanny precision, the pattern and alignments of the three Giza pyramids!"[28] It was probably no coincidence that this was the same time frame that West had suggested for the beginning of Ancient Egypt, roughly twelve thousand years ago.

This year, Bauval suggests, represented the First Time, the Egyptian moment of creation, and this was what the pyramid builders sought to immortalize in stone. It was also the moment when the constellation Orion was at its lowest point in its twenty-six-thousand-year cycle up and down the sky. At the remote date, the stars in the sky were one with the pyramids on the ground. A viewer standing at Giza could look south (to the Egyptians, south was "up") and see before him (if he were psychic or planning ahead) the colossal bulk of the three pyramids below the awesome splendor of Orion's three most recognizable stars spreading majestically from south to north. Heaven and earth were one in the perfection of the Orion Correlation. This was the Orion Mystery . . .

Wait a second. Giza faces south, and Orion faces north? That can't be right.

Ed Krupp, the Griffith Observatory astronomer and famous author, noticed right away that the Bauval theory was logically flawed. The problem, it seems, was that the constellation of Orion was aligned north to south, but the pyramids were arranged south to north. Recalling the controversy, Krupp described his observation:

> [A] direct projection of stars to earth cannot produce the pattern of monuments encountered on the ground at Giza. When you project the stars from the sky directly to the earth, the "Belt" of pyramids is angled the wrong way. Obviously this kind of mapping, which preserves the directional relationship between earth and sky, can't work at Giza. The geometry is compromised.[29]

In short, if the Orion Correlation were real, Bauval would have to explain why the pyramids were upside down. The BBC used Krupp's claim to challenge Bauval's theory in a pair of *Horizon* documentaries in 2000, *Atlantis Revisited* and *Atlantis Reborn*, ironic since a BBC/A&E documentary called *The Great Pyramid: Gateway to the Stars* helped build Bauval's reputation when it presented Bauval's theory uncritically in 1994.[30] Bauval, in turn, challenged this documentary (along with colleague Graham Hancock, whom we shall encounter soon) with a formal complaint to the British Broadcasting Standards Commission, and the BBC reedited it after the British watchdog group found against the network, the first such finding in the BBC's history. Bauval explained his reasoning: "I argued that the Giza-Orion's belt correlation theory worked because the similarity in patterns between the three pyramids and the three stars had to be observed by looking towards the south, such that the Nile and the Milky Way were to the left of the observer."[31] Since the constellation of Orion is in the southern sky and Ancient Egypt held south to be "up," this seemed like a logical point of view.

Of course, it was only logical if the Orion Correlation Theory were true, and for it to be true it had to be supported by evidence. That evidence lay primarily in the correlation of the ground to the sky, since Bauval's other proof, the Pyramid Texts and such, was supplemental to the visual correlation, the first proof in *The Orion Mystery*. The evidence he amassed he was able to find because he believed the correlation true and tried to support the idea. This evidence, not surprisingly, seemed to confirm his theory. So the visual correlation is true if the visual correlation is true. The arguments were thus reduced to a tautology. Therefore, the argument about upside-down or right-side-up was no argument at all. It was merely a debate on the limits of circular logic. The Orion Correlation Theory, like Temple's correlations before it, seemed ultimately to be a case of circular reasoning, though Bauval's circles seemed wider than Temple's and more difficult to see.

It may seem that we have now strayed far from Lovecraft country, into strange lands and odd theories. But let us not forget that Bauval's theories arose from Robert Temple's ancient-astronaut speculations, and Temple's theories derived ultimately from H. P. Lovecraft's "Call of Cthulhu." Of course, when in 2001 I asked Bauval about Temple's theories, he dismissed my question by denying that he supported Temple's theories: "[While] I also know Robert Temple personally, it also does not mean that I support his ideas." More fully, he explained to another questioner that *"The Sirius Mystery* is just that, a great mystery well-worth exploring. Temple may be wrong, only time will tell. But he's not dishonest. He is a brave man who stuck his neck out and stood up to be counted among original thinkers of his time."[32] Bauval did not reply to my requests for a more extensive interview. Yet, as we have seen, he embraced Temple's radical speculations about stellar correlations in the ancient world, and these speculations provided the basis for his Orion correlation. It was all there in *The*

Orion Mystery, itself named after *The Sirius Mystery*, for all to see. Only when Bauval became famous did he begin to disassociate himself from Temple's less acceptable theories, though he still recognized "inspiration" and "influence" from Temple and his band of extraterrestrial amphibians.

Therefore, we are not that far from where we began, and Robert Bauval would stray back into Lovecraft country soon enough when he came to embrace (temporarily) the possibility that aliens were our ancestors. But he did this only in 1998, after he had met another researcher into ancient mysteries, Graham Hancock, a man who would become internationally famous as the most important author of "alternative history" since Erich von Däniken.

12

DUSTING FOR
FINGERPRINTS

Before we explore Robert Bauval's foray into the ancient-astronaut theory, we must first meet his comrade-in-arms, Graham Hancock, international best-selling author and alternative historian of the first magnitude.

As we have seen, for generations scholars of both mainstream and fringe science had puzzled over the strange similarities that ancient monuments seemed to bear to one another. So great is the temptation to link the temples and tombs of the forgotten past that an entire subgenre of nonfiction had arisen to extol the theory that far-off places like Tiwanaku, Easter Island, and Egypt were part of a great and ancient global design. First among these controversial authors was Graham Hancock, who has sold millions of books by asking his readers to believe the seemingly impossible: that humanity is a "species with amnesia" that has forgotten the greatest episode in its history, the destruction and near-complete effacement of an antediluvian civilization whose tiny, scattered remnants form the "fingerprints of the gods," which was the title of his 1995 best-selling book.[1]

Hancock is an Englishman with a soothing voice that bears the culture and learning of the Victorian professors romanticized in too many bad novels and worse films. His hair has begun to gray, and his small, round glasses make him look more learned than his fifty or so years. A journalist by trade, Hancock worked for the renowned newspaper *The Economist* for many years and wrote several critically acclaimed books, including *AIDS: The Deadly Epidemic* and *Lords of Poverty*, before making a "life-changing" trip to Ethiopia, where he became a convert to a new faith based on a great legacy allegedly handed down from the most ancient times.

Because of his nose for news and the allure of a large sum of money from the corrupt government of dictator Mengistu Haile Mariam, Hancock undertook to write a history of Ethiopia in 1983. To glorify himself and his country, Mengistu granted the author free access to any site in the country, and he asked Hancock to emphasize the ancient cultures of Ethiopia and their achievements. Hancock later wrote that "I was under no illusions about how the project was viewed by senior figures in the regime."[2] Mengistu wanted to justify his oppressive government and the greatness of Ethiopia to the world. Perhaps to no one's shock, Hancock made a sensational discovery during his stay at the ancient city of Axum, home to Ethiopia's most ancient rulers: the city housed the Ark of the Covenant.

"I did not come to the book with any sense of moral mission," Hancock later conceded. "What drew me to it was a journalistic instinct that I had stumbled upon a good story that no-one had yet told properly. I decided to tell that story."[3]

Hancock picked up rumors and traced them backward in time, delving deeper and deeper into the murky underbelly of African and Jewish histories to produce a convincing, if sometimes speculative, argument that the Ark of the Covenant had been taken from the Temple in Jerusalem in the seventh century BCE to the city of Axum by way of the Jewish colony in Elephantine, Egypt. Treading much of the ground other writers of ancient mysteries had covered, Hancock related the Ark story to that of the Holy Grail, the legendary chalice used by Christ at the Last Supper. He believed that the Grail was an esoteric symbol for the Ark of the Covenant and that medieval epics of Europe and Ethiopia about the Grail (notably *Parsifal* and the *Kebra Nagast*) actually laid out a treasure map leading to its hiding place in Ethiopia. He capped off his research with firsthand accounts of his travels to the places described in the legends of the Grail.

In the final part of his book, he speculated about the Ark. Covering some of the same ground that Erich von Däniken tread in his failed speculations about the Ark, Hancock wondered at the Ark's amazing powers. Taking literally the biblical story of Exodus, he marveled at tales of the Ark's ability to strike people who touched it dead, and the apparent radiation burns Moses suffered coming down from Mount Sinai after encountering God. He began to believe that the Ark was a powerful piece of technology misinterpreted by the Jews as divine. This technology, he speculated, came from Egypt, where it may have been the legacy of a lost civilization.[4]

However, Hancock did not press the case, clearly labeling such thoughts as speculation and thought experiments when he sat down to compose his first best-seller. The resulting book, *The Sign and the Seal*, debuted in 1992 and sold millions of copies. It also planted in Hancock's mind the germ of an idea: "I began to realize just how many anomalies and enigmas there were in the past which either were not adequately explained by the orthodox theory of history or which could be equally adequately explained by an alternative theory."[5]

Here Hancock stopped being the objective journalist of his newspaper days and changed roles; he began to formulate an alternative theory to explain the enigmas he previously had been content merely to catalogue, a lost civilization. This powerful revelation in the heart of Africa set the stage for the rest of Hancock's career.

As we have seen, the centuries-long buildup of resistance to a perception of scientism in Western society produced a flurry of antiscientific thought in the middle of the twentieth century, something unseen since the Romantic resistance to the Enlightenment a century and a half before. Out of this chaos, a new breed of thought emerged from the postmodern anarchy, a type of Romantic view of history championed by Swiss author Erich von Däniken. He argued that extraterrestrials were the true "gods" of ancient times and through their artifice ancient man wrought great marvels. His theories lacked what would conventionally be called "proof," but like any great story, this modern myth took on a life of its own. By the mid-1990s, a new wave of spirituality, antiscientism, and millennial anxiety conspired to create a large market for anyone who could make a case against established thought. Enter Graham Hancock.

With the success of *The Sign and the Seal*, Hancock had begun to suspect that something was wrong with the human past. He began to explore the works of ancient-astronaut and alternative history authors and came to the conclusion that they were on to something, but that something was not aliens. In 1995 Hancock published his seminal work, *Fingerprints of the Gods*, in which he attempted to show that the end of the last Ice Age saw the demise of a technologically and, more important, spiritually advanced civilization whose few survivors carried the light of knowledge and wisdom for eight thousand years before depositing it wholesale in the laps of the Egyptian pharaohs and Bolivian priests. Unlike his disgraced predecessor von Däniken, Hancock attempted to provide solid, if controversial, proof of his claims. Unlike von Däniken, Hancock also avoided the extraterrestrial hypotheis.

Fingerprints of the Gods was arguably the most successful and most important work of "alternative history"[6] in the twentieth century. Told in the exciting style of an archaeological adventure like Indiana Jones, *Fingerprints* depicted Hancock's thrilling journey around the world in search of ancient mysteries. This tale was read by millions and featured in newspapers, magazines, and television documentaries. More people around the world were exposed to and believed Hancock's theories than with any previous author in the genre. Therefore, we need to take a close look at his book and what it says to understand exactly what happened in 1995. Hancock's most important claims surround his evidence in Egypt, but let us start where Hancock does, at the beginning of his "mystery."

The book begins with a dizzying array of ancient maps dating back to the sixteenth century that apparently show Antarctica long before it was officially discovered in 1818. Hancock uses this evidence to support his claim that the Ice Age produced a great civilization advanced enough to map the world and leave a legacy. That civilization, he believes, must have flourished around 10,500 BCE. Clearly that number is familiar, and it is no coincidence, as we shall see. The most famous of these maps is the Piri Reis map of 1513. As we discussed in our chapters on von Däniken and Robert Temple, the map was drawn from what Reis, a Turkish admiral, claimed were ancient source maps from the Library of Alexandria. The map seems to show the coast of Queen Maud Land as it appeared beneath the ice. The correlation is at first striking, especially in light of other sixteenth-century maps from such men as Mercator and Oronteus Finaeus that seemed to show Antarctica gradually glaciating. But all is not well because as we recall, these maps appear superficially accurate only if it is assumed that the source maps were accurate to allow us to mentally "correct" obvious errors.

If we take the Piri Reis map (famous since the 1950s) at its face, Paul V. Heinrich says, "the Piri Reis Map itself is grossly inaccurate."[7] Never mind that this was all worked out decades before Hancock when disgraced Prof. Charles Hapgood put forth his theories of ancient sea kings. Hancock uses it anyway, along with other maps. Antarctica in the Finaeus map shows mountains and rivers beneath the ice, and the depiction of Antarctica, while flawed, does conform to the continent's general shape in a way coincidence is hard-pressed to explain. There may be something to the ancient maps, but there is no proof that they date back to Hancock's 10,500 BCE. An ambitious fourteenth-century traveler could easily have surveyed the coast of the continent, and mapmakers could have used imagination to fill in the interior, much the way a previous generation populated the North Pole with Hyperboreans. Or perhaps it was all a coincidence. The ancients believed that the southern hemisphere would be a mirror image of the north, so the ancient concept of the "Antipodes" could have generated a perfectly reasonable southern continent. What mattered, though, was that this evidence looked so good to the untrained eye.

The imposing and austere ruins of Tiwanaku stand as mute witnesses to the ravages of time and man. Spanish missionaries stood in horror before the ruins of the city and ordered the idols smashed. We have seen the city used as a strange test case for an alien base camp and for claims of its great antiquity. Graham Hancock writes that this city was the seat of the Viracocha, the South American civilizer-god described in Spanish accounts of native legends as white of skin and long of beard. This Caucasian, he says, could only have been a memory of a lost white race that colonized South America fifteen millennia ago. Scholars had long ago concluded that these legends of white skin were a Spanish invention to make the natives accept white rule, but Hancock chose to believe these were authentic traditions.[8]

Much of Hancock's evidence is often lacking in solid background. He claims that a carving on the Gate of the Sun, a large archway in Tiwanaku, depicts a type of elephant extinct since

10,000 BCE. From one angle, the drawing does look something like an elephant, but it is ambiguous. Hancock wonders how could the ancients who carved that image have known about these elephants if they had not been told of them from time immemorial or carved them when the elephants still walked the earth. Prof. James Bailey offered an answer with Occam's Razor, the principle that the theory that requires the fewest unproved assumptions is most likely to be correct:

> This is a carving of a parrot. It looks like an elephant until you are told that it is a parrot and then it is very obvious that it is a parrot. . . . What's more likely, that it's an incongruous, extinct elephant . . . or a more recent carving of an existing, common indigenous species?[9]

But Hancock said he saw an elephant, and he believed the elephant more likely since he concluded that Tiwanaku is seventeen thousand years old.[10] He based this number on surveys of the site taken by Prof. Arthur Posnansky in the 1940s. As we saw, Posnansky based his date on an assumption that Tiwanaku was a solar observatory accurately aligned to the sun. Using an arbitrary point, he determined the sun was eighteen degrees off perfect alignment, so therefore the site was laid out when sun and stone aligned, roughly fifteen thousand years ago. Why Hancock added two thousand years is anyone's guess. Perhaps he confused fifteen thousand years ago with 15,000 BCE and thus added two thousand years of the Common Era a second time.

Yet there would be other evidence still at Tiwanaku. In a later work, Hancock would try to bolster his damaged claims about the city. Tiwanaku is one of only three places in the ancient world to use metal I-clamps to join cut blocks together, the others being ancient Egypt and Angkor Wat, Cambodia—both of which we shall see figure prominently in Hancock's cosmology. Those I-clamps at Tiwanaku are made of a particular alloy of iron, copper, and arsenic that requires a smelter operating at very high temperatures. A scanning electron microscope determined that the clamps were poured into place, necessitating a portable smelter.[11] All this occurred in an area where current theory denies an Iron Age. While Hancock argues baselessly for intervention from outside, at the very least one must concede that Tiwanaku's citizens had a high level of technology. Of course, it has been known for a long time that the ancient South Americans were master metalsmiths, a fact confirmable in most books on South American prehistory.[12]

As one critic put it, "The gullible investigator in this detective story has been led down a blind alley by a clever guide, and he has come up empty-handed. Rather than stumbling upon an archaeological mystery, [Hancock] has merely created one."[13]

We now move up the coast of South America and into the valley of Mexico. The colossal heads of the Olmec cannot fail to draw the attention of the archaeological tourist. Carved from enormous balls of stone, the heads depict helmeted figures with broad noses and thick lips. We saw that Robert Charroux liked to think of these faces as those of helmeted space travelers. Erich von Däniken preferred to think of them as evidence of Africans in Mexico because their broad faces and flat noses looked like a stereotype of African features. That the faces might just look like the Olmec people of Mexico, native to the Americas, was too horrible to contemplate, despite the clear evidence that it was true.[14] Like von Däniken before him, Hancock claims that the unique features of the Olmec heads are distinctly African and thus prove a transoceanic ancient culture. Or does he?

Throughout his writings on the Olmec, Hancock deploys rhetorical questions like "If [a lost civilization] left a legacy of high culture in Egypt and Mesopotamia, why shouldn't it have done so in Central America?"[15] This is a neat way of skirting the need for evidence because Hancock merely raised a question; he did not pose a hypothesis. The same goes for his use of the conditional tense and subjunctive mood to pull off the neat rhetorical effect of saying something without really saying it. For example, Hancock says in *Fingerprints* that by the Olmec Horizon, the beginning of their culture (c. 1500 BCE), "it is by no means impossible that these great works preserve the images of peoples from a vanished civilization which embraced several different ethnic groups."[16] Of course, Hancock did not really say that this was the case, only that it could have been.

Ironically, there is real evidence of some contact between Mexico and the Old World, not across the Atlantic as Hancock thought, but across the Pacific. The strongest, and indeed only, hard piece of evidence for trans-Pacific contact is the use of a particular technique for the manufacture of bark paper, common to China, Southeast Asia, Indonesia, and Meso-america.[17] But interesting facts like this were lost in the glitz and glamour of the more visually interesting Olmec heads.

Hancock claims the Olmec heads date back to the days of the Viracocha (c. 5000 BCE) because there is no accurate way of dating stone. Therefore Hancock argues that this date must be every bit as accurate as the standard 1500 BCE date. He is right that there is no way of saying when the stones were carved, only when they were buried in the Mexican jungles and forgotten to history. However, the context of Olmec civilization clearly places their achievements in the 1500 BCE time frame, so until the heads can be dated with any certainty, the safest and simplest assumption (Occam's Razor) is that they descend from those who buried them since no other artifact survives from the hypothetical pre-Olmec civilization.

But Hancock uses his rhetorical flourish to turn the fact that both the Old and New Worlds had cultures into a stunning coincidence: "Certain cultures of the Old World and in the New World may both have received a legacy of influence and ideas from a third party at some exceedingly remote date."[18]

Once again there is little solid evidence to back up the "may have."

Hancock then visited Palenque, a Mayan city in Mexico, where he viewed Pacal's tomb, which we saw Erich von Däniken compare with a spacecraft. Compare Hancock's reaction with Erich von Däniken's thirty years before. Hancock's *Fingerprints of the Gods*: "The structure Pacal reclined in resembled a technological device."[19] Von Däniken's *Chariots of the Gods?*: "Today any child would identify his vehicle as a rocket."[20] Hancock at least considered the mainstream interpretation that the lid represented the transition of the king into the underworld, but he rejected it on the basis of appearance: it looked too technological to him. It is an irrefutable argument; one cannot argue with perception. However, with no surviving piece of ancient supertechnology in Maya land and plenty of known drawings in the same style, it seems more likely that the lid was a piece of art and not a diagram of any ancient science other than the science of the afterlife.

Hancock tried to find corroborating evidence for an ancient civilization in Mexico on the basis of a site at Cuernavaca where a step pyramid lay beneath a volcanic lava mantle, which geologists had dated to eight-five hundred years ago. Thus the pyramid was older than this ancient date.[21] Unfortunately for Hancock, this sensational claim was a mistake. The geology was proven wrong, and Hancock had to retract the claim in a subsequent edition of the book. He never did any actual research into the myth of the ancient temple, reiterating a mistake made by Prof. Charles Hapgood, the same man who advocated the Piri Reis map.[22]

And yet . . . something about Hancock's view of Mexican civilization rings in part true because there are occasional glimpses of similarities almost too great to be coincidence—like a ceremony common to Egypt and Mexico in which the facial orifices of a corpse are struck open by bent metal rods to free the soul. Beyond any buildings or artifacts, it is the similarity of ideas in ancient civilization that make Hancock's view more palatable than von Däniken's ever was. But this need not imply an ancient lost civilization, only a human mind capable of creating fascinating edifices of religious belief and myth from a set number of archetypes in the human mind. It is possible that early humans shared certain belief systems, and the remains of these were incorporated into humanity's first recorded religions. Yet since thought is free, these philosophies did not necessarily need a lost civilization attached to them, only a few smart people with a lot of time on their hands.

Speaking of time, Hancock next turns his attention to the timeless guardian of Egypt's pyramids. The centerpiece of *Fingerprints* and its sequels, *Message of the Sphinx*[23] (1996) and *Heaven's Mirror* (1998), stands guard over the pyramid complex at Giza, positioned exactly on the border of the ancient Two Kingdoms of Egypt. For centuries the Great Sphinx stood guard over Giza, which the ancients knew as Rosteau. The head of this statue has long puzzled some archaeologists because it seems out of proportion with the rest of the creature's body. Simply put, it is too small.

Building on an actual scientific theory that the head had been recarved at a later date, Hancock makes a baseless assumption that the Sphinx was once a full lion with the head of the animal to match the body. No document or evidence confirms this; in fact, the theory was first put forward during that 1993 NBC special with John Anthony West that claimed Atlantean origins for the statue. However, this assumption is vital for Hancock's theory to work.

Hancock used the work of maverick amateur archaeologist and tour guide John Anthony West to bolster his claims of ancient civilization. We saw that West did extensive work on the statue, measuring and photographing all the weathering on the body of the lion and the walls of the "Sphinx enclosure" surrounding it. His conclusions were mind-blowing. West had concluded that the weathering occurred by falling water, not blowing wind. This meant that extensive rainfall must have weathered the statue before the desert sands had buried it. Since the last Egyptian rainfall of that magnitude was more than seven thousand years ago, this meant that history as we know it needed an overhaul. This was bolstered when geologist Robert Schoch agreed. Schoch had presented his findings to the Geological Society of America, where the story went that "[s]everal hundred geologists" gave their support to Schoch.[24] Apparently GSA meetings feature booths like science fairs. The geologists passed by Schoch's booth and said his research seemed interesting. It did not, as many claimed, imply an endorsement.

Egyptologists, in fact, fired back at Schoch with a theory that the Sphinx was weathered by "salt crystal exfoliation" where Nile salts were sucked into the sand-covered enclosure surrounding the Sphinx statue and performed a leeching of the limestone walls.[25] But the water-weathering theory is a seductive hypothesis, much simpler to understand and agree with than an obscure "exfoliation." While the burden of proof falls on West to prove the antiquity of the Sphinx, the exfoliation reaction sounded to many nonspecialists like the last gasp of Ptolemaic theory adding epicycles upon epicycles to compete with the simpler heliocentric universe. West told me that the weathering pattern on the southern, or side, wall of the enclosure surrounding the Sphinx could have been made only by water overflowing from the road, or causeway, running beside it:

> The salt crystallization theory does not and cannot account for the indisputable fact that the southern enclosure wall of the Sphinx is drastically more weathered at its western end than at its eastern. Only long periods of rainfall runoff spilling over the wall at its rear and bouncing off the causeway at this western extremity can account for this. Salt crystallization is not, as you suggest, a plausible theory, it is actually just plain stupid. Other alternative theories posed are equally derisory. . . . Occam's Razor has to be put inside the Great

Pyramid for a night for a good sharpening, I'm afraid. It's much too dull in the hands of archeologists to provide alternatives to our indisputable evidence.[26]

The last part of his response is a reference to the unproven theory that pyramid-shaped structures generate a force that can sharpen razor blades left beneath them. I've tried it, but nothing happened. For those who learned of the Sphinx-dating controversy only from NBC or Graham Hancock, there could be only one conclusion.

By the time this argument came to a boil in mid-1990s, Hancock had arrived fresh from his success with *The Sign and the Seal*. While researching the controversy for *Fingerprints of the Gods*, Hancock met former surveyor and amateur archaeologist Robert Bauval, now the famous author of *The Orion Mystery*, and history changed again.

Hancock and Bauval then teamed up to become coauthors of *Message of the Sphinx*, in which they elaborated Bauval's theory, showing a correlation between the three Giza pyramids and the three belt stars of Orion. To explain a discrepancy between the pyramids' position at the time of construction in 2500 BCE and the position of the stars, the two authors were obliged to rotate the sky backwards through the slow changes in position wrought by the precession of the equinoxes to find a match, which Bauval had already calculated in *The Orion Mystery* to be around 10,500 BCE, the date Hancock was already toying with as the end of the Ice Age and the date West favored for the Sphinx's construction based on the heavy rains at the end of the Ice Age. Hancock and Bauval turned the cosmic clock backward to align the pyramids with Orion circa 10,500 BCE, which they claim was the date of the lost civilization's entry into Egypt. That time falls within the astrological "Age of Leo," when the sun rose in the constellation of Leo on the spring equinox due to effects of Precession. What a wonderful match it made, a veritable dog pile of endless coincidence, that it could not possibly be the result of chance. Lo and behold: we have a giant lion, the Sphinx, dating from that same time! What's more, on the equinox of 10,500 BCE, the Sphinx would have stared eastward at its own celestial image while the pyramids reflected the setting of Orion and the Nile mirrored the Milky Way. Thus the entire heavenly host at dawn of the spring equinox at 10,500 BCE was reproduced in miniature at Giza. It was a very neat and seductive hypothesis indeed, and for a time I was more than convinced.

But, like any new theory, there are many problems to sort out. As I would discover, there is no evidence that the ancient Egyptians had any constellation called Leo. In fact, the only constellations we know they shared with the modern zodiac were Orion and Draco. Other correlations are unproven. Even if it were true, there is no clear evidence that the Sphinx represented Leo or a lion at all. Robert Temple, for instance, thought the Sphinx resembled a dog more than a lion, since the dog-god Anubis guarded most sacred spaces. Also, there is no hard evidence that the Egyptians knew about the Precession of the Equinoxes, let alone had the ability to calculate it to fix pyramid positions.

However, we recall that Giorgio de Santillana and Hertha von Dechend wrote an elaborate and dense study of ancient myth called *Hamlet's Mill*, in which they chronicle the use of numbers derived from the Precessional figures (i.e., 72, 144, 216, 432, etc.) in ancient mythology, like the 72 conspirators who killed Osiris or the 432,000 warriors of Valhalla. They discovered that most ancient myths carried what they considered to be antediluvian star knowledge. Their study, written before *Chariots of the Gods?* brought aliens into the equation, concluded that ancient man had advanced knowledge of the stars from generations of observation, but it stopped short of claiming proof for any advanced civilization to account for the knowledge.

This puts the researcher in a bad position. Even if *Hamlet's Mill* were true, how does it apply to the structures ancient man created? The answer was once again: we don't know. But Hancock tried to find out.

Hancock's research assistant, John Grigsby, brought something interesting to Hancock's attention in the summer of 1997. While running a check on the temple layouts at Angkor Wat, the twelfth-century CE Hindu and Buddhist temple complex in Cambodia, the assistant discovered that the fifteen "principal" temples of the seventy-two at Angkor corresponded roughly to the constellation of Draco as it appeared in 10,500 BCE. A look at the "correlation" at first appears to be amazing because the temples align so perfectly in the drawings produced for Hancock's book *Heaven's Mirror*.[27] But upon further inspection the industrious researcher discovers that the correlation is achieved by ignoring the majority of the temples. There is no specific reason for the selection of the fifteen temples chosen other than their similarity to the layout of Draco. Hancock justifies this by claiming that only the largest and oldest of the temples deserve to be counted, since the others were built later by people unfamiliar with the master plan handed down from antiquity.

But even without the faulty veneer of a twelve-thousand-year-old civilization, the pyramids of Giza did seem at first to line up with Orion and the selected temples of Angkor seemed to bear an uncanny resemblance to Draco in the maps and charts the public saw. There was always that exciting shred of a chance that this might just be true. While there was no proof that Angkor had anything to do with Egypt (dating some 3,600 years apart), somehow it seemed to many readers too much of a stretch that these buildings would line up by coincidence. Of the two, the Orion correlation was the stronger. We saw the desert of quicksand on which it was erected, and we can thus judge the Draco correlation accordingly.

Clearly, there seemed to be problems with the type of proof

Hancock was using. This was not the boring, tedious evidence piled up by methodical researchers over decades or centuries. It was instead the exciting revelation of sudden inspiration. But above all, it was selective evidence. When critics pointed this out,[28] Hancock responded by portraying himself as a lawyer defending the lost civilization as he would a client:

> Of course I'm selective! It isn't my job to show my client in a bad light. Another criticism is that I use innuendo to make my case. Of course I do—innuendo and anything else that works. I don't care about the 'rules of the game' here—because it isn't a game and there are no rules.[29]

The BBC's flagship science program, *Horizon*, sought to demolish Hancock's theory on these very grounds, much the same way another BBC program built up Bauval a half decade earlier. That program, *The Great Pyramid: Gateway to the Stars*, was shown on A&E in America in 1995 and was the first major documentary on alternative history I had ever seen. From the show, I had no idea that the Orion Correlation was controversial or "alternative." That was the power of the media, and so it is easy to imagine how much damage the more critical *Horizon* programs would do to Hancock's theories in 2000. As we saw, the show picked apart the lost-civilization hypothesis point by point, and in it astronomer Ed Krupp presented his opinion that for the Orion Correlation to work, the pyramids would have to be flipped upside down. This is because the pyramids are arranged with the smallest and "uppermost" pyramid located at the southernmost point of Giza. The smallest and "uppermost" star of Orion is in the northern extreme of the belt.

Neither Bauval nor Hancock was allowed to present a rebuttal that the Egyptians saw south, not north, as up and therefore arranged their pyramids to face "up" the way Orion does. So, like any good postmodern individual, Hancock filed a complaint. After months of adjudication, the verdict was in.

The *Daily Telegraph* reported that the BBC reedited the show after the Broadcasting Standards Commission agreed with the authors that *Horizon* was unfair.[30]

If the media could be manipulated into agreeing with Hancock, science was not so easy to change. Yet all through the mid-1990s, Hancock's book sales piled up, he appeared on television and radio dozens of times, and he became the spokesperson for a renewed interest in a fringe science now known as "alternative archaeology." By the time he and Robert Bauval decided to join forces and work together to further what became "their" idea of a lost civilization of the Ice Age, Hancock was already a global superstar.

Much of *Fingerprints of the Gods'* appeal stemmed from its surface plausibility, the grand Indiana Jones–style adventure, and Hancock's undeniable writing talent. Also, it capitalized on a feeling of resentment among laypeople who could no longer understand the complex mechanisms of institutional science, and it dared to bring up genuine anomalies and mysteries that mainstream science dismissed or relegated to the back burner. Ancient-alien theorists tried to do this years before, and Hancock repeated the task, though he dispensed with the need for extraterrestrial intervention.

Borrowing John Anthony West's conclusions about a lost civilization, Hancock located this lost culture in time and space, proposing that at the end of the Ice Age a very human civilization located in Antarctica had been destroyed by the environmental devastation accompanying global climate change around the 10,000 BCE transition from the Pleistocene to the Holocene. He provided what seemed like reasonable suspicions, drawn from *Hamlet's Mill* and ancient-astronaut books, that something was amiss in the human past, and he gave these thoughts a new respectability by dumping the aliens in favor of the lost civilization. Where the former theory was ridiculous, Hancock's ideas had a reasonable chance of being true.

Then, in 1996, Hancock and Bauval made a startling claim: Mars may have had an ancient civilization that gave rise to Earth's prehistoric cultures. It seemed that the pair had renounced the lost civilization and had embraced the ancient-astronaut theory. What on earth had happened?

13

THE LEAGUE OF EXTRAORDINARY GENTLEMEN

As I discussed in the introduction, Graham Hancock's theories made good sense to me at the time I first heard them in 1996. I was young, and in my rush to rebel against authority, I embraced ideas that should have seemed odd even then. But the media had given Graham Hancock an aura of credibility. A&E's *Ancient Mysteries*, hosted by Leonard Nimoy (himself a veteran of the 1970s ancient-astronaut fad with his series *In Search of . . .*), featured Hancock as a guest one evening, and the broadcast made me think. At the time I was deeply interested in the ancient-astronaut theory but was sure that despite its promise of mystery and excitement, extraterrestrials probably did not lurk in humanity's past. As I listened to him talk, Hancock provided an alternative theory that seemed to dispense with all of the problems of the extraterrestrial hypothesis.

Hancock had tapped into the resurgent New Age movement, which was returning to prominence after it had largely disappeared from the public consciousness with the end of the 1970s. But millennial angst, the end of the cold war, and a booming economy had provided a potent medium for the return of strange beliefs that had declined in popularity during the conservative 1980s. Instead, the 1980s saw a different form of belief on the ascendant. In that decade, a religious revival movement in rural America had led to a new rise in evangelical Christianity, often called the "Religious Right." Led by leaders like Rev. Jerry Falwell and the Rev. Pat Robertson (who ran for President of the United States in 1988), evangelical Christianity had become a powerful reactionary force in American politics, seeking to overturn two centuries of increasing separation of church and state and reinstitute Christian virtues and biblical authority into American public life.[1]

Largely a process of cultural revitalization among rural white men, evangelical Christianity espoused its own flavor of pseudoscience in the form of creationism, the belief that mankind did not evolve but was created by God. Though the story of the creationist movement is much beyond our current study, we must note that evangelical Christians tried to have creationism included in science curricula in schools across the country under the name "creation science," and their opposition to evolution became an article of faith, regardless of evidence.[2] This trend continued with increasing fervor into the twenty-first century, when creationism returned in the guise of "intelligent design," the theory that evolution was somehow guided by an unnamed higher power.

Many creationist authors wrote books arguing that Charles Darwin was wrong, that science as we know it was a lie, and that God was the living truth. Books with titles like *Darwin on Trial* and *Forbidden Archaeology* argued that the current scientific understanding of the human past was flawed, and a special creation was the first cause of human life. God, of course, was responsible for this creation. The Christian (or, in the case of *Forbidden Archaeology*, Hindu) authors gave each other their uncritical and unwavering support. Though their ideas were often contradictory or mutually exclusive, creationist authors considered their goal (destroying evolutionary theory) more important than evaluating the truth of their own or each other's claims. Thus the creationists had formed a mutual-

defense league of sorts, hoping to overturn the scientific consensus in favor of biblical literalism and a return to "traditional" values and power structures.

For the large number of Americans who could not take
comfort in biblical literalism or evangelical Christianity, some
found comfort in less dogmatic forms of religion; some found
solace in the promise of science, but a large number sought
their truth in a revival of the New Age beliefs of the 1970s.[3]

Sir Isaac Newton had proposed that every action had an
equal and opposite reaction, and it seemed that the cultural
sphere tried time and again to prove the validity of his thermo-
dynamic axiom. If the creationists had challenged science in
order to forward a conservative agenda and had formed a
united front for their mutual defense, authors of the "alternative archaeology" movement would form a mirror image of the
creationist forces. They would also challenge science, but their
fight would push a more liberal agenda, though they, too,
would form an armed camp for their mutual protection.

The first to join up were Graham Hancock and Robert
Bauval. Hancock described and popularized Bauval's Orion Correlation Theory in *Fingerprints of the Gods,* and he used it to lend
credence to his idea that a supercivilization handed out the blue-
prints for civilization at the end of the Ice Age in 10,500 BCE.
The two became fast friends and shared animated discussions
about the origins of Egyptian civilization. Eventually they
decided to write a book together combining Bauval's Orion Correlation with Hancock's lost civilization to make a new synthetic
theory that would explain the Orion Correlation and make a
startling new prediction. That book was *Keeper of Genesis,* published in the United States as *The Message of the Sphinx* (1996).

In that book, the pair of alternative-archaeology authors
formed a united front to blast Egyptology as a close-minded,
conservative profession more interested in keeping the tidal
wave of grants and research funding flowing than in exploring

the truth, which for them is a lost civilization. In particular, Hancock and Bauval heap scorn upon Zahi Hawass, then director-general of the Giza pyramids, and Mark Lehner, one of America's most prominent Egyptologists. In their eyes, Hawass was blocking attempts to properly determine the "true" age of the Great Sphinx and attempts to explore the door Rudolph Gatenbrink found in the shaft of the Great Pyramid.[4]

For Lehner they reserved a particularly harsh judgment. Lehner began his career as a fan and follower of America's "sleeping psychic" Edgar Cayce, who was famous for the prophecies he uttered while in a trance. Cayce believed he had lived past lives in the fabulous Atlantis of Ignatius Donnelly's imagination, and he told his followers that Atlantis would rise again beginning in 1968. That year, the Bimini Road, believed to be an ancient causeway but actually a geologic formation, was uncovered, seemingly confirming the Cayce prophecy. Cayce may not have been entirely wrong, for in that same year *Chariots of the Gods?* was published in its first edition, and it did resurrect Atlantis, at least in the popular mind. Cayce also predicted the existence of a "Hall of Records" underneath the Sphinx in Egypt where the records of the lost civilization of Atlantis were supposed to be housed.

By the time Mark Lehner had entered the University of North Dakota, he was a member of Cayce's Association for Research and Enlightenment (ARE), an organization that tried to "prove" the truth of Cayce's predictions. Lehner went on to study archaeology at American University in Cairo beginning in 1973, and he gradually came to discover that what he had heard from Cayce and from the books of ancient mysteries did not match what he learned in school. Carefully weighing the evidence of archaeology against the speculations of Cayce, he concluded that archaeology had it right. Thereafter he became a scientist.[5]

For Hancock and Bauval, this was tantamount to heresy, and they complained that Lehner had "veered further and further away" from the Cayce teachings to embrace a hard-core orthodoxy.[6] They implied a level of intrigue at Giza surrounding the "Hall of Records" under the Great Sphinx. They noted that much of the funding for Lehner's research came from Cayce's ARE, and they imply through innuendo that Lehner is acting as a double agent, publicly proclaiming a strict scientific orthodoxy while secretly searching for the Hall of Records. Lehner denied the charges in a letter to Hancock, and he tried to explain why there were no fingerprints of the gods:

> In archaeology, many dilettantes and New Agers want to be on the trail of a lost civilization, aliens, yes, "the gods," without having to pay attention to the real people behind time's curtain and without having to deal with the difficult subject matter upon which so-called "orthodox" scholars base their views.[7]

He noted the futility of John Anthony West arguing that Egyptologists did not know the true meaning of the sacred science in Egyptian writings when West himself could not read Egyptian hieroglyphics, comparing it to discussing the true meaning of Shakespeare without knowledge of English. Yet this was precisely the appeal of the genre. Increased specialization in professions had rendered much of human knowledge incomprehensible to those outside a given field, and few could understand the complexity of science or any rigorous program of study. As a result, popularizers could find a massive audience by providing a simple, easy narrative that did not require a doctorate to understand or years of expertise to ponder. Indeed, as the education system gradually broke down in the twentieth century, ever-larger numbers of people were leaving school ignorant of methodology and indoctrinated only in diversity and political correctness. They lacked the tools to understand or to think, and they resented the educated elite who told them what was right or true. It would take many years before the literati began to understand.

But Hancock and Bauval had by then joined with John Anthony West to explore the situation and conduct their own investigation of the Sphinx. Building on Professor Schoch's work redating the Sphinx, the team of alternative historians concluded that the Sphinx dated from 10,500 BCE and was a monument designed to reflect the constellation of Leo in that year, just as the pyramids reflected the stars of Orion's belt in that same year. Because the Sphinx was a lion, this seemed an obvious conclusion, especially since 10,500 BCE marked the start of the astrological "Age of Leo," when the sun rose in that sign of the zodiac at the spring equinox.[8]

Further, if they projected the Sphinx over an image of the constellation Leo on that spring day, they found an amazing discovery. Leo lay on the horizon a few hours before dawn, March 21, 10,500 BCE. If one were to project the sun's position below the horizon at that moment, it would appear to be about twelve degrees below the rear paws of Leo. Translating that to Sphinx and the ground at Giza, this implied that there was a hidden chamber beneath the rear paws of the Sphinx—the Hall of Records: "It is a map, not buried in the earth but cunningly concealed in time, where 'X' almost literally marks a spot directly under the rear paws of the Great Sphinx of Egypt, at a depth, we would guess, of about 100 feet."[9] They accompany this revelation with a fanciful diagram depicting the scale and location of this "chamber," a chamber that would several years later be uncovered and shown by Zahi Hawass on a Fox-TV live special. It did not, however, contain the records of Atlantis, but a cult chamber of a later period serving as a symbolic tomb for the god Osiris. This was the message of the Sphinx . . .

At the time that all of this was going on, a revolution of sorts was taking place on the Internet. The World Wide Web had made finding information and connecting with like-minded individuals fast and convenient. Authors in the "alternative history" genre were among the earliest adopters of this technology, putting up sites to bring their unique views of the world (and their products, of course) to the eyes of a global audience. Soon, alternative history was one of the Web's hottest topics (though always behind pornography and celebrity searches). Graham Hancock, Robert Bauval, John Anthony West, Robert Temple, Erich von Däniken, and countless others set up their Internet headquarters years before the mainstream point of view found voice on the Web. They linked to each other's pages and reinforced each other's views. For an entire generation of young people surfing the emerging Internet, the ancient-astronaut or alternative-history point of view was likely the only one they got. By the mid-1990s, more than a third of incoming college students believed aliens had visited Earth in the remote past.[10]

But the Internet did manage to bring together hundreds of individuals who supported "alternative" positions, and it provided an echo chamber that helped both confirm and amplify these beliefs in the minds of believers. Over the years, Graham Hancock's Web site became the leading destination for alternative history, and its message board registered hundreds of posts in a never-ending discussion of ancient mysteries. As with so much in the Internet age, these discussions rarely elucidated or expanded the discourse but instead became shouting matches and playgrounds of taunts and insults. At one point in 2001, Hancock threatened to shut down his message board due to the vicious personal attacks and bitter invective on his site.

Skeptics, too, came together on the Internet, and they set up rival Web sites that challenged the "alternative" historians. The Center for the Scientific Investigation of Claims of the Paranormal,[11] publisher of *Skeptical Inquirer*, set up shop on the Web, as did the famous magician and debunker of the paranormal James "the Amazing" Randi. A group of skeptical posters left the discussion on the Graham Hancock site to found In the Hall of Ma'at: Weighing the Evidence for Alternative History. That site presented a skeptical view of alternative theories and challenged Hancock, Bauval, and others. In 2001, I launched my own site, Lost Civilizations Uncovered, to present my own ideas about ancient history, the result of which you are reading now.

Of course, the sites presenting sexy, alternative viewpoints received many more visitors than skeptical sites, so in all, the Internet, like the book industry and television, in the end forwarded the cause of alternative history at the expense of mainstream or skeptical views. Its echo-chamber effect let people search and read only those views with which they already agreed, and this seemed only to confirm their opinions.

And with public opinion turning in favor of alternative theories of human origins, television was not far behind. With the expansion of cable from a cultural backwater to a major force in the television industry, by the late 1990s there were a large number of cable channels devoted to science and history. By the new millennium, the Discovery Channel and its siblings, the Travel Channel and TLC, broadcast science documentaries[12]; A&E and its sister station, the History Channel, broadcast historical programming; and a host of niche channels aped their larger rivals. Faced with twenty-four-hour days to fill, the gaping maw of television sought cheap, sensational programming, both to fill time and to get attention. What better way to do that than "alternative history"?

Given the success of NBC's *Mystery of the Sphinx* documentary in 1993, the cable channels commissioned a series of documentaries exploring "mysterious" topics; their favorite subjects were UFOs and Atlantis. At one point, the History Channel showed UFO documentaries almost as often as the World War II programs that had given it its dubious nickname, "The Hitler Channel." Nevertheless, these programs aired on networks that seemed dedicated to science or history, giving an air of credibility to sensational claims. The major networks, too, got involved once they saw how these programs played on cable. Fox broadcast an "alien autopsy," and ABC revisited *Chariots of the Gods?* One could be forgiven for assuming from the high representation of aliens on these programs that extraterrestrials were a major subject of research in the scientific world. For the general public, unschooled in science and by the year 2000 receiving most of their news and information from television, it was hard not to conclude that extraterrestrials or Atlanteans had bequeathed civilization to our ancestors. But nonfiction wasn't the only place these theories held sway. Television shows like Showtime's revived *The Outer Limits* and Sci-Fi's *Stargate-SG1* (based on the movie *Stargate*) and *Stargate Atlantis* presented in fictional form a world where aliens hid in the ancient past and were responsible for humanity's greatest achievements. Surveys found that college students got nearly all their information about archaeology from these broadcasts, and consequently more than one-fourth believed in Atlantis, and almost half believed Europeans (excluding the Vikings) or Africans had arrived in the Americas before Columbus.[13]

Thanks to this media saturation in books, Internet, and television, independent researchers and amateur historians began to imitate the major authors' theses in a slew of books on the subject, though few sold as well as Hancock's or Bauval's. By 1998, Graham Hancock, Robert Bauval, Robert Temple, and a pair of lesser-known authors joined together to stop the publication of Nigel Appleby's *The Hall of the Gods*, which the authors claimed plagiarized important parts of their works, specifically their ideas about the ancient Egyptian "Hall of Records" and its alleged construction by a lost civilization at the end of the Ice Age.[14] I wondered how the supposedly true history of Egypt could be plagiarized, for if the theories of these authors were true, then should they not be public domain? After all, in most jurisdictions, copyright protects only the expression of certain ideas, not the ideas themselves; they are free. Appleby's book was withdrawn, and he did not receive his £750,000 advance.

Others bypassed traditional publishing and went straight to the public. Mark and Richard Wells posted to the Internet in 1998 their theory that little-known pyramids in China reflected the constellation of Gemini based solely upon "Graham Hancock's ideas in *Heaven's Mirror* and *Keeper of Genesis.*"[15] They chose the date they would match to the pyramids by borrowing from Hancock, too—that magical year 10,500 BCE. Unfortunately, there is only the slightest similarity between the Chinese pyramids and Gemini, as far as I could tell. The findings seemed to be another case of wishful thinking and hopeful emulation.

Much of this explosion in ancient aliens occurred because in 1996, a sensational discovery from Mars would catapult the idea of ancient aliens back into the spotlight, and Graham Hancock and Robert Bauval were there.

In August 1996, NASA announced at a breathless press conference that analysis of a Martian meteorite recovered from Antarctica in 1984 had bacteria-like microfossils. In other words, there was once life on Mars. Though skeptics contended that contamination from earth bacteria or other natural processes could have produced the alleged fossils, which were many times smaller than the smallest known earth bacteria, others held that the meteorite (and a second tested in October) proved that the Red Planet had once had life. The debate continues today, but in 1996 an official organ of the United States government had confirmed for the first time the existence of extraterrestrial life.

Graham Hancock and Robert Bauval seized upon this to produce a series of articles for the London *Daily Mail* in which they announced their belief that Mars once housed an

advanced civilization that could have influenced or bequeathed Earth's first cultures: "Could there be some sort of
bizarre interplanetary connection, not yet understood,
between the story of civilization on Earth and on Mars?"[16] The
pair specifically built upon the work of science writer Richard
Hoagland, who in his 1987 book *The Monuments of Mars* proclaimed that the *Viking* expedition to Mars in the fateful
summer of 1976 captured a picture of a monument on Mars,
the so-called face. Dismissed by NASA as a "trick of light and
shadow," believers contend that the face represents an actual
monument, a carved figure of a crowned humanoid face,
bearing a passing resemblance to the face of the Great Sphinx
at Giza. Hoagland came to believe that one side of the face was
human and the other side feline, making the monument half
man and half lion, like the Sphinx.[17]

The original photograph of the "face" was a low-resolution
image taken accidentally by the *Viking* and discovered only by
accident when a NASA worker saw an eroded hill resembling a
face while poring over photos sent back to Earth. A second image
of the face emerged from the *Viking* files in 1980. A lynchpin of
both the UFO and ancient-alien theories, the face has generated
endless speculation with little proof. By the time NASA repho-
tographed the "face" in 1998 and demonstrated that it was
nothing more than an eroded hill that the human instinct to see
faces misconstrued, researchers into alien archaeology like
Richard Hoagland saw a full range of "cities" and "pyramids" on
Mars, and no amount of new photographs would stop them
from crying conspiracy and claiming that the new pictures were
doctored to hide the truth about aliens on Mars.

The *Daily Mail* articles concluded by arguing that Egyptian
authorities and American government officials were working
together to secretly excavate beneath the Sphinx for links to
Martian archaeology. Of course, neither author specifically said
any of these things. Instead they asked rhetorical questions and

presented the research of others. Yet the impression was clear: Egyptian civilization came from Mars.

Here now was the ancient-astronaut theory from authors who had specifically rejected it when launching their alternative history careers. Hancock and Bauval then turned their series of articles into a book written with research assistant John Grigsby and released in 1998. Called *The Mars Mystery: The Secret Connection between Earth and the Red Planet*, the book expanded on the same themes as the 1996 articles, appending a final section dealing with the risk of meteorite or asteroid impacts on the earth and speculating that such disasters may have been responsible for developments in the ancient world.[18] The book was logically flawed and intellectually sloppy, repeating itself again and again and making few strong points.

The Mars Mystery, however, began to backtrack slightly from the uncritical endorsement of Richard Hoagland's Martian archaeology given in 1996. The book is tepid; it describes the mysteries of Mars: the face, the pyramids, and the possibility of microbial life. But it does not draw conclusions with the same vim or vigor as either Hancock or Bauval did in the *Daily Mail* or even *Fingerprints of the Gods* or *The Orion Mystery*:

> Moreover, we ourselves are far from certain—and have remained dubious throughout—about the true provenance of the Martian monuments. They could just be weird geology. They really could. Or they could have been intelligently designed.[19]

Instead, the authors talk about the decline of Western civilization and accidentally reveal the true reasons for their work. Alternative archaeology was nothing more and nothing less than a way to reconnect to the primal magic of better days. The promise of scientific progress had faded in the twentieth century, and the egalitarian ideals of Western democracy clashed with the elitist, specialist nature of industrial science. Therefore, Hancock and Bauval say, humanity is equipped with "rapidly evolving technology but a stunted spirituality."[20]

> What has happened to the human soul when adults—men and women—are so in love with evil that they gain sexual pleasure from the kidnap, torture, rape, and murder of children? Such horrors had become routine in Europe and the United States at the end of the second millennium. . . . We simply wish to suggest that a species that is so drawn toward the darkness is unlikely to be able to meet the challenge of the galaxy.[21]

This then is the ultimate revelation of the secret of alternative archaeology. Like creationism, it is a cultural revitalization movement of sorts. It is a replacement belief system, a faith in the greatness and goodness of the mysterious ancestors, be they human or alien, for a salvation through a return to the past, to childhood, to innocence. As such it is immune to facts, reason, or science because it is not science. It is instead antiscience, for science represents change and relativity with no absolute truths and thus no absolute good or evil. Alternative archaeology of any stripe can provide those absolutes in a fixed, unchanging cosmos, restoring for believers the comfort that biblical creationism provides to the more religiously inclined.

Once it becomes obvious that the alternative history movement and the ancient-astronaut theory are really nothing more than an appeal to the golden age, a way to find comfort and order in a world slowly going mad and a culture slowly on the decline, it becomes easy to see the appeal of this kind of thinking. It is comforting to believe in something. If you cannot believe in God or angels, then aliens and Atlantis are the next best thing. This is the true Mars mystery . . .

The rest of the story of alternative archaeology is a gradual fade into the background. The cult archaeology movement hit its peak in the mid-1990s, and as the scientific community began to react and argue against the lost-civilization theory or the ancient-astronaut theory, these books gradually lost their prominence. They instead became a large niche market catering to the same audience. Both Hancock and Bauval continued to write books into the twenty-first century, but each successive book made less of an impact. Bauval wrote *The Secret Chamber* in 1999 to link Hermetic traditions to Egyptian knowledge, an unorthodox but hardly radical idea. Hancock abandoned ancient aliens and returned to the lost civilization in 1998's *Heaven's Mirror*, focusing on the spirituality of the ancients. The accompanying television series, *Quest for the Lost Civilization*, was enormously entertaining, but watched by relatively few people in the United States. Unlike the heady days of 1995 and 1996, when stores could not keep *Fingerprints* on their shelves (I had to wait six weeks for my copy), his later books did not move as fast, though they eventually sold millions of copies.

By 2002, Hancock had effectively abandoned many of his earlier positions with the publication of his longest book on the search for the lost civilization, *Underworld*. In this book, he claimed that the remains of the lost civilization would be found underwater, on the continental shelf, which sank beneath the waves at the end of the last Ice Age. He also now believed that this lost civilization was a spiritually rather than technologically sophisticated culture.[22] Through dives around the world, Hancock tried to find traces of temples and stone structures on the continental shelf, though he turned up little direct evidence. In my review of *Underworld* for Lost Civilizations Uncovered, my Web site, I noted the problems that the book posed for fans of *Fingerprints of the Gods*:

I find myself compelled to say a few words about Hancock's thesis because it directly impacts the book as a whole. In fact, this new version of the lost civilization theory is the single largest problem with an otherwise compelling and readable *Underworld*. Graham Hancock has done the unthinkable: he has effectively abandoned much of his charmingly quirky earlier theory that Paleolithic Ice Age humans were technologically advanced super-men.

Even if we accept every shred of Hancock's evidence without question, he has done nothing more than propose that over the course of the 5,000 years people spent living through the Ice Age meltdown people managed to raise some stone monuments, develop a spiritual system of great complexity, and (most controversially) somehow manage to map the world. While many conservative archaeologists will disagree with at least the last of these things, it is not hard to conceive it possible. Since ancient humans arrived in Australia by boat before 50,000 B.C., it is not that hard to imagine that Ice Age peoples did explore their coastlines, trade maps and information with neighboring groups and produce after thousands of years a decent and close to accurate map of most of the world. If Europeans could do it in two centuries, then Ice Agers could have done it in five millennia.

Hancock's other position, that ancient peoples lived along the coasts that the end of the Ice Age sent underwater is neither new nor original. Hancock claims, however that it is being ignored: "Marine archaeologists have barely begun a systematic survey for possible submerged sites on those flooded lands. Most would regard it as a waste of time even to look." Yet Hancock fails to recognize two important facts. First, that many (if not a majority) of archaeologists would very much like to explore the old coastlines where early humans once lived. Second, the funding is not there because the archaeologists cannot guarantee to financers that they will find anything down there. It is the funding system Hancock should attack, not the archaeologists' integrity.

So what is the bottom line on *Underworld*? It is an ambitious and largely solid book that makes a compelling case that the areas once occupied by Paleolithic man may hold secrets that we do not yet understand. It is also a book that, while always taking the most extreme view the scientific facts make possible, does not often go beyond published literature. What we have is a work of alternative history that tries so hard to be credible and factual that it comes across at times like the very archaeological literature it aims to replace.[23]

In other words, Graham Hancock had gone almost mainstream. By 2002, Hancock had had enough of the battle to save his lost civilization. He conceded that much of *Fingerprints* was unfounded speculation—("Had I known the scrutiny . . . I may have written a different book"[24])—and he decided to give up writing about the lost civilization. He said his quest in search of the fingerprints of the gods had helped erode his atheism, and he now believes in life after death. He said he wanted to look into human origins and intelligent design.[25] Of course, he would not stay retired long . . .

In August 2003 I asked Graham Hancock about his quest and about how he came to his ideas. He was kind enough to answer my questions, but he insisted that his answers be presented in full. Therefore, here is the full question-and-answer session conducted via e-mail. I have slightly edited my questions to remove superfluous background material:

JC: *In your book,* The Sign and the Seal, *you describe the process by which you came to believe the impossible about the ancient past. Though you rejected the extraterrestrial visitation hypothesis, to what degree were you inspired by "ancient astronaut" books like Erich von Däniken's* Chariots of the Gods? *or Robert Temple's* The Sirius Mystery?

Hancock: I don't think I was "inspired" by Robert Temple's *Sirius Mystery* during the years before *The Sign and the Seal*. I did eventually read the book, but much later. One of the readers of the *Sign and the Seal* kindly sent me a copy of the English translation of *The Pale Fox* in 1992 or 1993 and I think I may have read that before I read Temple. Of course I was well aware of Temple's general thesis from the background literature.

As to Däniken's *Chariots of the Gods?* I had read it and browsed similar books long before I wrote the *Sign and the Seal*. I found the general subject area exciting—the notion that there were major unanswered questions, and enduring mysteries, about the past. I never understood why some people felt that those mysteries and unanswered questions about the past absolutely had to involve aliens/ETs. Nevertheless it was nice to know (contrary to what I had been taught in school) that mysteries and unanswered questions were out there. In the years since then I have not come across a single mystery or unanswered question about the past that can only be explained by recourse to aliens/ETs. Everything I've seen (I think) can be explained in terms of human civilisation, which makes the aliens/ETs explanation unnecessary. If I ever come across an anomaly that can only be explained by aliens/ETs I will be willing to change my view but until then I think a lost civilisation (or lost civilisations) to be the much more likely "alternative" hypothesis.

This is not to say that I have anything against aliens/ETs! On the contrary, I'm sure the universe is full of life of which we on this planet are but one tiny spec. But I still don't think we need aliens/ETs to explain the mysteries of our past.

JC: *Having researched the lost civilization topic, you are undoubtedly familiar with the 1960 work* Morning of the Magicians *by Louis Pauwles and Jacques Bergier . . .*

Hancock: Amazing as it may seem to you, I have never read *Dawn of the Magicians* [sic] by Louis Pauwles and Jacques Bergier.

JC: *Were you aware that Pauwles and Bergier came to their conclusions based on the horror fiction of American author H. P. Lovecraft . . . ?*

Hancock: To repeat, I have never read the Pauwles and Bergier book. Unsurprisingly therefore, I am not aware that it was based on the horror fiction etc., etc. work of H. P. Lovecraft. And no, I haven't read Lovecraft.

JC: *If the fictional work of Lovecraft is the major inspiration for the alternative archaeology movement, as channeled through* Chariots of the Gods? *how does this impact the credibility of alternative archaeology?*

Hancock: The fictional work of Lovecraft has not been an inspiration of any kind for me, whether channeled through *Chariots of the Gods?* or not. I can't speak for the "alternative archaeology movement" since I am not aware of the existence of any such entity. But if for the sake of argument I accept your hypothesis that Lovecraft has been a source of inspiriation for whoever you define as members of the alternative archaeology movement, you still don't seem to me to be making much of a point. Surely the credibility of the "alternative archaeology movement" should be assessed on the basis of its ideas/hypotheses and work today rather than on the sources of its inspiration?[26]

Undoubtedly, Hancock is, of course, right. Alternative archaeology should be judged on its merits and not on its inspiration. However, as we have seen, there is ample evidence that the merits of alternative archaeology are not compelling.

Alternative history, in the final analysis, was not so much about facts as about an attitude and philosophy. It was an attempt to bring to elite science the democratic and egalitarian values that animated the politics of liberal democracies for two centuries. It was an attempt to bring science back to the masses and return to the public the lead role in defining our shared sense of culture and the past. To that extent, it was no different than the concurrent political upheavals of the 1990s or the economic boom of those same years. All of these tried to democratize their respective fields and loosen the grip of entrenched power and react against the calcifying forces inherent in institutionalized authority. If political changes in the 1990s freed record numbers from authoritarian regimes, and if the long bull market brought wealth and investment power to the masses, then alternative archaeology was one facet of the social manifestation of these forces. In its pages, alternative historians had the lost civilization bring peace and prosperity, just like the political and economic forces of the world in which they wrote.

As an attempt to create a coherent worldview, alternative archaeology had to make itself relevant to what was going on in the here and now. After the September 11, 2001, terrorist attacks, alternative history began to see the ancients in a darker, less beneficent way, in tune with the dark times of the War on Terror. To that end Hancock teamed up with Robert Bauval to write *Talisman: Sacred Cities, Secret Faith*. In their minds, the influence of the lost civilization extended, like the secret Cthulhu cult of Lovecraft, straight through from 10,500 BCE to modern times and may have played a role in the occult design of world capitals and the September 11, 2001, terrorist attacks on New York and Washington.[27] Now even current events were part and parcel of the same worldview first proposed to give coherence to ideas of the past: "In the light of the confusion of current events—the 'War on Terrorism,' the 'Liberation of Iraq,' the 'Israel/Palestine Road Map,' and the paranoia that has gripped the Western world since 911 [*sic*]—TALISMAN puts forward a completely new view of 'history' that is as unconventional as it is disturbing."[28] Why be confused by facts when you can have a new ideology to make sense of it all?

In line with this conspiratorial view of world history, Bauval also believed that the scientific establishment, especially CSICOP, was using its power to stop the truth of his and Hancock's theories from being made known: "Eventually an uncoordinated campaign and pulling-ranks began to be seen [as] aimed against us, with CSICOP agents and science editors of journals and newspapers unleashing, on the one hand, systematic attacks and, on the other hand, forming a wall of fire to stop our work [from] entering the academic and scientific arena."[29]

Since the academic mainstream rejected alternative theories as groundless, the authors decided it was the academics who were part of the conspiracy, one that stretched from the lost civilization through Egypt and the secretive society of Freemasons (a favorite target of the conspiracy fans) down to the confusing, astounding events of the War on Terror. In order to make sense of events that seemed out of control, the authors found a secret cult dedicated to control; it was all one big conspiracy. In troubled times, people seek out answers in established authority: the Bible, the elders, ancient wisdom, etc. It is an unchanging force in our society. In 2005 Hancock turned to the Shamanistic origins of religion with another new book, *Supernatural*.

Now we must return to 1976 and trace a different path from the one followed by alternative archaeology. If the Romantic visions of a lost civilization were heartfelt nostalgia for the good old days of the past, then the extraterrestrial-genesis theorists represented a frightening vision of a terrifying future. Their prophet was Zecharia Sitchin, and their Bible, *Twelfth Planet*.

PART FIVE

HUMAN CLONES FROM THE TWELFTH PLANET

14

ANCESTORS FROM NIBIRU

Zecharia Sitchin's unique contribution to alternative archaeology and the ancient-astronaut theory began with the publication of his book *The Twelfth Planet* in 1976. Though he made many outrageous claims, notably that human beings were genetically engineered by aliens in the remote past, it is most instructive to begin our survey of Sitchin with a look at one of his more scholarly claims, that the Great Pyramid was not built by Khufu and that evidence attributing the monument to him was forged. Graham Hancock and dozens of other "alternative" writers eagerly accepted this and incorporated it into their works to help "prove" that the pyramids were really the work of aliens, Atlanteans, or other demigods. Though his theories earned him a cultlike following and the status of prophet to thousands of so-called Sitchinites worldwide, to see the extent of Zecharia Sitchin's influence across the spectrum of both alternative archaeology and extraterrestrial-genesis theorizers, we should start at the end and work backward.

Up until now, I have used the terms "ancient-astronaut theory," "alternative archaeology," and "alternative history" fairly interchangeably, since what we have discussed until now has largely been the outgrowth of Robert Temple's archaeological and anthropological musings. Now, with our focus shifting to Zecharia Sitchin's more philosophical and less archaeological claims, our terminology must also shift. For Sitchin and his followers, I prefer the term "extraterrestrial genesis" to describe their work, for they claim that humanity was created by aliens who were the first gods. This is hardly distinct from the ancient-astronaut theory, but I have chosen to emphasize the archaeological claims of the ancient-astronaut theory over the philosophical and/or technological claims of the extraterrestrial genesis, and I believe there is at least a degree of distinction between them (see Appendix). But, on with our story.

For millennia, the Great Pyramid has stood in mute testimony to the architectural genius of its builders. Within its walls no hieroglyph proclaims the name of the architect and no cartouche celebrates the life of the pharaoh for whom it was built. When the caliph Mamum forced his way in more than a thousand years ago—the first person to enter since antiquity—he found no record of who had built the massive structure. Not in the Subterranean Chamber, nor the so-called Queen's Chamber or even in the much-vaunted King's Chamber. Not until 1837 did any marking or identifier turn up within the pyramid's walls, and only then deep inside the secret relieving chambers above the King's Chamber that keep the pyramid's bulk from crushing the room's flat roof. The first relieving chamber came to light in the eighteenth century, and Col. Howard Vyse uncovered the remaining four chambers in 1837, after tunneling upward and using gunpowder to blast apart parts of the pyramid. Vyse found in those hidden chambers painted hieroglyphics that indicated that the pyramid was built for Pharaoh Khufu.

Computer programmer and part-time amateur pyramidologist Tim Hunker gave his version of what happened next on his Web site:

'Quarry Marks' exist in the relieving chambers above the King's Chamber, including one mark which is reported to indicate Khufu, the pharaoh under whose reign the Great Pyramid was built. One source suggests that these quarry marks were faked by Howard Vyse in 1837. . . . There are problems with the hieroglyphics in that they are a mixture of styles and syntax/usage from differing time periods of Egypt. And finally, in the marks bearing Khufu's name, mistakes were made. Those same mistakes occur in the only two hieroglyphics references that would have been available to Vyse at that time.[1]

In other words, Vyse faked the inscriptions. Of course, even if the inscriptions were fake, that alone does not disprove Khufu's ownership. If the "Made in China" sticker fell off a pair of sneakers, that does not mean that they suddenly sprang from Mexico instead. Nevertheless the inconsistencies seemed to prove to many that the pyramid was actually the work of a lost civilization or aliens instead of Khufu's minions.

Hunker goes on to espouse a firm belief in pyramidology, the belief that the Great Pyramid holds profound meaning in its measurements. But where did he get this strange idea that the quarry marks are fakes? He says only in the text that "one source suggests" this is the case. Turning to the notes at the end of his article, he informs the reader that he gleaned this information from "*The Message of the Sphinx*, 1996, Graham Hancock and Robert Bauval, ISBN 0-517-70503-6."[2]

As we have seen, *Message of the Sphinx* represents the first joint book by *Fingerprints of the Gods* author Graham Hancock and *Orion Mystery* coauthor Robert Bauval. Together they combined their theorizing about a pre–Ice Age advanced civilization into a unified theory of ancient man. Briefly stated, the two men came to believe that an advanced culture disappeared during the Ice Age, and its survivors gained footholds throughout the world, establishing ancient cultures like the Egyptians, the Maya, and the Easter Islanders.

The two authors devoted three pages to questioning the validity of the Vyse find, elaborating on the information summarized above. They then say the Egyptological acceptance of Vyse's quarry marks "verges on intellectual chicanery."[3] They claim that while they raise troubling questions about the Vyse find, they "are frankly puzzled that such questions are never asked."[4] They say, however, that the questions are irrelevant to their larger argument about who owns the pyramids:

> [E]ven if the quarry marks were not forged by Vyse, what do they really prove? Isn't attributing the Great Pyramid to Khufu on the basis of a few lines of graffiti a bit like handing over the keys of the Empire State Building to a man named 'Kilroy' just because his name was found spray-painted on the walls of the lift?[5]

But Hancock and Bauval were not the first to market these theories. Turning to the notes in the back of *Message of the Sphinx*, it becomes patently obvious that the authors drew their criticisms of Howard Vyse from none other than Zecharia Sitchin, the author who was most famous for believing that humanity was spawned by aliens who genetically engineered them.[6] We will return to Hancock's acceptance of the quarry marks in a moment.

As we shall soon see, Zecharia Sitchin is one of the most famous proponents of the extraterrestrial-genesis theory today, second only to the first popularizer of the theory, Erich von Däniken, in importance to true believers. Sitchin claims to be the only person who can "correctly" interpret ancient Sumerian writings. While many have disputed his translations and conclusions, Sitchin maintains that the Sumerian writings show that aliens called Annunaki visited Earth and created humanity to mine gold for them. Sitchin debunker Ian Lawton:

In order to support his revised chronology of mankind, and his contention that these pyramids were built as 'ground markers' for the Anunnaki's incoming space flights, it was Sitchin who first suggested that Colonel Richard Howard Vyse faked the hieroglyphics in the Relieving Chambers in the Great Pyramid, some of which include the name Khufu.[7]

Like von Däniken before him, Sitchin needed the Great Pyramid to represent something greater than a pharaoh's magnificent construction. To "prove" the theory of alien intervention, it must be a construct of the alien visitors, and the hieroglyphics claiming Khufu as creator got in the way. Therefore they had to be effectively dismissed. The hieroglyphics, he said, were misspelled and therefore likely to be fakes. Sitchin argued that Vyse had faked the hieroglyphics from erroneous nineteenth-century books of hieroglyphics, unknowingly copying mistakes in those books.[8] Experts, like Martin Stower on his now-defunct Web page, were able to show that the hieroglyphs' "misspellings" and errors were actually imperfections in nineteenth-century knowledge of hieroglyphs projected onto the correctly spelled hieroglyphs themselves.

Nevertheless, the authority of Zecharia Sitchin gave free license to more than a dozen alternative authors to cite the "forged" quarry marks as proof that Khufu did not build the pyramid. Further, it gave reason to say that the Great Pyramid had not a single inscription, rendering the work ownerless.

For this reason von Däniken could still say in 1996's *Eyes of the Sphinx*: "[T]he Great Pyramid is a huge, *largely anonymous* work. . . . The pyramid itself features no hieroglyphics at all" (emphasis in original).[9] As we have seen from the earlier discussion of the quarry marks, this is patently false. Whether they are genuine or not, the quarry marks do exist, and they are hieroglyphics.

While von Däniken stuck to the forgery line, Graham Hancock changed his mind in the light of "new" evidence known to Egyptology since the nineteenth century. As the years went by, Hancock became more mainstream as he tempered the more radical aspects of his theory in the hopes of finding greater acceptance:

> Cracks in some of the joints reveal hieroglyphs set far back into the masonry. No 'forger' could possibly have reached in there after the blocks had been set in place—blocks, I should add, that weigh tens of tons each and that are immovably interlinked with one another. The only reasonable conclusion is the one which orthodox Egyptologists have already long held—namely that the hieroglyphs are genuine Old Kingdom graffiti and that they were daubed on the blocks before construction began.[10]

Hancock wrote those words in 1998, just months before the launch of his high-profile television series *Quest for the Lost Civilization* and his book *Heaven's Mirror*. Hancock seemed to be seeking credibility as a serious researcher at the time, and he revised his beliefs accordingly:

> Although I was still open to the erroneous forgery theory while *Keeper/Message* was being written, I was also very much open to the orthodox theory that the Giza pyramids were Fourth Dynasty work—irrespective of the provenance of the quarry marks.[11]

And so we have come full circle, from the Egyptological acceptance of Vyse's findings, to alternative history's rejection and then, in some quarters, acceptance of them. Along the way, each author's acceptance of the Sitchin theory compounds the damage done. A Google search in 2004 turned up more than one hundred pages that repeat some iteration of the Sitchin theory.[12]

As Ian Lawton said, "Bearing in mind that it was this original attack by Sitchin which prompted so many other 'alternative Egyptologists' to repeat his accusations without question—although fortunately now most of them have seen the light—this saga perhaps more than any other tells us a very great deal about Sitchin and his work."[13]

Naturally, I wanted to talk to Sitchin and see how he would respond to these criticisms of his work. However, Sitchin declined to be interviewed, citing a lack of time. Therefore, I had to make do with the next best thing, Sitchin's published works and comments.

The Russian-born Zecharia Sitchin does not seem at first glance like one of the leading forces in the ancient-astronaut debate, a latter-day prophet with a cultlike following, or someone who would try to paint Howard Vyse as a forger. He looks like a kindly old man with thinning gray hair and thickening glasses poised above a gently mustached mouth. By 2004 he was the author of nine works on the influence of ancient astronauts on the emerging human race, starting with the 1976 best-seller *The Twelfth Planet* and proceeding through *The Lost Book of Enki*, the "autobiography" of an ancient astronaut. He grew up in Palestine, where he says he learned Hebrew, Semitic, and European languages before attending the University of London, where he graduated with a degree in economic history. He worked as a journalist in Israel for many years before moving to New York City. There he began to discover anomalies in the human past, and, like so many others, became taken with the ancient-astronaut theories circulating in the popular press. Sitchin combined the ancient-astronaut theory with his own interest in Semitic languages, and he reached a startling conclusion. Building on a suggestion in Erich von Däniken's *Gods from Outer Space*, Sitchin believed aliens genetically engineered humanity.

Sitchin says that he first realized aliens colonized Earth when he discovered that the mythology of the Sumerian people spoke of real places and real things. They were not mere allegories or products of a fertile imagination; instead they were the literal chronicle of fantastic happenings. Like the creationists who took literally every line of the Bible, Sitchin believed each word of every ancient text was an accurate portrayal of high-tech history seen through the eyes of primitives. For him the moment of discovery arrived when he came to a stunning conclusion about our familiar solar system: the ancient Sumerians from 6000 BCE knew there were not only the nine familiar planets:

> Once I realized that this was the answer, that there is one more planet, everything else fell into place. The meaning of the Mesopotamian *Epic of Creation* on which the first chapters of *Genesis* are based and all details [about how the aliens] traveled from their planet to Earth and how they splashed down in the Persian Gulf and about their first settlement, their leaders and so on and so on, everything became clear![14]

Sitchin was then able to read through the ancient texts, from the Bible to the Mesopotamian epics, and develop his vision of human history. Sitchin speculates that a race of extraterrestrials visited Earth almost half a million years ago. This planet was known to the ancient Mesopotamians (in succession, the Sumerians, Akkadians, and Babylonians) as the planet "Nibiru." These aliens came to Earth not of their own good will or beneficence but to mine the earth for minerals that were rare on their own planet. Specifically, they needed gold to protect their atmosphere.

The Nibiru aliens genetically engineered humanity from the primitive hominids of the earth by infusing them with their own genes to create a subservient class to do the hard work of mineral mining. After thousands of years and several wars between the "gods," the Nibirunians took off in the ships and returned to their planet, which orbits our sun every 3,600 years. Because the ancient Mesopotamians called the sun and moon planets, Sitchin says they counted eleven planets in our solar system. Nibiru, therefore, was the twelfth planet.[15] And of course, like all good saviors, the aliens, led by Enki and his rival Enlil, promised to return when their planet completes its orbit of the sun. On that glorious day, humanity can rejoice in the return of its saviors.

Sitchin described once what led him to these remarkable conclusions, spelled out in his first six books, known collectively as *The Earth Chronicles*: "My starting point was, going back to my childhood and schooldays, the puzzle of who were the Nefilim, that are mentioned in *Genesis*, Chapter six, as the sons of the gods who married the daughters of Man in the days before the great flood, the Deluge."[16]

Fascinated by the Nefilim,[17] Sitchin delved into his knowledge of Semitic languages to provide a translation for this odd word. Sitchin translated Nefilim as "those who from heaven to earth came." Standard translations have it as "fallen ones," which Christian mythology links to the angels cast out of heaven during Lucifer's rebellion. Sitchin instead takes the meaning literally and holds that going from heaven to earth was the Sumerian way of indicating descent to Earth from outer space.

He also holds that the meaning of Nefilim is identical with that of the Sumerian Annunaki, the fifty anonymous gods whom we met briefly in our discussion of Robert Temple and the fifty-year orbit of Sirius B. For Temple, the Annunaki represented the number of Earth years it took Sirius B to circle Sirius A, but for Sitchin, the Annunaki would have a far less esoteric meaning. For him, his "discovery" that the Nefilim were synonymous with the fifty mysterious gods of fate in Sumerian mythology led him to a startling conclusion. The Annunaki were the aliens from Nibiru: "If Nibiru exists, (and this is the planet that astronomers nowadays call planet X) then the Anunnaki exist."[18] Planet X was the name some astronomers gave to a hypothetical planet that they once thought may have existed in the solar system. There was little evidence for Planet X then and there are few believers today. There was a brief revival of interest in Planet X in 2002, and again in 2004, when a trans-Plutonian "planet" was discovered, but due to its small size, it was reclassified as a large asteroid. Pluto itself was briefly shelved from the list of planets in 2002 because of its small size, though it was returned to the roster upon reconsideration. This new planetoid hardly constituted Sitchin's mysterious Nibiru.

Sitchin wrote an article for his Web site in May 2001 claiming that this mysterious planet has been located by astronomers. He cited an "alternative theory" proposed to explain the oddly eccentric orbit of a large "super" comet named 2000 CR/105. While one theory had it that Neptune exaggerated the comet's orbit, the alternative theory said that a hidden or unknown Mars-sized planet could possibly affected the comet's orbit. Sitchin gleefully noted that *Science* magazine had reported that a "Supercomet following an unexpectedly far-flung path around the sun suggests that an unidentified planet once lurked in the outermost reaches of the solar system, an international team of astronomers reports. What's more, the mysterious object may still be there."[19] Since it "may" still be there, it obviously *was* there, and further it clearly was the home of aliens that mine precious metals with genetically engineered slaves. After all, there wasn't any evidence that this was untrue.

Sitchin believed this closed the case on his ancient Annunaki astronauts. Clearly, they had to be real because the planet was (well, might have been). However, even if this planet does exist, it is a vast leap of logic to assume that it is the home of alien builder-gods. Sitchin may believe that if Nibiru exists the Annunaki must, but there was no evidence that one led to the other.

But, in fact, Sitchin's theory was vastly more ambitious than merely adding one more planet to the solar system's roster. He provided an entire history for this planet, based mostly upon his unique reading of ancient myths and legends:

> According to the ancient texts as interpreted by me, Nibiru was a planet ejected from some other planetary system in outer space that was captured into our Solar System as it passed near Neptune. It became involved in a collision with a pre-existing planet where the debris of the Asteroid Belt are [sic] now. As a result of that collision, some 4 billion years ago, the Earth and the Moon came to be where they are now.[20]

Leaving aside legitimate theories about the existence of a planet where the asteroid belt now is, of course, the main condition to accepting this theory is that Sitchin has a special expertise in interpreting ancient texts. Others are not quite ready to give him so much credit. One researcher looking into Sitchin's claims talked to a bona fide Sumerian linguist, who requested anonymity to avoid the onslaught of hate mail from ancient-astronaut believers. The linguist confirmed that Sitchin's "special" understanding of Sumerian is not that special:

> [Sitchin] demonstrates a consistent lack of appreciation of even some of the most basic fundamentals of Sumerian and Akkadian grammar, even to the extent of regularly failing to distinguish between the two entirely different languages, and mixing words from each in interpreting the syllables of longer compound words.[21]

This mixing of languages allows Sitchin to make amazing "discoveries." Robert Carroll of the famed *Skeptics Dictionary* was not impressed with Sitchin's scholarship, sarcastically noting, "Sitchin stands alone, on nobody's shoulders, as a scholar nonpareil. . . . He alone knows how to correctly translate ancient terms allowing him to discover such things as that the ancients made rockets."[22] Carroll further noted Sitchin's dubious translations are used to deceive: "Sitchin weaves a compelling and entertaining story out of facts, misrepresentations, fictions, speculations, misquotes and mistranslations."[23]

Yet Sitchin's presentation of his interpretations left many believing that this kindly old man had hit upon the most one of the most momentous discoveries in human history. In an era when trust in science was on the decline, when faith in government and authority had faltered, it was all too easy to believe that a maverick individual could trump the calcified establishment of science and find what so many others had missed. Hundreds of followers attended his lectures, and a traveling group of "Sitchinites" attended several lectures at venues around the United States. They held him as their prophet, hung on his every word, and some even composed poetry to celebrate Sitchin's achievements.[24]

Further, Sitchin allowed readers the chance to participate in these discoveries in a way that institutionalized science did not. One could not readily walk into a laboratory and watch a DNA extraction, nor could most people have their thoughts and ideas entered into a prestigious scientific journal. Sitchin appealed to America's anti-intellectualism, and he offered a shortcut to knowledge. No longer did you need years of education and decades of research to make major discoveries; you simply needed to read Sitchin's books, for he had all the answers.

In fact, Sitchin fans had their own alternative educational system. As we shall see, he called the program "Sitchin Studies," and the author handed out certificates at the end of a few hours' lecture fully accrediting paid customers in extraterrestrial genesis. Combined with a thorough reading of all Sitchin's books, the "scholar" was now equipped with all available knowledge about the gods who created humanity. This said much more about the rigor of Sitchin's theories than it did about mainstream scholarship.

Robert Hafernik is one of Sitchin's most vocal critics, and his work debunking Sitchin is one of the few detailed critiques of Sitchin available. An aerospace engineer, Hafernik worked for NASA and knows all about orbital dynamics and the workings of the universe and rockets. His excellent scholarship serves as a useful guide through the (frankly, unreadable) works of Zecharia Sitchin. Hafernik said he found a problem right from the beginning of *Twelfth Planet*:

> Instead of quoting standard translations for Biblical verses, Sitchin makes up his own translations, based on his interpretation of 'the parallel Sumerian and Akkadian texts/tales.' Unfortunately, he is using those verses to support his interpretation of those texts.[25]

In other words, his own translation is used to prove his "discoveries" about the texts themselves. Like so many alternative theories we have studied, Sitchin's "translations" were simply another case of circular logic. He could make them say whatever he wanted. Hafernik says bluntly, "Right away, we're in deep academic doo-doo. [Sitchin]'s let us know he's going to twist the translations around to support his thesis."[26] In other words, Sitchin uses his own translation to prove his presupposed conclusion. He made the evidence fit the theory, something he and other alternative authors are quick to criticize in mainstream science, especially evolutionary biology.

These cases of circular reasoning highlight the difference between science and pseudoscience. In true science, the investigator notes a phenomenon and comes up with a hypothesis, a guess really, about why that phenomenon exists. He or she then creates a test to try to prove that guess wrong. Most of the time, the hypothesis is incorrect and quickly discarded. If after repeated testing it cannot be falsified, it becomes a theory and is likely to be correct. Of course, if a new test ever shows that the theory is not true, it is quickly discarded. We all know that this is not the way it always works, but it is the ideal.

Pseudoscience, on the other hand, notes a phenomenon, in this case the ancient texts, which *may* record alien visitation. Pseudoscience then comes up with a hypothesis, a guess really, about that phenomenon. Here, Sitchin guesses it is because the ancients knew all about extraterrestrial visitors. Then *assuming the hypothesis is true*, pseudoscientists collect selective evidence to back up the hypothesis and manipulate or interpret other evidence in light of the hypothesis. The researcher does *not* attempt to refute, test, or disprove his or her theory or consider contradictory evidence. After gathering the supporting "evidence," the pseudoscientist then declares that the hypothesis is true, even though it was the assumption at the beginning of the equation.

This is what Sitchin has done.

On the basis of this reasoning, Sitchin also makes sweeping statements about the technological development of the Sumerians based on a few subjectively interpreted drawings of the inscribed cylinders Sumerians used as seals. Hafernik says, "He goes too far, however, when he claims that one of the Sumerian tablets 'shows, without question, a man lying on a special bed; his face protected by a mask, and he is being subjected to some kind of radiation.'"27 Quite simply, there is no way to verify this bizarre assertion. Hafernik says there is very little chance that anyone could challenge this interpretation, not because it is right (it isn't) but because there is no way of tracking down the source for the hand-drawn copy of the Sumerian tablet. There is no citation and no reference. For this claim, we have only Sitchin's word and a poorly drawn reproduction with no evidence that an original ever existed.

In another section of *Twelfth Planet*, Sitchin shows a drawing without citation or photograph of a presumably Sumerian cylinder seal, which depicts wings topped by a bird. He related this to the Sumerian legend of Etana, who was brought up into the heavens by an eagle. Of this he asked:

> What or who was the Eagle who took Etana to the distant heavens? We cannot help but associate the ancient text with the message beamed to earth in July 1969 by Neil Armstrong, commander of the *Apollo 11* spacecraft: Houston! Tranquility base here. The Eagle has landed.[28]

This argument is patently ridiculous. By this measure, then, the Greek myth of Ganymede borne to Olympus on the back of Zeus in his guise as an eagle is also a prediction of the *Apollo* mission. Nevertheless, Sitchin's musing eventually took on the aura of gospel among the true believers. Sitchin further argued that the Sumerian texts, in his translation, clearly indicate that the alien visitors rode back and forth to heaven in rockets, just like the Saturn V used in the *Apollo* space program.

But why should Sitchin have a rocket fetish? After all, advanced civilizations should logically have moved beyond the need for fuel-inefficient rockets. Were they not supposed to have antigravity devices, saucer-shaped ships, and other whizbang technology? However, when *Twelfth Planet* was written, rockets were state of the art. But all the rockets landing in ancient Sumer apparently did not impress the jaded residents of that civilization. Citing standard works on Sumer, Hafernik says there is no record of these visitations:

> Here we are at the heart of the matter. These Sumerians, direct descendants of the gods from the skies, privy to the creation of the solar system, eye witnesses to rockets coming and going, didn't record enough astronomical observations that even a single tablet (out of many tens of thousands) has made it to the present day.[29]

Sitchin argues the reverse, claiming that his special and unique ability to understand and decipher Sumerian texts proves the visitation of the Annunaki. Remember, Sitchin claims to be the only person in the world capable of accurately translating the ancient texts; therefore, all other translations and interpretations are prima facie invalid. Sitchin says his unique Sumerian comprehension led him to Akkadian Seal VA243, which he claims shows an accurate view of the universe through the use of small dots to represent the planets. He says that all the known planets are present, in exact proportion, a perfect scale model of the universe. Yet his evidence is not the seal itself, or even a photograph of it, but is instead a "redrawing," done by him in his own hand. Comparing the drawing with the actual photograph of the cylinder shows an immediate problem: Sitchin's hand drawing changes the size and location of the seal's original configuration. Unfortunately, even the most cursory examination of the size of the dots, which I did, using a photograph of the actual cylinder, shows that their relative sizes do not correlate to the size of the planets at all. Clearly, this is a problem.

But thanks to the rise of the Internet during the 1990s, Sitchin supporters were able to band together to defend their belief system. Sitchinite William Saylor supported Sitchin's theories and on his Web site claimed that the seal described above accurately shows the universe by relating the size of the small bumps to the logarithm of each planet's orbit, thereby correcting the mismatch between planet size and the size of the carved image through advanced mathematics.[30] Unfortunately, there are problems with this theory. Saylor bases his theory on the drawing from Sitchin's *Twelfth Planet* that claims to reproduce the Akkadian original, and his drawing is admittedly "not to scale." Consequently, measurements taken from it are suspect, especially given the fact that most Sumerian cylinder seals were only a few inches long. Last, Saylor concludes based on his logarithmic studies that the Akkadians "[k]new the precise diameters of the Sun, nine major planets, Titan and the Moon." Yet he also says that the sun is not accurately portrayed and claims that as evidence that the Sumerians knew what they were doing, since they "purposely" got it wrong![31]

Sitchin wrote seven other books after *Twelfth Planet*, each building upon the theory he first laid down in 1976. Over decades, Sitchin has claimed that the Annunaki genetically engineered humanity, that the space invaders tried to destroy humanity in a flood, and that someday the aliens will return and bring a biblical-style judgment on mankind. Recent lectures by Zecharia Sitchin have taken on the air of a religious revival meeting. He does not discuss extraterrestrials and aliens in any real, scientific way. Instead they are props for a religious experience that transcends science and reunites believers with the Other that the decline of religion had left behind. A look at the topics for a 2003 lecture in Philadelphia, part of a "reunion" with Sitchin Scholars, demonstrates how far from science this philosophical system has come:

> Why are there wars?
> How did wars begin?
> When did they begin?
> Was Man born to be a warrior, or was he taught to make war?
> Will there be a Final War, an Armageddon?[32]

The answers are yours for the asking, for just $21 for a two-tape set.[33] Though Sitchin's answers to these questions are extraterrestrial, they really represent a religious yearning, a need to understand the nature of being human. In an age when religion no longer holds those eternal truths and the essence of humanity is mutable through chemical and genetic manipulation, Sitchin's "truths" represent an attempt to find a stable belief system amid the ever-changing world around us.

One concerned critic worried about the impact of Sitchin's work:

> Over the last quarter of a century, Sitchin's books have made a considerable worldwide impact, and have persuaded a great many people that the "gods" were flesh and blood visitors from elsewhere. This idea has become extended by many into the belief that they will return to "save" the human race. I believe this is a fundamentally dangerous proposition.[34]

As we shall see, the Heaven's Gate cult committed mass suicide in 1998 to meet up with the "gods" from outer space who were supposed to return in a UFO flying behind the comet Hale-Bopp. Other groups, like the Raëlian Revolution, have embraced Sitchin's work and used it as a basis for their own UFO cosmology and even as a justification for human cloning. After all, if the Annunaki made man in their image, they ask why man should not do the same with clones.

Zecharia Sitchin's books have become best-sellers wherever they are published and in seventeen languages, from German to Greek. In 2004 the Google search engine found more than forty-five thousand Web sites devoted to Sitchin and his theories.[35] Sitchin is only too happy to tell people that he is more popular than ever:

> There are two dozen or more books that are based on my books. These are in theology, astrology, and so on and so forth, and I am sure there are many more about which I don't know. They refer to my writings or are based on them. I provide the facts as I see them, and everyone is free to interpret them as they wish.[36]

As we have seen, one of Sitchin's "facts" concerned the quarry marks that showed Khufu built the Great Pyramid. Sitchin claimed years ago they were fake to bolster his theory that space aliens built the Giza pyramids as beacons for their rocket ships, and many people believed him without question. Today, almost no one takes this seriously, but many readers of Sitchin's books still believe. At a 2002 "Sitchin Studies" conference in Los Angeles, Sitchin spoke to two hundred audience members and about two dozen "alumni," true believers who attended at least three "Sitchin Studies" seminars.

They gathered to listen to their hero discuss his latest discoveries and the publication of his new book, *The Lost Book of Enki*, which Sitchin wrote in the Sumerian alien-god Enki's voice by weaving together eight hundred fragments of unrelated ancient texts to tell the story of his battle with fellow god Enlil, the war in heaven, and the creation of human beings. Each audience member, known as a "Sitchinite" for his or her devotion, received a "Sitchin Studies certificate," signed by Sitchin himself.

> As the session ended, it was kind of sad as people had to say goodbye to others with whom they shared thoughts and ideas. Then, group by group and one by one, the Sitchinites slowly left, clutching their certificates (all individually signed by Zecharia), plenty of e-mail addresses and much enthusiasm.[37]

For Sitchin's critics, their greatest concern is that many people are unable to separate fact from fiction and eagerly consume Sitchin's work as gospel truth. For Sitchin's followers his word is Truth, and in their desire to await the return of the Annunaki, we see echoes of Millennial Christians who awaited the Second Coming of Christ. Sitchin is not a scholar; instead he is a latter-day prophet.

Like the followers of Cthulhu, liberated into a future of ecstacy and freedom, Sitchinites, too, found a world of wonder, unconfined by facts, reason, or evidence. It was a Romantic notion, irrational, wild, and exuberant. It is a return to the primal excitement of ancient religion, made new by modern archetypes and made real by the trappings of science. Thus aerospace engineer Robert Hafernik misses the point of Sitchin's work when he sums him up:

> Clearly, Sitchin is a smart man. He weaves a complicated tale from the bits and pieces of evidence that survive from ancient Sumeria to the present day. Just as clearly, Sitchin is capable of academic transgressions. . . . Worst of all, he is almost utterly innocent of astronomy and other assorted fields of modern science. . . . In the end, he's just another nut making a living selling books that treat folks to a tale they want to believe in.[38]

But it is that need to believe that animates Sitchin's followers. He is the prophet of a new faith, boldly asserting the Truth of his doctrine in the face of skeptical heathens, and that is in essence his appeal. He weaves bits and pieces of old texts together not to prove a point but to provide a history and a detailed background for his philosophy and his vision. He uses the myths as a mine to give legitimacy to his prophecies about the return of the Annunaki. Arguably, it is this quasi-religious hope for the aliens' return that marks the true appeal of Sitchin Studies and perhaps the real reason they line up for Sitchin's messianic lectures and buy his bizarre merchandise like his line of *Twelfth Planet* playing cards.[39]

In our next two chapters, we will take a look at the two major groups who follow Sitchin's path. One group, the metaphorical believers, used Sitchin as a guiding philosophy for their spirituality and to find a literal religious revival. But first we shall explore the literalists, who believe in Sitchin the way he believes in the Sumerian texts. They attempted to use Sitchin's theories to prove "scientific" truths.

15

TAKING OFF FROM NIBIRU

O f course, Zecharia Sitchin was not writing in a vacuum. Despite the cult of personality he and his followers built around him, Sitchin spent the greater part of his career playing second banana to the number one man in the ancient-astronaut movement: Erich von Däniken. Though Sitchin would participate in von Däniken's Ancient Astronaut Society and write for its newsletter, *Ancient Skies*, he borrowed little from his predecessor other than the conceit, first expressed in *Chariots of the Gods?* and *Gods from Outer Space*, that aliens had genetically manipulated hominids into modern human beings in an extraterrestrial genesis. Von Däniken, however, borrowed liberally from the work of Sitchin, citing him time and again as his source for important revelations in his later books. And so it was that Sitchin's ideas entered into the New Age mainstream, for while few outside his immediate cult had read Sitchin, many still had a residual respect for von Däniken and came to know Sitchin and his works through the popular books of Erich von Däniken. In the pantheon of the Ancient Astronaut Society, von Däniken and Sitchin were the twin lights that guided the (space)ship.

In the years after Zecharia Sitchin released *Twelfth Planet*, world reaction to his revelations was decidedly tepid. With the end of the 1970s, paranormal studies and the occult were in eclipse, and most scholars never bothered to read Sitchin, and few bothered to comment on him when they did. Since the ancient-astronaut theory was in decline thanks in part to a concerted scholarly effort to debunk and refute Erich von Däniken, Sitchin received something of a free pass. His works sold under the radar through the 1980s, building up impressive sales figures but rarely reaching the level of public prominence that other "alternative" or "fringe" authors achieved. Sitchin was no Robert Temple.

In fact, I had not heard of Sitchin until long after I had already begun to question the fundamental principles of the ancient-astronaut theory. As a result, during my period of belief I never fell for his extraterrestrial genesis. Whatever odd beliefs I had stumbled across and half-heartedly explored, his was not one of them. I was more consumed by H. P. Lovecraft, whose work was in the 1990s starting to come into a prominence it had never before seen. Del Rey books printed the complete works of Lovecraft in handsome paperback volumes, Sam Remi made use of the *Necronomicon* in his popular *Evil Dead* movies, and "Call of Cthulhu" had become a best-selling role-playing game from Chaosium. With the advent of NecronomiCon, a gathering of Lovecraft aficionados, and several small publishers dedicated to printing Lovecraftian fiction, the Cthulhu Mythos had never been more popular. Several important authors like Stephen King, Ramsey Campbell, Brian Lumley, and T. E. D. Klein produced first-rate fiction inspired by and building upon H. P. Lovecraft. There was clearly something about times of angst and uncertainty that brought out a florescence of interest in the Old Gent from Providence. More often than not, periods of strong interest in Lovecraft coincided with a renewed interest in the occult, the paranormal, and the supernatural.

When the millennial angst of the fin de siècle caused an occult revival in the mid-1990s, Zecharia Sitchin's obscure and dense theories slowly wormed their way toward the surface. While the man himself remained something of a cult figure, his ideas permeated those of alternative researchers. As we have seen, alternative historians like Graham Hancock embraced some of Sitchin's logic to help bolster their archaeological cases for a lost civilization, and Erich von Däniken borrowed many of Sitchin's arguments for his own books. Others embraced his theories of an extraterrestrial genesis and worked to document and prove his assertions that aliens bearing Sumerian names created humanity in their own image.

By Sitchin's own count, at least two dozen books by other authors built upon his theories. Since so many of these books were derivative rehashings of the same arguments, they did little to further the extraterrestrial genesis idea. Some, however, made bold new claims that took Sitchin's and von Däniken's thesis to strange new levels hinted at previously only in the fictions of Lovecraft. We will examine three of these authors, David Hatcher Childress, Alan Alford, and Laurence Gardner, by looking at a key issue from each one to see how the potent parascientific team of von Däniken and Sitchin have driven their ideas and led to truly bizarre conclusions.

David Hatcher Childress is a member of the Ancient Astronaut Society, and he works closely with Erich von Däniken to further the extraterrestrial-genesis theory. He is perhaps at present the most famous proponent of the theory that the ancients used nuclear weapons, and he goes by the title "lost science scholar." He strongly supports the ideas of both von Däniken and Sitchin, and he has produced numerous glossy volumes providing supporting "evidence" for these beliefs. I wanted to talk with Childress about the ancient-astronaut and extraterrestrial-genesis theories, but Childress did not return requests for an interview. The Ancient Astronaut Society chairman, Giorgio Tsoukalos, whom we met in Part Three, had warned Childress not to speak to me. After I tried to talk to Erich von Däniken and Tsoukalos stopped me, he read some critical articles I had written on Childress's ideas in Lost Civilization Uncovered, and he warned the author.[1] It was clear, though, that Childress's research methods share much in common with the tactics of creationists.

One of the key tenets of creationism, extraterrestrial-genesis, and alternative archaeology theories is the belief that ancient scriptures are the literal testament of what has gone before. For this reason young-earth creationists still claim that the earth is only six thousand years old, and others take literally the harrowing adventure the Hebrew patriarch Enoch had in heaven. Oddly enough, none of these biblical or mythological literalists accept Greek mythology at face value. For them the voyage of the *Argo* was nothing more than a flight of fancy (or a retelling of a story written in the stars, as *Sirius Mystery* author Robert Temple would have it). There is neither Medusa nor Zeus hurling thunderbolts from on high. Yet these same people wish us to believe that ancient Indian Vedic literature is every bit as true as a modern-day news report. "Researchers" like David Hatcher Childress fervently argue that the Vedic flying machines and powerful weapons were actual airplanes and even nuclear weapons.

Among his unique ideas, Childress claims that pyramids, domes, and spaceports are clearly visible on the moon and on other planets, even though no scientists have been able to see them. He also believes that the famous scientist Nikola Tesla invented a death-ray and time machines, which world governments conspired to keep secret, and that the Smithsonian is covering up a lost civilization in the Grand Canyon. According to a 1909 newspaper article from the Arizona *Gazette*, which is highly dubious, Smithsonian archaeologists supposedly found a Tibetan or Egyptian tomb in the Grand Canyon, complete with mummies. The tomb has never been seen since, and the Smithsonian denies any knowledge of the story, which was likely a hoax.[2]

Childress wrote a series of *Lost Cities* books in which he compiled anomalous, questionable, and apocryphal stories to prove his thesis that extraterrestrials influenced early humanity and that current governments are suppressing this fact. It appears that Childress discovered the *Gazette* article while researching *Lost Cities of North and Central America*, in which he repeated apocryphal stories of pterodactyls alive in Texas. He took the official denials of the *Gazette* story as proof of a cover-up. He included the story and the denials in a chapter of *Lost Cities*, and he excerpted that chapter for the alternative publication *Nexus* magazine in 1993.[3]

After publication in *Nexus*, the article was posted on KeelyNet BBS on May 8, 1993, under the inauspicious heading of CANYON.ASC. KeelyNet issued the disclaimer that anything it published was free to copy, and an Internet revolution was born. Soon the Childress article appeared all over the Internet and hundreds of Web sites carried the news that ancient Egyptians had lived in the Grand Canyon. By the turn of the millennium, the dubious story was firmly embedded in the alternative community as proof that the Smithsonian covered up parts of history. But while this would be Childress's most widely repeated theory, it was another, his claim of ancient atom bombs, that showed best how far extraterrestrial-genesis theories had gone in the years since *Chariots of the Gods?*

In 2000, to promote his new book, *Technology of the Gods*, Childress released a chapter on ancient nuclear weapons to *Nexus*, the alternative magazine founded in 1987 to report unconventional and occult stories, or what owner Duncan Roads calls "suppressed information."[4]

Childress begins his article on ancient atomic weapons by discussing a geological anomaly: the same glasslike fusion of sand that occurs on the land beneath a nuclear blast can also be found in ancient strata dating back eight thousand years. Childress provides the scientific explanation, and then he rejects it: "The general theory is that the glass was created by the searing, sand-melting impact of a cosmic projectile. However, there are serious problems with this theory."[5]

Childress rejects the theory because he says there is no evidence of an impact crater, but he himself admits that there have been impacts that did not produce craters. One was the Tunguska Event of 1908, of which mainstream science holds that an asteroid hit Siberia and vaporized without leaving any trace except flattened trees and an explosion so loud it could be heard in Moscow and so bright that midnight was light as noon as far off as London. A whole mythology has grown up around the Tunguska Event. Many explanations exist, ranging from the scientifically accepted asteroid theory to the crash of a UFO and the resulting detonation of its nuclear reactor. How anyone knows whether UFOs are nuclear powered is not explained. One fringe theory that fits well with Childress's conspiratorial view of Tesla is the Tesla ray. Some believe that Nikola Tesla invented a powerful ray in the early twentieth century and that its first test went awry when Tesla directed an energy ray across the globe to blow up a relatively uninhabited section of Siberia. So what does the Tunguska Event have to do with ancient atomic warfare?

Childress needs the Tunguska Event to be something other than an asteroid impact to bolster his theories that such technologies as the Tesla ray not just are possible but actually existed in ancient times. Childress is also prone to seeing conspiracies, arguing in his book *The Fantastic Inventions of Nikola Tesla* that the US government conspired to suppress the discoveries made by Tesla to protect big business. Incidentally, Childress claims to be the coauthor of *Fantastic Inventions*, with Tesla as the posthumous main author.

In the course of his work, Childress became convinced that Tesla had only "rediscovered" technology that had existed in ages past, much as Ignatius Donnelly asserted in his *Atlantis:*

The Antediluvian World. Therefore, when confronted with the anomaly of green glass from melted sand found buried deep in the Libyan desert—the so-called vitrified desert dismissed by scientists as a natural result of a meteor impact on silica-rich sands—Childress asked: "[I]s it possible that the vitrified desert is the result of atomic war in the ancient past? Could a Tesla-type beam weapon have melted the desert, perhaps in a test?"[6]

Decades before, Erich von Däniken had argued in *Chariots of the Gods?* that atom bombs destroyed Sodom and Gomorrah, the biblical cities of sin: "[s]ince the dropping of two atomic bombs on Japan, we know the kind of damage such bombs cause. . . . Let us imagine for a moment that Sodom and Gomorrah were destroyed according to plan, i.e. deliberately, by a nuclear explosion."[7] From his offhand remark, asked as a question rather than stated as fact, a whole subgenre of ancient warfare grew. In *Gods from Outer Space*, von Däniken says, "[I]t is the old Indian and Tibetan texts in particular that teem with science-fiction weapons. I am thinking of the divine lightning and ray weapons . . . and of the texts that seem to be referring to bacteriological weapons."[8]

Childress built on this to develop his own "evidence" from the same sources: "If one were to believe the *Mahabharata* [one of the ancient Indian epics], great battles were fought in the past with airships, particle beams, chemical warfare and presumably atomic weapons. . . . [B]attles in the latter days of Atlantis were fought with highly sophisticated, high-tech weapons."[9] He eventually degenerates into incoherence, claiming that Atlantis was not alone: "The Rama Empire, described in the *Mahabharata* and *Ramayana*, was supposedly contemporaneous with the great cultures of Atlantis and Osiris in the West. Atlantis, well known from Plato's writings and ancient Egyptian records, apparently existed in the mid-Atlantic and was a highly technical and patriarchal civilization."[10]

Needless to say, there is neither proof of Atlantis existing outside of Plato's mind nor any evidence that the Atlanteans had high-tech weaponry. I know of no ethnographies describing the familial relations of Atlanteans. Osiris, we are told, is predynastic Egypt. Childress's source? "Esoteric doctrine" unrevealed to the reader. As for the Rama Empire, Childress says it began with "Nagas (Naacals) who had come into India from Burma and ultimately from the 'Motherland to the East'—or so Colonel James Churchward was told."[11] As we saw in Part One, Colonel Churchward wrote about the lost continent of Mu in the early twentieth century. His books sold well but were quickly shown to be a hoax when he could produce no evidence of the tablets where he read of the continent or the monks who gave them to him. Of course, this is good enough evidence for Childress. He identifies Mu with Lemuria and uses material from the Lemurian Fellowship lesson manual to tell how the Ramas and the Atlanteans fought a great war that resulted in nuclear holocaust. Never mind that Lemuria was a nineteenth-century fiction supported by Madame Helena Blavatsky.

None of this made it into Childress's story, though he tells how the Atlanteans were angry that the Ramas had beat them in battle: "Assuming the above story is true, Atlantis was not pleased at the humiliating defeat and therefore used its most powerful and destructive weapon—quite possibly an atomic-type weapon!"[12] As has been shown, the above story is not true, and there was neither Atlantis nor Lemuria to fight with any weapons at all, let alone nuclear ones.

Childress cites L. Sprague de Camp's assessment of ancient oil-based weapons like Greek Fire to bolster the claim of sophisticated stone-age weapons.[13] De Camp, aside from his books on ancient history, was the biographer of H. P. Lovecraft, whose mythos of Great Cthulhu spawned the very ancient-astronaut theory Childress is using him to support! Finally, we learn from another Indian epic, the *Vymaanika-Shaastra*, that ancient peoples had plasma guns powered by electrified mercury.

Remembering what von Däniken said about Sodom and Gomorrah—that they were destroyed by a vengeful alien race —Childress asserts that the story of Sodom and Gomorrah is the most famous of the "ancient nuke 'em stories."[14] Childress apparently does not think it is that well known, for he then quotes it in full. He then claims there is but one hypothesis to explain the disappearance of the two cities, the "popular theory" that the destruction was caused by human or alien atom bombs.[15] But the theory was popular only because the echo chamber of extraterrestrial-genesis authors repeated it!

So where does this leave the theory of ancient nuclear activity?

On the one hand, there may be scattered pieces of evidence that do not yet fit into the standard model. This is to be expected. On the other hand, there are ridiculous amounts of speculation, like the silly and childish stories Childress professes to believe: "If we accept the Lemurian Fellowship stories as fact, then Atlantis wanted to waste no more time with the Priest-Kings of Rama and their mental tricks. In terrifying revenge, they utterly destroyed the Rama Empire, leaving no country even to pay tribute to them."[16] There is no basis in fact for these empty assertions, but they are repeated by so many who read authors like Childress that they take on a verisimilitude that endangers a rational view of the past. They are the mythology of a belief system that wants desperately to believe in Zecharia Sitchin and Erich von Däniken as prophets of a higher power. If one cannot have God, one can have extraterrestrials.

For David Hatcher Childress, the idea that aliens came to Earth and created humanity in their image was only common sense. Researcher Alan Alford agreed.

Alan F. Alford spent most of his writing career with a single goal in mind: to prove that Zecharia Sitchin and Erich von Däniken were right. He wrote a book providing additional "evidence" that the Annunaki of Sitchin's *Twelfth Planet* were responsible for humanity's extraterrestrial genesis. Then in 1996, he had a change of heart and decided that something was not quite right with Sitchin's worldview. A considerate man of obvious intelligence, Alford explained to me how he came to reject Sitchin's unique interpretation of ancient Sumerian texts:

> Suffice to say that the more I have seen of these writings, the more horrified I have become at the interpretation that Sitchin has dragged out of them. I regret very much not researching this properly prior to 1996. I was young, enthusiastic, perhaps a little naive. Now I am older and wiser. Too wise to call Sitchin a charlatan—I have no idea whether he knows his theory is bogus or not. As far as I'm concerned, it doesn't really matter one way or another. The important thing is to know that his theory is completely wrong. I should emphasise, though, that this does not mean that all ancient-astronaut theories are wrong—just Sitchin's particular "brand."[17]

However, Alford's replacement paradigm was every bit as bizarre.

Alford calls himself the "voice of common sense" on his Web site, where he published many articles about his books, which include *Gods of the New Millennium* and *The Phoenix Solution*. On the surface, Alford seems unique. Because he has repudiated Sitchin, he is one of the few authors in the alternative-history genre to say that he firmly rejects the extraterrestrial genesis concept after doing extensive research in the field. Instead, he believes that the "gods" were used as a religious metaphor for an exploded planet: "I have argued that the religions of the ancient Near East were 'exploded planet cults' and that the priests popularised their religion by telling the celestial story with human-like imagery. In other words, the ancient priests 'dumbed down' their religion."[18] Of course, appearances can be deceiving, and the ancient-astronaut theory does not die such an easy death. Although he rejected Sitchin's Sumerian gods, he still supports the idea that humans were the genetic legacy of alien beings.

While there exists no scientific evidence to back up the claim of planets blowing up as Alford suggests, it is his lack of knowledge about evolutionary theory that has led many of his readers to believe that our own species, *Homo sapiens*, was the genetic legacy of advanced residents of this hypothetical exploded planet, a process he calls Interventionism. The ancient aliens are back again in force.

Alford became interested in ancient mysteries by reading alternative literature, according to his Web site: "The Ancient Astronaut Hypothesis has intrigued me for 15 years, ever since I read the books of Erich von Däniken. It was the writings of von Däniken, Sitchin and other ancient astronaut writers which really got me hooked on the subjects of religion and ancient history."[19] While he supposedly rejected this philosophy, even today he claims on his Web site to show that man is not descended from apes but is the product of Interventionism from above. Whether the product of God or aliens is for the reader to decide.

Alford uses selective quotations from scientists like the late Stephen J. Gould (called "America's evolutionist laureate" by Alford) to build a case that science has no firm concept of human origins. He quotes Gould as saying humanity is "an awesome improbability" without mentioning that Gould does not treat this as anything other than a mathematical fluke; winning the lottery is an awesome improbability, but someone wins somewhere in America every week.

Of the earliest of man's ancestor species, Alford says, "It is also important to emphasise that many of these finds have skulls more like chimpanzees than men."[20] Far from being a strange fact, this is precisely what one would expect from ancient ancestors, that they would be most like the apes from which they diverged millions of years ago. There is no mystery here.

Alford then cites a newspaper article as evidence that the human family tree baffles scientists, who he says cannot find a connection between the mysterious chimplike creatures and modern man. However, new fossil finds are often confusing and cause scientists to revise theories about the exact sequence of human evolution. Yet, while the human family tree is complex and often incomplete, it is not without the general trend of apelike to manlike creatures. Australopithecines gave way to *Homo erectus* and then modern man. This is fairly well established, and Alford offers no evidence that this is wrong; therefore, we must conclude this argument does not hold water.

Alford, however, has further arguments in favor of alien intervention, namely, hair: "Today, four out of ten Americans find it difficult to believe that humans are related to the apes. Why is this so? Compare yourself to a chimpanzee. Man is intelligent, naked and highly sexual—a species apart from his alleged primate relatives," Alford says.[21] This is demonstrably false.

But this is not important for Alford because human sexuality sets us apart from the chimps. Alford says that humanity is different from all other animals because *Homo sapiens* has "unique human features such as extended foreplay, extended copulation and the orgasm."[22] Unfortunately for Alford, foreplay, copulation, and orgasm are not uniquely human. The bonobo (pygmy chimpanzee) engages in near-constant foreplay, with frequent and sometimes homosexual sex, much to the embarrassment of early researchers who were shocked by their free love. The rhinoceros copulates for hours at a time. Finally, if animals had no orgasms, why would they have sex? Obviously and biologically sex is enjoyable for most mammals.

Alford goes on to say that hidden ovulation, the fact that human women do not advertise their periods of fertility with swollen, red buttocks as other apes do, cannot be explained by natural selection. Once again he is wrong. Concealed ovulation and open ovulation are used variously by different species, and evolutionary histories suggest that species go back and forth between the two as environmental situations warrant. Concealed ovulation leads to constant sex and a reinforcement of pair bonds. There is nothing unnatural about that.

For much of the above, Alford relied on the work of Desmond Morris, the famed author of *The Naked Ape*. Morris, however, is not an evolutionary biologist but a zoologist with no special training in evolution. In fact, the biography Morris's agent provides says specifically that Morris "reminds us that man is relative to the apes—is in fact, the greatest primate of all."[23] This is a far cry from the implication in Alford's work that Morris finds faults with the relationship between man and ape.

Alford's showstopper argument is that the complexity of the human brain shows that evolution could not have led to it. He even says that "it is so complex and unique that there is no chance of reverse engineering the evolutionary process that created it."[24] He oddly enough holds the contradictory position that this miracle of complexity was bestowed by the aliens, who apparently were able to grasp this self-same process of complexity creation. Of course, one wonders whence came the aliens.

Alford holds that the true evidence that aliens created humanity comes from the sudden transition from *Homo erectus* to *Homo sapiens*, which he believes defies the laws of evolution. Here again his ignorance shows. He obviously ignored the previously quoted Steven J. Gould's theory of punctuated equilibrium, which shows that great changes in a species happen very rapidly, followed by long periods of stasis. Thus, a lack of smooth transition is expected. This theory built Gould's reputation; that Alford could quote Gould and be ignorant of the theory that made him famous is astounding. Alford also denies that the division of species—speciation—can be observed, though there are seagulls in Canada that are a prime example of such division.

Clearly Alford inhabits a territory that is the secular equivalent of creationism. Like that theory, Alford denies evolution and tries to argue that Darwinism is an enemy of true research. For both creationists and extraterrestrial genesis proponents, it is of paramount importance to disprove Darwinism in their followers' eyes, or at least demonstrate that it does not apply to human beings. Only this way can they pave the way for their larger claim that the creationist God or the extraterrestrials "really" created humanity. In both cases, this belief transcends evidence and forms an article of faith necessary to perpetuate a belief in a higher power of some kind.

Thus Alford plays numbers games and makes many other arguments derived from "creation science" literature, but at this point we see how his thinking goes. It should not surprise us then that he finishes his essay by claiming, "Clearly everything is not 'hunky dory' with Darwinism."[25] He calls for an "alternative" to Darwinism, which is his label for science with which he disagrees. He even says that evolution's "general principles are of great value in explaining the evolution of animals and specific organs such as the eye, but severe doubts surround its practical application to man."[26] If it can explain all of man's organs, then, pray tell, why not man? The answer for Alford is that an "intelligent extraterrestrial species migrated to the Earth."[27] He believes that this is much more scientific than a century and a half of evolutionary research. Needless to say, he does not say whether the aliens evolved.

But I do not mean to be overly harsh toward Alan Alford, no matter how vociferously I disagree with his ideas. He has made significant progress in distancing himself from Zecharia Sitchin's theories, and he continues to evolve and adapt his thinking. I am confident that over time he will move still closer to the mainstream. His ability to change his mind and reject an erroneous belief system when confronted with solid evidence of its untruth places him in a unique position among ancient-astronaut theorists. With time, I am sure he will eventually decide that extra-terrestrial genesis is a seductive theory lacking evidence.

I asked him what he thought of this book's thesis that the ancient-astronaut theory originated in the works of H. P. Love-craft and what this meant for the idea of extraterrestrial genesis:

> My own view is that if this is how the idea originated then it doesn't matter one jot. All sorts of theories are inspired by other strange and often non-related happenings. The impor-tant thing is that each theory, in whatever field, be judged according to its inherent merits.[28]

Of course, Alford is right. If the ancient-astronaut theory were true, it wouldn't matter whether it derived from Lovecraft or the *Love Boat*. That, of course, is why I have endeavored to show some of the weaknesses and flaws in extraterrestrial-genesis speculations, so the reader can see that the theory has few inherent merits. When we realize how little solid ground the ancient-astronaut theory rests upon, we can see how much more important it becomes to recognize its origins so we can under-stand the source and appeal of this sociological phenomenon.

Meanwhile, all did not go well for Alan Alford, especially as the twenty-first century began and extraterrestrial-genesis the-ories were on the decline. Each of his books sold fewer copies than the one before, and by the time he published his fifth and sixth books, he no longer had a professional publisher. He released his most recent works through Eridu Books, which was Alan Alford self-publishing. A much bigger publishing phe-nomenon was Sir Laurence Gardner, a historian who came to embrace extraterrestrial genesis.

In October of 1996 Laurence Gardner, the self-styled Histogra-pher Royal to the House of Stewart (Stuart) and a prominent sovereign and chivalric genealogist, published a speculative volume tracing the lineage of modern royalty back to the alleged children of Jesus. In *Bloodline of the Holy Grail*, he had claimed that Christ married Mary Magdelene (a theory repeated in the best-selling novel *The Da Vinci Code*[29]), and he argued that their children carried the royal blood of the House of David; therefore, anyone descending from these people had the blessing of the divine powers to rule.[30] Unlike Graham Hancock, who saw the Holy Grail as an esoteric symbol for the Ark of the Covenant, Gardner saw it as an esoteric symbol for the bloodline of Christ, through a sacred pun in the French language: the Medieval French words for "Holy Grail" and "Blood Royal" used the same letters: *San Greal* versus *sang real*. Therefore, the grail legend was really a legend about Christ's descendents.[31]

In complex genealogical discussions, he traced the lineage of Jesus from Mary Magdelene's children, through the Merovingian kings of France and King Arthur, down to a modern dynasty. It almost goes without saying that the historian to the House of Stuart, deposed kings of England, discovered that the Stuarts were the last lineal descendents of Christ![32] Of course, I did not know when I first read the book that Gardner's boss, Prince Michael of Albany, was in reality Michel LaFosse, a Belgian national whose "de jure" claims to the throne of Scotland were based on forged documents and apparent falsehoods.[33]

Though I did not know it in 1997, Gardner's *Bloodline of the Holy Grail* was obviously inspired by the 1982 best-seller *The Holy Blood and the Holy Grail* by Michael Baigent, Richard Leigh, and Henry Lincoln, the first book to claim that Christ had children by Mary Magdelene. When first I read it, Gardner's book seemed highly convincing to my younger self. Of course, at the time I had no background in genealogy or medieval history. Laced with pages of complex genealogical charts and reams of historical details—names, places, dates—it provided a compelling and fascinating journey through medieval history.

When I first discovered the book in 1997, when Barnes & Noble republished the volume in an inexpensive edition, I was hooked. Gardner's book especially appealed to me because he rejected the religious version of Jesus' life and presented instead a view that, while still taking literally the events of the Bible, was rooted much more in history and in materialism. He portrayed Jesus as the last descendent of the bloodline of King David of Israel, whose very earthly mission was to carry on the royal house into the Roman era.[34] I should have realized that something was amiss when the bibliography listed Erich von Däniken's *Chariots of the Gods?* and Robert Bauval's *The Orion Mystery* as sources.[35] By the time I was halfway in, it was too late. Parts of the book, like a claim derived from Louis Charpentier's *Mystery of Chartres Cathedral* that the Cathedrals of Notre Dame scattered across France formed an image of the constellation Virgo, seemed too much like the Orion Correlation Theory to be a coincidence.

I eagerly anticipated his next book, unaware that his research methods were increasingly moving away from what few facts *Bloodline* used and toward extraterrestrial genesis. By the time he prepared to release *Genesis of the Grail Kings*, the self-styled Chevalier Labhràn de St. Germain seemed to have gone from alternative history to all-out Sitchinite. I say "seems" because Gardner himself disagrees with this. A kind man who graciously consented to answer some questions about his work, Gardner comes across as a chivalrous gentleman, polite to a fault, a distinct contrast to many of his colleagues in alternative history. In 2004, Gardner told me that he is only conditionally convinced in extraterrestrial beliefs: "I have not come to that conclusion, since I actually have no way of knowing. What I have said is that it is a possibility, and that a lot points to it having been likely. I can think of no good reason to discount the idea."[36] Nevertheless, there was a distinct Sitchinite bent to Gardner's intellectual journey.

In his first book, Gardner had traced the lineage of Jesus from Bethlehem down to modern times. In 2000, Gardner continued his quest for the ultimate origins of Jesus, this time tracing Jesus' lineage backward in the murky depths of prehistory, and he made controversial claims that stretch the power of imagination and slip into the dangerous realm of extraterrestrial genesis. In *Genesis of the Grail Kings*, Gardner claimed evidence that the royal bloodline descends ultimately from the biblical Cain, whose sons were of extraterrestrial persuasion. To promote his book, Gardner took the show on the road. He shared the main points of his book in a lecture that made the rounds of the Internet. Though the book was not the best-seller the original was, Gardner's lecture became one of the most readily available Internet texts on the extraterrestrial genesis theme.

In that lecture, Gardner made an astounding claim about Jesus' ancestors:

> They were the true Sons of the Gods, who were fed firstly on Anunnaki Star Fire from about 3800 BC and, subsequently, on "high-spin" metal supplements from about 2000 BC. In short, they were bred to be leaders of humankind, and they were both mentally and physically maintained in the "highward" state: the ultimate dimension of the missing 44 per cent—the dimension of the Orbit of Light, or the Plane of Sharon.[37]

The meaning of those enigmatic statements will become plain soon enough. Gardner developed his thesis with almost encyclopedic detail, and nary a verifiable fact to be seen. He informed the audience that though his first book dealt with New Testament themes, he had moved on to the Old.

Already we have a problem because Gardner took the biblical stories to be something more than fable and something less than truth. Once more we begin to slip down that slope toward biblical literalism, the belief that the Bible's text is an eyewitness account of events as they happened. Gardner seems to see these events as a conspiracy designed to obscure the truth with a quasi-religious message superimposed over an ancient record of alien visits: "the Old Testament scriptures were designed to uphold the emergent Hebrew faith, rather than to represent historical fact."[38] He says that the Old Testament does not accurately portray the ancient past, yet paradoxically, he claims to know what that hidden past is.

Gardner described the origins of the Hebrew faith as a mixture of heretical Egyptian sun-worshipers and remnants of the ancient Sumerian belief system. He believes that the Sumerian gods Enki and Enlil, the two gods whom Zecharia Sitchin most directly discussed, were fused together by the early Hebrews into the composite god Jehovah (YHWH). From the biblical Cain, everyone from David to Jesus to the self-styled Prince of Albany descend. Cain, of course, was the son of Adam and Eve, who "were purpose-bred for kingship by Enki and his sister-wife Nîn-khursag. This took place at a 'creation chamber' which the Sumerian annals refer to as the House of Shimtî." There, Gardner says, Adam and Eve "were created from human ova fertilized by Lord Enki."[39]

Needless to say, there is no evidence to support the idea that Enki was in any way real, nor is there evidence that Adam and Eve, if they existed at all, were genetically engineered by Enki. By linking the biblical God to the Sumerian pantheon, Gardner can then equate the Judaic Elohim to the signature assembly of the Sumerians, the Annunaki, whom we remember from Zecharia Sitchin, who claimed that they were aliens from a trans-Plutonian planet and created man as a slave race to mine gold. For Gardner, the Annunaki provide the crucial link between the mythological gods of Sumeria and the Old Testament narrative, identifying the Annunaki with the Elohim, as described in Psalm 82.

That the psalm is a remnant of Sumerian myths may well be justified, but whether this implies a reality to the Annunaki legend is doubtful. To seal the alleged connection between the bloodline of the Grail and the Sumerians, Gardner claims the Sumerian word for the Mark of Cain is *"Gra-al,"* which he implies sounds a lot like the Holy "Grail," identified in his previous book with the blood of Jesus. As we saw, he argued this identification came from an imagined medieval French pun: *Sang real* (royal blood) vs. *san greal* (Holy Grail). *"Real"* sounds like *"greal,"* which sounds like *"Gra-al,"* so everything fits. Of course, the Latin word *homo* (man) sounds like the Greek word *homo* (same), so Gardner's logic would predict that the Romans must have viewed all men as identical. This, of course, is wrong. Without proof that a French pun derives from a Sumerian word (unknown, of course, to the medieval French, who could not read the Sumerian written tongue, cuneiform) this argument is nothing more than innuendo.

Gardner then asks a rhetorical question: "[S]ince it is known that the Chalice is a wholly female symbol which has been emblematic of the womb from the earliest times (as discussed in *Bloodline of the Holy Grail*), might this Messianic lifeblood (now symbolized by wine) have been an extract of menstrual blood in original times?"[40] For him the answer is a solid yes because the Sumerians drank menstrual blood in rituals. However, many authorities disagree and argue that any menstrual rituals were connected not with the Annunaki but with the moon-god Sin, who controlled fertility cycles. The Annunaki were merely a blank, faceless council.

But this is not the point. Gardner has a "scientific" explanation for why the Sumerian would want to drink menstrual blood. Gardner claims that the Annunaki's menstrual blood stimulates the pineal gland in the brain, providing an infinite source of melatonin to stop the aging process. Of course, there is no medical evidence that melatonin has any effect on aging, despite press reports in the 1990s claiming it as a wonder drug.

Yet Gardner insists that the menstrual blood of the Annunaki was special: "In addition to being the Gold of the

Gods, the Anunnaki menstruum was also called the Vehicle of Light, being the ultimate source of manifestation and, in this regard, it was directly equated with the mystical Waters of Creation—the flow of eternal wisdom."[41] He called the Annunaki's menstrual blood "Star-Fire" and said that it was the source of kingly power and is why the patriarchs and ancient aliens lived hundreds of years, he said. Later, when this blood was no longer available, they ate ground gold crushed into a white powder.

Of course, there is no proof whatsoever that eating gold or metal of any kind produces eternal youth. Nor is there proof that the ancients consumed metal. Gardner says that eating the mysterious "white powder of gold" stimulated the pineal gland, identified in esoteric lore as the seat of the soul.

Gardner says this metal is similar to a science experiment that reduced metal to monoatomic white powder (m-state gold) through complex stimulation of atomic nuclei. As the nuclei are stimulated, the atoms lose weight and seem to disappear: "Moreover, its optimum weight is actually 56% of the metal weight from which it was transmuted. So, where does the other 44% go?" Gardner, as always, has an answer: "It becomes nothing but pure white light and translates to another dimension beyond the physical plane."[42] Beyond this, the powder also made objects like the stones of the Great Pyramid fly.

The Great Pyramid, therefore, was a giant superconductor that the ancients used to transport the pharaoh to an alternate dimension to meet with the "gods." This alternate dimension is obviously the home of the Annunaki, who are more accurately described as transdimensional rather than extraterrestrial, not unlike Yog-Sothoth in the Cthulhu Mythos. In fact, all of these strange claims strike me as highly derivative of Lovecraft, where ancient rites and rituals actually describe unknown laws of physics and open portals to other dimensions and past times, as in *The Case of Charles Dexter Ward* or "The Dreams in the Witch-House."

I had to ask Mr. Gardner where he obtained insights that other historians seemed to have missed for thousands of years. "There is a good deal of evidence," he told me, "in ancient writings, that M-state gold was manufactured and ingested—just as is happening again today. Records indicate that the manufacture was performed by priestly characters in temple workshops."[43] But, I protested, how can we trust that ancient texts are true accounts of the past and not figments of the ancients' imaginations? After all, Gardner himself claimed that the Old Testament was Hebrew propaganda:

> I have never suggested that ancient texts are literally true—nor any other texts for that matter. What they are, however, is documented evidence from the era in question. My premise is that any report from someone at the time of an event stands [a] more probable chance of being correct than an interpretation by someone centuries later. . . . History is not the event, it is the chronicle of the event—and chronicles will always depend on viewpoints and vested interests. Whether true or not in content, therefore, the ancient documents do constitute history.
>
> All history is based on the reports of its writers, whether ancient tablets or yesterday's news. Today we have film footage, etc. to aid correct record keeping, but we have nothing comparable from ancient times—just inscribed tablets and the like. There is nothing to prove that these documents contain truths but, for now at least, they are the closest we can get to knowing what went on at the time.[44]

And what went on was the advanced manufacture of complex life-extending chemicals. It seemed that Gardner's thinking was heavily dependent on Zecharia Sitchin, especially the material on Sumerian "gods" as aliens; that is classic Sitchin, who we know is obsessed with Sumeria. But Gardner disagrees and believes that his work is more about what happened *after*, not who ultimately started the Grail bloodline. For him von Däniken and Sitchin are not important: "Their books were of no influence at all really—although I've read most of their works. Both Sitchin and von Däniken are ufologists (to coin a term), whereas I am a pretty straightforward historian, albeit a revisionist historian. Those writers know more about their individual areas of subject interest than I do—so I have never tried to encroach in their domain as such."[45] Whither then the Annunaki and Jesus' alien origins?

Nevertheless, like Sitchin, Gardner's work represents an attempt to find a replacement faith for a Christianity that no longer inspires the same devotion its medieval incarnation compelled.

Medieval Christianity was a doctrine of hierarchy, status, and power. In its organization and development, the Church had become a surrogate for the fallen Roman Empire, and its members formed part of an elite governing class. Until the French Revolution of 1789, the clergy were still represented as one of the Estates General, and until the late nineteenth-century empires like Austria-Hungary and Russia ceded significant control to the organs of institutionalized faith, so much so that Marx was forced to declare religion the "opiate of the masses" because of its ability to stamp out resistance and drug the ignorant into complacency and compliance.

The opposite force gave us the modern world, beginning with the Protestant Reformation and moving steadily toward secularism. This philosophy was inherently linked to capitalism and liberal democracy. But as this belief system matured, it lost much of the spiritual trappings that made the institutional Church a source of mental safety and security. Especially in Europe, the old faith lost its attraction, and surveys showed belief reached a low point during the late 1990s. Books like Sitchin's and Gardner's were a way to recapture that lost spirituality and recast it in modern terms. Gardner specifically ties

Jesus to Darwinian evolution and to democratic values in his attempt to revitalize Christianity in Europe:

> The Grail quest is governed by an overriding desire for honest achievement. It is the route by which all can *survive* among the *fit*, for it is the key to the harmony and unity at every social and natural station. The Grail Code recognizes advances by merit, and acknowledges community structure— but above all things it is entirely democratic.[46]

It is therefore a belief system to fit the age, a belief system that can cast aside the detritus of Western civilization's systems of class, race, and hierarchy and embrace the anarchic democracy of liberty, equality, and fraternity. In short, it is an attempt to create a faith for a new world order. As he told me, "Today we still live in a feudal environment of laws instead of codes. Hence our system is thoroughly undemocratic. The Quest prevails as a search for enactment of the Code—i.e. Government *by* the people *for* the people, as against what we have: a feudal system based on government *of* the people."[47]

Others, however, would carry this quest further. Instead of finding a substitute *for* religion, they would instead find a substitute religion. Inspired by Zecharia Sitchin and by the burgeoning UFO movement, these groups would go on to create the ultimate legacy of the Great Cthulhu, contributing to that time when mankind would be "beyond good and evil" that would herald the Old Ones' return.

16

THE UFO CULTS AND HUMAN CLONING

Near the end of March 1997, the spectacular comet Hale-Bopp blazed across the night sky, and with its arrival, the wave of extraterrestrial speculation accidentally inaugurated by H. P. Lovecraft turned deadly. Thirty-nine followers of the Heaven's Gate cult rejoiced at the news broadcast on Art Bell's *Coast to Coast AM* radio show that a strange, unidentified object had been spotted following in the tail of the comet and that this object was possibly an alien spacecraft, a UFO. This was their signal to prepare for the end, for this was the sign that extraterrestrials had returned and the cult needed to shed its flesh-and-blood containers to meet the aliens.

In their spacious nine-thousand-square-foot Spanish-style mansion in Rancho Santa Fe, California, the cultists dressed in flowing black shirts, black sweatpants, and brand-new black Nike sneakers. They placed on their arms *Star Trek* "Away Team" badges, emulating their favorite science fiction show's interstellar travelers.[1] Following the orders of their leader, Marshall Herff Applewhite, they consumed a cocktail of drugs, vodka, and applesauce; placed plastic bags over their heads; and died en masse, in groups of fifteen, fifteen, and seven. Before the end, the last two men scheduled to die laid out the cultists' bodies on bunk beds and mattresses and covered their faces with purple shrouds. Then they, too, prepared for death in the mansion decorated with posters of *The X-Files* and *E.T.*, though there was no one left to put purple shrouds over their faces. It was the largest mass suicide in United States history.[2]

When the authorities found the bodies of the twenty-one men and eighteen women, aged twenty-six to seventy-two, they at first thought they were all young men because they all had short hair, smooth skin, and had no identifying sexual characteristics. Some of the men had even been castrated to overcome their humanness.[3] The dead had left videotapes explaining what had happened. One cultist took issue with those who criticized her choices in life: "People in the world who thought I'd completely lost my marbles—they're not right. I couldn't have made a better choice."[4]

Another cultist explained Heaven's Gate's strange belief system, relating it to the "beam me up" transport system used on the *Star Trek* science fiction TV show:

> We watch a lot of *Star Trek*, a lot of *Star Wars*, it's just, to us, it's just like going on a holodeck. We've been training on a holodeck . . . [and] now it's time to stop. The game's over. It's time to put into practice what we've learned. We take off the virtual-reality helmet . . . go back out of the holodeck to reality to be with, you know, the other members on the craft in the heavens.[5]

The Heaven's Gate cult members believed that by committing suicide, their souls would ascend to a UFO trailing in the wake of the Hale-Bopp comet, which would take them to a type of paradise, the "Level Above Human," which served as a way station on the path to yet higher levels outside this universe. Some said the UFO was actually Sitchin's twelfth planet, Nibiru, while others claimed it merely heralded its imminent arrival. When a photograph surfaced on the Internet claiming to show this UFO, the cult took action. Astronomers later confirmed that the alleged UFO in the photograph of Hale-Bopp was nothing more than a star.[6]

Heaven's Gate began in 1975, in the heady days when the ancient-astronaut theory was in its first florescence and UFO abductions first garnered public attention. At the beginning, as at its end, extraterrestrials had saturated the media and gained a large share of legitimacy. Applewhite and his consort, Bonnie Lu Trusdale Nettles, known as "Bo and Peep" or "Ti and Do," were eventually able to attract between two hundred and one thousand followers at the cult's peak. Their philosophy was a strange mix of Christianity, gnosticism, and science fiction, a perfect recipe for a millennial group awaiting salvation on a flying saucer.

Applewhite and Nettles held that Jesus Christ was a messenger of this Level Above, sent by the extraterrestrials to preach their coming, and reactionaries murdered him for his radical doctrines. Only by following Christ's path, freeing oneself of all that is human, can one ascend to the flying saucer and the Level Above Human. While this is bizarre, in my mind it drew strong parallels to a story by H. P. Lovecraft, "The Whisperer in Darkness," the first alien abduction tale. While there is no evidence that the Heaven's Gate cult directly borrowed from this story, it is by now obvious that much of the ancient-astronaut theory supported by Heaven's Gate derived in the first instance from Lovecraft.

In the story, Lovecraft describes how a race of aliens, the Mi-Go or Fungi from Yuggoth, terrorize a scholar named Henry Akeley in his home in rural Vermont. The aliens do not want their presence known, and Akeley suspects that they will "kill me or *take me off the earth to where they come from*."[7] These creatures came from a planet called Yuggoth, "at the rim of the solar system; but this was itself merely the populous outpost of a frightful interstellar race whose ultimate source must lie far outside even the Einsteinian space-time continuum or greatest known cosmos."[8] Gradually, the aliens close in on Akeley and cut off every route of escape. The aliens eventually take Akeley from Earth, ripping his brain from his body and placing his consciousness in a cylinder for transport to Yuggoth.

Lovecraft identified Yuggoth with "the new planet Pluto," just discovered at the time of his writing.[9] With some speculating that the object behind Hale-Bopp was either Nibiru or a taxi to it, the parallels with Heaven's Gate were unmistakable.

If Heaven's Gate was focused on the here and now, other cults would look deeper into the past to find communion with their alien gods. As we shall see, one such cult would eventually cause a public outcry when it claimed to have cloned a human being because the ancient aliens told them to. Of course, cults are not recent phenomena and have been part of the religious landscape as long as there have been religions. Some have even taken their beliefs to dangerous extremes, like the Jim Jones in Guyana People's Temple, whose 938 members committed mass suicide in 1978. However, cults devoted to the worship of space creatures became a decidedly modern phenomenon, growing out of the middle twentieth century's paranoia over modern technology and the space race. As we have seen, some in the Satanist community went so far as to take H. P. Lovecraft's fictional mythos literally and worship the Old Ones as though they were real. Others revered flying saucers.

UFO cults were nothing new in the 1970s, when "Bo" and "Peep" founded Heaven's Gate. They had existed almost since the beginning of the modern UFO era, and they continued into the twenty-first century as a technological faith recasting outdated religions into modern molds. As we have seen, the Aetherius Society was one such group, believing that Venusians held the key to human fate. Other groups like Christ's Brotherhood and the Association of Sananda and Sanat Kumara held that UFOs had quasi-divine powers, and on the other extreme, fundamentalist Christians began to believe that UFOs were manifestations of the devil.[10]

The most successful of the pure UFO cults was Unarias, a group that worships flying saucers and awaits their return. Founded in 1954 by Ernest and Ruth Norman, who believed themselves incarnations of the Judeo-Christian archangels Raphael and Uriel, Unarius stands for the Universal Articulate Interdimensional Understanding of Science. According to the group, human beings have an evolutionary mandate to seek higher levels of consciousness with the aid of communion with extraterrestrial beings, who are actually humans living on other planets.[11] The "Unarias Academy of Science" attracted only a small following between its foundation and the death of Ernest Norman in 1971. Thereafter, under the flamboyant Ruth Norman (Uriel), Unarius grew into a worldwide network of "study centers" spanning the globe from Florida to Poland.[12] The Unarians revere the scientist Nikola Tesla for his attempts to build an energy transmission tower, which David Hatcher Childress said caused the Tunguska Event of 1908.[13]

Dressed up in the guise of science, Unarius denied that it was a religion or a philosophy and proclaimed that its teachings about reincarnation and extraterrestrial life were verifiable facts in a new science of life.[14] The Unarians believed that humanity would be saved from its millennia-long spiritual regression by extraterrestrial saviors from the Pleiades, the constellation best known as the "seven sisters" of the night sky. This was to happen in 1974, but when this did not occur, the date was moved to 1975, then 1976, and finally 2001, when the first alien ship, from the planet Myton, was to land on the lost continent of Atlantis.[15] The Unarians held that, according to the "space scientist" Alta of the planet Vixall, 2001 would be the time when the "Space Brothers" would come to save Earth:

The reason will be that in 2001 A.D., those individuals who have been working for many, many years to wake up man; those individuals who have functioned in the communities in the space societies and who have been working silently, behind the scenes, will have helped to change the psychological current, the atmosphere of planet Earth, as to the reality of space being occupied by other human beings on other terrestrial planets.[16]

The Unarians prepared for the arrival of the aliens, but they were sorely disappointed. They had suffered from high attrition rates over the decade before the prophesied return of the aliens, and this failed prophecy surely did little for recruitment. When the beings from the planet Myton did not arrive, Unarian leaders announced they had made "mental contact" with them, and the aliens said they would not arrive until humanity was prepared to accept the reality of extraterrestrial beings.[17] Given the prevalence of aliens in our media, one wonders how much more acceptance is needed.

But the Unarians were essentially a futurist group, using their extraterrestrials as a prop for their deification of a strange form of science. As such, their claim that the Unarian plan was a million years old does not really make them an ancient-astronaut religion.[18] Stranger cults would instead use the extraterrestrials as gods who could provide a divine origin for group members and raise them above the common mass of humanity through their revealed knowledge of the human past. In this, these groups were little different than early Hebraic groups who claimed a covenant with God, or Mormonism claiming a special revelation from an archangel.

The Nuwaubians are one such cult, one that draws more heavily from the work of Robert Temple and Zecharia Sitchin than UFO literature. The Nuwaubians are an African-American cult that grew out of a 1960s-era Sufi group emulating the success of the Nation of Islam. Over time, their religion grew more eccentric and came to embrace ancient-astronaut beliefs and the history of Earth presented by Zecharia Sitchin. The Nuwaubians hold that African-Americans are actually Native Americans who came from Nubia in the distant past but whose ancestral memories of this are kept repressed by an oppressive white culture. The Nuwaubian leader, Dwight York, claims to be the representative of the Annunaki, who, as in Sitchin, came to Earth in the distant past and created humanity through genetic engineering. He teaches that Nuwaubians can become gods through following his teachings and communing with the Annunaki, who, again as in Sitchin, will return to usher in a golden age.[19]

The Nuwaubians number around five hundred and function as their own nation in rural Georgia, complete with their own passports and licenses. Under the title "The United Nuwaubian Nation of Moors," they claim the sovereignty rights due to Native American groups. They use ancient Egyptian garb and Plains Indians' insignia like feather headdresses as their costume and speak their own language, Muskogee. Though an Afrocentrist movement providing a black reaction against white cultural hegemony, Nuwaubians uniquely merge Afrocentrist views with ancient astronauts and extraterrestrial genesis.[20] Nuwaubians have been accused of several crimes, including fraud and child molestation.[21]

By far, however, the Raëlian Revolution was the most successful, most famous, and most controversial of the ancient-astronaut religions. It, too, has roots in the 1970s, and it combined the ancient-astronaut craze with the UFO movement in a final apotheosis of our themes. In Raëlianism, all the major themes of our study come together in a final reckoning with science and society.

On December 13, 1973, French race-car driver and magazine journalist Claude Vorilhon was visiting a French volcano when an extraterrestrial spacecraft descended before him. A four-foot-tall pale green humanoid creature with almond-shaped eyes and dark hair emerged from the craft and spoke to him in fluent French.[22] The creature took Vorilhon onboard the ship and explained to him the mysteries of the universe. The aliens ordered Vorilhon to form a movement to spread the aliens' message, and they bestowed a new name upon the journalist, who was from then on known as Raël.[23]

Vorilhon's abduction came only a few years after the 1966 publication of *The Interrupted Journey*, the book detailing Betty and Barney Hill's terrifying and involuntary "abduction." As we have seen, in the years that followed the book's release a veritable wave of alien abductions swept the globe; however, Vorilhon's abduction has far greater similarities to George Adamski's meetings with creatures from Venus during the 1950s, where friendly Venusians treated Adamski as a cosmic equal, or to George King of the Aetherius Society, who claimed the Venusians had come to appoint him Earth's ambassador to a galactic counsel. Then, as here, the extraterrestrials were beneficent, loving creatures who wanted to act as intercessors in the process of saving mankind. Vorilhon took the Adamski-King model a step further and added a rich and textured background drawn from the ancient-astronaut frenzy, which had taken Europe by storm several years before it went mainstream in the United States thanks to the works of Robert Charroux, Louis Pauwles, and Jacques Bergier, from whom Erich von Däniken would derive many of his ideas. Significantly, Charroux, Pauwles, and Bergier were all French authors whose views were well known in France at the time of Vorilhon's abduction. Though it is impossible to confirm, it is not unreasonable to assume that Vorilhon had at least a passing familiarity with these works. The Raëlian Web site officially endorsed

Charroux's 1967 work *Masters of the World* as well as Zecharia Sitchin's *Twelfth Planet*, so we know books of this type are not unfamiliar to Vorilhon.[24]

However, the presiding bishop of the US Raëlian Movement, Bishop Ricky Roehr, disagreed. Roehr told me that he did not know what books Raël had read before meeting the alien creature, but he felt that it was uncertain that Raël could have been exposed to ancient astronaut works or the fiction of H. P. Lovecraft: "I doubt it since Raël was living in a very rural area of France and wanted only to be a race car driver."[25] I had wanted to find out more about Raël and the Raëlian belief system, so I contacted the movement and asked questions. I was surprised that the group's representatives were kind, generous, and helpful, very different from the image of them I had formed from media coverage. Nevertheless, I found it difficult to believe that there was no influence from the ancient-astronaut theory, then so popular, during the formative years of the Raëlian faith. After all, as we shall shortly see, the things the alien told him sounded remarkably similar to passages from *Chariots of the Gods?* or *Twelfth Planet*.

While Vorilhon was onboard the ship, the alien told him that the Bible actually formed a record of the alien creatures' activities on the earth. The creatures called themselves Elohim, meaning those who came down from the sky, and later generations mistook the word to mean God; therefore, the God of the Bible is really the alien Elohim. The aliens told Vorilhon during their meetings over the next five mornings that they genetically engineered humanity in their own image, and they deigned that humanity should remain blissfully ignorant of science lest it corrupt and kill them. Then they changed their mind and made scientists out of humans. The aliens bequeathed civilization to humanity and gave them the tools to learn all knowledge. Further, they held that humanity should be run by a "geniocracy," that is, a rule by geniuses, to create good government. All of this could be proved by reading the Bible carefully, noting that passages like "God created the heavens and the earth" really meant that the Elohim aliens had discovered the planet.[26] The story of Adam and Eve's expulsion from the Garden of Eden was nothing more than the aliens kicking humanity out of their zoolike laboratory habitat in the Holy Land after the humans' aggressive nature manifested and became too much for the aliens to take.[27]

They also revealed the ultimate secrets of existence. The earth, they said, was a mere atom in an infinitely larger being, whose own planet was an atom in another, still larger, being. This process went on infinitely upward. Each atom on earth was itself a planet teeming with intelligent life, whose own atoms were still smaller planets, on and on, to infinity. Moreover, according to Raël, "There is no 'God' but there is the Elohim, our Creators. . . . Also there is no autonomous soul flying from the body after death, but there is the genetic code which allows access to eternal life."[28] This genetic code would become an obsession for the Raëlians.

Further, the extraterrestrial told Raël that he had an important mission to fulfill. Like Mohammed for Islam and Joseph Smith for Mormonism, Raël had been chosen to receive the dictated works of a higher power. He was charged with creating a new religion to spread the word of the alien gods and prepare the world for their arrival. He was to build an embassy for the space voyagers in the heart of Jerusalem when the time was right. The extraterrestrial creature told Vorilhon that the aliens could not show themselves to masses of humanity because they feared that mankind was not prepared to accept their reality. Further, they feared that landing their craft in a particular spot would imply an endorsement of either a capitalist or communist government, and this was something they wanted to avoid.[29]

And the alien also told him that they had impregnated his mother and erased her memory of the event. "She had a boyfriend. She thought her boyfriend was my father," Raël explained.[30] Half-alien, Raël was uniquely qualified to start his faith, which he christened the Raëlian Revolution. He announced his beliefs in his book *The Message Given by Extra-Terrestrials* in 1974. That year he stopped auto racing to focus on his movement, which he claims has fifty-five thousand followers in eighty-four countries.[31] Experts, however, say there are only around twenty thousand to thirty thousand members, the majority of whom live in Europe's Francophone countries, Quebec, and Japan.[32]

Raël is not shy about his status in the worldwide Raëlian community, openly comparing himself to Jesus at seminars he holds for believers:

> You are being offered the most extraordinary opportunity—to have the experience of a lifetime—by coming to the seminars. This year, I will probably still be there. I can never be sure that I will be there next year, nor in the years to come. So, this may be your last chance to attend. Perhaps you have dreamed of attending a seminar given by Jesus, Buddha, or Mohammed. Well it's too late. With me, it is still possible . . . but not for long.[33]

The Raëlian organization attracted many followers who were seeking a replacement faith that could incorporate materialistic science into a spiritual system. Raëlianism seemed to offer such a faith, and with its appeal to an ancient past filled with alien beings, it offered a historical richness that UFO cults like Unarias could not quite match. Unarias and its kin seemed increasingly like science fiction relics of the whiz-bang future of the 1950s. By contrast, Raël's system of belief still offered the same hope for the future inherent in the UFO movement, but he tempered it with an appeal to a glorious past courtesy of the ancient-astronaut theory. According to one Raëlian bishop,

> Our primitive ancestors wave the "tradition flag," claiming
> that the past is always better. Nothing could be more false.
> Our ancestors were primitive and barbaric. The only thing we
> should learn from most of our ancestors is what *not* to do.[34]

Nevertheless, the past still held import because it was the time
when the aliens came to Earth and created mankind, the glorious first time of creation. Thus, Raël synthesized Erich von
Däniken's appeal to a mysterious and wondrous past with
Zecharia Sitchin's quasi-religious evocation of the aliens'
return. Taken together, these streams formed the center of the
Raëlian religion, and the religion had a powerful attraction to
scientists. Even some in the scientific community fell under the
Raëlian spell, seeing in the ancient-astronaut theory a creation
myth more satisfying than the cosmic nothingness of atheism,
materialism, and evolution. The Raëlians claim scientists in
several fields among their members.[35]

Raël further gave his movement the trappings of organized
religion. He opened cult centers, conducted seminars, and
taught "sensual meditation" techniques to awaken the mind.
The Raëlian faith encouraged free love and sexual exploration.
Raël began wearing a distinctive all-white uniform much like
those worn in *Star Wars*; he tied his hair in a Jedi hairdo. Combined with neatly trimmed jet black facial hair, he gave the
appearance of a pope from the year 3000. Around his neck, he
wore a pendant of his group's new logo. Raël is said to have
"received" from the aliens the symbol for his faith, a Star of
David inscribed with a swastika, a symbol that meant infinity
or the sun millennia before Hitler adopted it for Nazism.[36] The
symbol, however, was changed in 1991. The swastika was
replaced with a swirl. It seems that Jewish leaders in Jerusalem
were not too keen on giving space for a UFO embassy to a
group using a swastika as its symbol. In 1997 Raël obtained the
"permission" of the Elohim to change the symbol if it would

facilitate the building of the embassy, for which he had raised $7 million. However, this change did not help much. Israeli leaders still refused to give him land for his embassy.[37] For now he has had to content himself with UFOland, the movement's extraterrestrial theme park in Canada.

The following year, the Raëlians began distributing condoms to high school students in Quebec after a local school board declined to install condom vending machines in their schools. The Raëlians said that they wanted wake up the school board to their responsibilities,[38] by which they presumably meant encouraging the Raëlian brand of "sensual" exploration. The media seized on this story of the Raëlian sensual meditation and ran salacious stories in the 1990s about Canada's UFO sex cult.

But the Raëlian Revolution had a more sinister aspect than the sex-and-UFO trappings the public saw. Behind the scenes the Raëlians were working to turn science fiction into science fact. In 1968 Erich von Däniken had written:

> Dim, as yet undefinable ages ago an unknown spaceship discovered our planet. . . . The spacemen artificially fertilized the female members of this [prehuman] species, put them in a deep sleep, so ancient legends say, and departed. Thousands of years later, the space travelers returned and found scattered specimens of the genus [sic] homo sapiens. They repeated their breeding experiments several times until finally they produced a creature intelligent enough to have the rules of society imparted to it.[39]

Or, more directly: "I put forward the speculative idea that 'God' had created man *in his own image* by means of an artificial mutation."[40]

Clearly, the parallels between von Däniken's ideas written down in 1968 and Raël's 1974 description of how the Elohim (also discussed by von Däniken) created humanity through genetic engineering are striking. More striking still is that this same argument would appear yet again in Zecharia Sitchin's 1976 work, *The Twelfth Planet*, which Raël would embrace, equating Sitchin's Annunaki to his own Elohim. Sitchin and von Däniken thereafter provided an important mythological backdrop to Raëlian belief.

But the ancient-astronaut authors had never taken their speculations to the next level. They did not act on their theories. Raël was different. Encouraged by the birth of the first test-tube baby, Raël began to harbor a notion that the extraterrestrials were not the only creatures that would create life. The Elohim seemed to tell him that humans, too, should create life in their own image. After the birth of Dolly the sheep, the world's first cloned mammal, proved in 1997 that it was scientifically possible to make genetic duplicates of living adult animals, Raël started to act. He heard on the radio that the pope denounced human cloning, so he decided to score a public relations victory by publicly opposing the Catholic Church, which he considered an enemy of his faith. He set up a shell company in the Bahamas, made a public statement about his desire to clone a human, and was off and running: "For a minimal investment of $3,000 in U.S. funds, it got us media coverage worth more than $15 million . . . I am still laughing. Even if the project had stopped there, it would have been a total success."[41]

As justification, Raëlians noted that cloning was an important tenet of their faith. As worshipers of science, they saw advancement in the sciences as a religious duty. According to Raëlian views, cloning was the only possible way to achieve immortality by perpetuating the individual's genetic code and "downloading" memories into new bodies.[42] Since there was no eternal soul, science would find a replacement.

Raël had enlisted French chemist and fellow Raëlian Brigitte Boisselier years before to help prepare the movement for the time to come when cloning would become a reality, and Raël wanted to be on the forefront of this new science in order to please the Elohim and prove that mankind had truly developed in the image of its alien ancestors. When Dolly was born, they were ready: "Raël told us this would happen," Boisselier told *Discover* magazine in 1998, "so when we heard the news we weren't shocked; we were organized."[43] Just one month after the announcement of Dolly's birth, the Raëlians launched Clonaid, the world's first human cloning company with Boisselier as scientific director. Within six months, more than one hundred people had signed up for cloning services at a price of $200,000 per clone.[44] The group also set up Clonapet to create genetic replicas of animals.[45]

A few other non-Raëlian researchers also attempted to clone a human, but they were not as well funded or as well organized as the Raëlians, at first. Despite the fact that at the founding of Clonaid the scientists responsible for Dolly had not yet made public the details of their work, Boisselier was confident she could apply the same technique to making a human being.

Roughly speaking, the process of cloning involves removing the nucleus, the part containing genetic material, the DNA, from the center of an adult cell and injecting it into an egg cell of the same species whose own nucleus has been removed. Then, the scientists bathe the egg in chemicals and jolt it with electricity to induce the egg to begin splitting and growing into an embryo. If all goes well, it will grow into a genetic duplicate of the adult whose DNA it contains.[46] Unfortunately, this happens rarely, and most clones either die or are born malformed for reasons not yet fully understood. Despite the deep risks to the cloned child, not to mention the psychological problems any clone would encounter, Bishop Roehr told me Raëlians considered it their duty to start cloning efforts

for the same reason proponents of IVF [in vitro fertilization], organ transplants, blood transfusions, surgery and countless other procedures supported new technologies in the past decades. The technology will need to be developed just as IVF etc. was, and when developed there will be only positive health consequences, namely a healthy, disease free eternal life! The first step in human cloning has taken place. Cloning has been achieved and will be more developed in the future into a technology that gives us eternal life. We will eventually be able to transfer our memory into a new fully-grown clone of ourselves (not just a baby), thus reaching eternal life.[47]

Clonaid set up a laboratory in an old high school in West Virginia and began work in an attempted resurrection of a dead eleven-month-old baby, whose parents desperately wanted a clone of their child.[48] By 2001, Clonaid said it was only weeks away from cloning a human being when the federal government stepped in. On March 27, 2001, the United States Food and Drug Administration delivered a letter to Clonaid's laboratory warning the group that it was in violation of FDA regulations. Later in the year, a federal grand jury in Syracuse, New York, launched a formal inquiry into Clonaid and the Raëlians. After the grand jury subpoenaed telephone records and other documents, the FDA raided the cloning lab and ordered all efforts to stop.[49] Boisselier then appeared before Congress to read a tearful letter from a man who had donated $500,000 to Clonaid to resurrect his dead son.[50]

The FDA would not confirm at the time how far along the Raëlians had come in their attempts, but the Raëlians continued their work in an undisclosed location to keep out of the law's reach. On December 27, 2002, the world woke to the shocking news that the group had cloned a human being. At a news conference in Miami, Florida, that morning, Brigitte Boisselier, pushing back her polychrome hair and dressed in a black jacket and Raëlian-symbol pendant, stood at a bank of microphones to tell the world that the first clone, baby "Eve," had been born in an undisclosed country. She also announced that a former ABC News science journalist, Michael Guillen, would lead a team of scientists to document and confirm that baby Eve was a clone.[51] "It's very important to remember we are talking about a baby," Boisselier said. "She is not a monster or some result of something that is disgusting. She is a very healthy baby with very happy parents."[52] However, Boisselier declined to provide a photograph or any proof that the baby existed, let alone was a clone.

By the next day, reaction had come in from all over the world. Bioethicists, traditional religious groups, and scientists had all condemned the cloning announcement. The White House released a statement saying President Bush "believes like most Americans that human cloning is deeply concerning, and he strongly supports legislation banning human cloning."[53] Congress set to work on a federal ban of reproductive human cloning, but debate stalled over whether so-called therapeutic cloning, the creation of clone cells for replacement organs, would be allowed. Eventually, building on the cloning ban in place in four states, the United States government banned reproductive human cloning within America's borders, ostensibly to protect the sanctity of human life and protect potential clones from medical complications. However, other scientists not affiliated with Raëlianism, like Dr. Panos Zavos and Dr. Severino Antinori, continued cloning efforts in other countries that had not yet banned the procedure. By 2005 the cloning of human embryos, if not whole humans, had been accomplished in South Korea.

Raëlian Bishop Ricky Roehr told me that the US and state government bans on cloning were hypocritical:

> [I]f the governments were really so concerned about protecting the sanctity of human life, they would not make every invention/discovery into another weapon. The auto was invented, they made it into a tank. The atom was split, they made it into a bomb. Biological discoveries were made into

biological weapons. Chemical discoveries were developed into chemical weapons. The list is long here. It's never the scientists but it's the governments that use technology in a bad way. These technologies—including cloning—*will* happen.[54]

Thus, of course, it must be, for science is the true subject that UFO religions actually worship, a science dressed in the guise of semidivine extraterrestrials. It is not the science that is evil, only the governments that use it. Of course, this invites the question of good and evil, which is itself a decidedly Western phenomenon. Though UFO groups claim that their morality and faith comes from the stars, it is surprising how very Western their dichotomous vision really is. Here again is the good and evil of Christian lore wrapped in the guise of good science and evil governments.

But all of that aside, skeptics quickly pointed out that Clonaid had not produced any evidence of a human clone, even as it promised that four more clone babies would be born within a month's time.[55] By January 2003, Boisselier had changed her tune. No longer would there be DNA testing of the cloned baby. Blaming a Florida lawsuit that threatened to take custody of a cloned child, Boisselier announced that the parents would not allow DNA testing.[56] The promised tests were never done, the baby was never seen, and the Raëlian cloning effort was widely condemned as a hoax designed to achieve maximum publicity, which is all Raël really wanted when he launched cloning efforts in 1997.

Interestingly, after most scientists and most members of the media decided the Raëlian cloning claims were a hoax, the Raëlian movement backed off its earlier support of Dr. Boisselier. Despite Raël's joint appearances with the cloning doctor on talk shows and news shows in the weeks following the event, the Raëlians denied sponsoring Boisselier's work when I asked Bishop Roehr about the skeptics who doubted the Raëlian cloning effort:

The "skeptics" you refer to are right in one thing that you state. The Raëlian Movement has not produced a clone. It is Dr. Boisselier and her private company that claim to have done so.[57]

This backtracking did not sit right with me. I remembered that Raël boasted that his initial investment of three thousand dollars had gained his group fifteen million dollars in publicity. I also remembered that Dr. Boisselier had said that she got the imperative to clone when Raël told her that it must happen. Bishop Roehr continued:

The Raëlian Movement has never tried to clone anyone. Nor has it claimed to. Dr. Boisselier is a Raëlian Bishop, and she is a scientist. The Raëlian Movement has never, nor will it ever, financially support her private company. When organ transplants or blood transfusions were the "fringe" technology of the day, and we know that among these brave scientists there were Christians and Jews, do you think that the media asked "why are the Christians developing this grotesque technology?" Or would they claim "Jews are destroying the sanctity of life!" Of course not! The fact that Dr. Boisselier is a Raëlian adds sensationalism to their articles.[58]

It seemed to me that the movement was trying to distance itself from Boisselier's failed cloning claims. From what I had read and heard, it seemed that the Raëlians were trying to regain their credibility as a religion by disclaiming involvement in a scientific adventure now seen as a hoax. Of course, that is only one explanation for the contradiction between earlier and current Raëlian statements. It is possible that "media sensationalism" was responsible for the linkage of Raëlians to Boisselier's cloning efforts, but based on statements by both Boisselier and Raël, I don't think so.

Just two days after my interview with Bishop Roehr, Dr. Boisselier made another startling claim. A British newspaper reported that Boisselier told it that "the cult" had set up a new company, Stemaid, to cure aging through the use of fetal stem cells, the controversial cells that differentiate into every kind of body tissue and that some believe could be coaxed into regenerating body parts. Boisselier also announced that a "second generation" of cloned children was nearing birth.[59] She planned to announce her stem cell discovery at a scientific conference in London, but it was canceled after organizers discovered the Raëlians had used a false name to get into the conference. Boisselier continued every few months to announce the arrival of more cloned babies, always without proof.

However, the fact remained that the Raëlian claims had affected US national policy and the global debate on the ethics of cloning. All around the world, governments and religious groups reacted to the events unfolding in Miami, Florida, on a timetable set by a UFO religion. For the first time, the Cthulhu Mythos of H. P. Lovecraft became an important player in government policy. Through the short fiction of Lovecraft to *Morning of the Magicians* and Erich von Däniken, and then to the UFO religions of Heaven's Gate and the Raëlian Movement, the mythology of extraterrestrials masquerading as gods in the ancient past grew ever larger. Now, in the twenty-first century, the consequences of Lovecraft's "sheer fun" are more dire than ever. Essential questions about who and what constitutes a human being, about what types of medical procedures can and cannot be performed are increasingly seen through a prism whose faces reflect back the tentacled octopoid creature called Cthulhu.

Ironically, Raëlian efforts to clone a human being may just bring about the fulfillment of a promise made in Lovecraft's fiction decades ago, when he made the mad Arab poet, Abdul Alhazred, sing his cryptic couplet, whose meaning takes on sinister shades when read in the light of the cloning debate:

That is not dead which can eternal lie
And with strange aeons, even death may die.[60]

CONCLUSION

17

A MODERN MYTHOLOGY
FOR TROUBLED TIMES

There probably is no used-book sale that does not feature at least a half-dozen copies of *Chariots of the Gods?* yellowing volumes rotting in the summer sun of too many garage sales, yard sales, and charity events. Though seldom selling for more than fifty cents, these moldering tomes represent a unique moment in Western culture, a turning point encapsulated in prose of the time when Western faith in science and Progress suffered a terminal shock. Though *Chariots* and its ilk were not the cause of this moment, they perfectly embodied the mood of a society unable to accept the authority of its political and corporate leaders. As the Raëlians noted, every scientific discovery led only to more pain; chemical research yielded toxic weapons, biological research yielded new toxins, and nuclear research yielded the potential of annihilation. Is it any wonder that so many turned away from an ideology that seemed to be in a dangerous infatuation with death to embrace instead the comfort of irrational belief? H. P. Lovecraft saw it coming in that great period of anxiety between the calamitous wars of the twentieth century:

> The sciences, each straining in its own direction, have hitherto harmed us little; but some day the piecing together of

dissociated knowledge will open up such terrifying vistas of reality, and of our frightful position therein, that we shall either go mad from the revelation or flee from the deadly light into the peace and safety of a new dark age.[1]

Following the nuclear devastation at Hiroshima and Nagasaki, it increasingly became clear during the course of the twentieth century that the new Dark Age was slowly arriving. The signs were everywhere. Like the first Dark Age, when the unifying force of Rome collapsed into tribal chiefdoms, fractured miniature states, and a Byzantine Empire as a much smaller medieval "superpower," so too did this new Dark Age see its own political fragmentation, as the number of sovereign governments grew from 55 in 1914 to 192 by the turn of the century. Just as the European empires of the nineteenth century served as modern analogs of Roman universal power, so too did the United States function as a renewed Byzantium in the fragmented political universe of the twenty-first century.

In the cultural field, the same process of calcification and stagnation had hit Western culture, halting in its tracks the centuries-long parade of Western innovation. Born into an endless cycle of reason and irrationalism, the interplay of science and Romantic notions fueled the fertility of the Western mind. But by the year 2000, the famed historian Jacques Barzun had proclaimed Western civilization had entered a phase of terminal decadence:

Many shrewd minds, accurately noting the condition of stasis, urged plausible remedies; nobody pretended that apart from science and techne [technology] advance was taking place. But some hesitation was shown about applying the word *Decadence* to the whole West and the whole era, as our distance from it now enables us to do without tremor.[2]

Barzun noted the similarity between the twilight of the West and the incipient Middle Ages, the twilight of antiquity. Then, as now, an educated elite ruled over the ignorant masses; then, as now, the finer points of high culture fell by the wayside as a general coarsening of society tore down the old forms of civilized life. Mysticism thrived in both periods. In its older form, mysticism built upon the one vital and active area of medieval life, the Catholic faith. In its modern form, today's mysticism embraces the one active and vital area of modern life: science. Modern cults, so similar to medieval sects and heresies, embrace science as the cover for their faith. UFO cults especially simply replace God and angels with aliens and extraterrestrials. In their worship of UFOs, they transfer to technology the fetish that earlier ages held for the dubious relics of plaster saints. But to some degree, all of Western society has come to embrace science as the ultimate arbiter of spiritual beliefs. A recent book phrased the problem eloquently:

> At the juncture in Western history, it is perhaps especially important to recall that spiritual values have long guided scientific endeavors, a fact that is clear from the history of alchemy, eugenics and more recent efforts to clone a human being following the religious tenets of the Raëlians. And now science is being employed to "prove" spiritual theories as well. In a culture that has trained itself for three centuries to trust the findings of science, such a procedure will certainly lend an advantage to the religious view that could enlist the largest number of scientists, or at least the most persuasive, in its support.[3]

And so it is not so different when believers in ancient astronauts go hunting for evidence of prehistoric extraterrestrial contact than it is when fundamentalist Christians try to use the methods of archaeological science to uncover traces of Noah's Ark or the cities of Sodom and Gomorrah. Both are, in essence, a concession that science is the ultimate arbiter of truth, and both seek to (mis)use science to give absolute authority to their beliefs. The Raëlians, for example, believe that their efforts to clone human beings will prove beyond doubt their fundamental belief that there is no God because humanity will have become equal to the Elohim. Creationists believe just as strongly that science will someday prove beyond doubt that God exists through evidence of His special creation. Both, of course, deny evolution, the cornerstone of modern science, even as they embrace the trappings and glamour of the laboratory.

But a more disturbing parallel to the Middle Ages can be found in the juvenile flavor of both ages. Self-taught historian Barbara Tuchmann, in her book *A Distant Mirror*, wrote that the primitive civilization of the fourteenth century felt like a society of adolescents: violent, impulsive, childish. One thirty-year-old living in twenty-first-century Chicago noted without irony that adults have increasingly come to embrace children's games, children's playthings, and children's holidays, like Halloween: "I think our generation is a little more hesitant to let go of childhood than past generations. We want to hang onto Peter Pan as long we can."[4] It hardly goes without saying that it is impossible to imagine Victorian statesmen appearing unkempt or discussing their preferred type of undergarment.[5] But today our society does not just tolerate but encourages such disclosures. The modern presidents of the United States have acted like teenagers writ large, and the policy consequences are self-evident. It seems likely that no Bismarck or Disraeli will emerge from this generation. Our education system has made sure that none in this generation will even know of Bismarck or Disraeli.

For every dedicated professor, like H. E. Legrand and Wayne Boese, who designed college courses to counteract the affects of the pseudoscientific revolution—and it is nothing less than a revolution—there are dozens of professional educators who will not or cannot do anything to stem the tide of irrational beliefs. In the twenty-first century, many of the top liberal arts colleges stopped requiring freshmen to learn the mainstream view of history at all, replacing traditional courses in the development of Western civilization with specialized offerings like "Gender and Nation in Latin America."[6] Without foundation courses, it was utterly impossible for many students to understand when reputed historians were offering them unevidenced views of history.

But if educators, taxed by poor training, violent and disruptive students, and shrinking budgets, did little, the media were much more to blame for the spread of pseudoscience and irrationalism. In love with ratings and sales, which, in turn, equaled profits, the mainstream media embraced the ancient-astronaut myth with a dedication seen only in the feeding behavior of sharks in bloody water. To appeal to the broadest audience, the media increasingly came to appeal to the uneducated, who watched ancient-astronaut programs and bought ancient-astronaut books. These sold well or got good ratings through an appeal to the sensational, the emotional, and the exotic. By contrast, when the media presented real science, especially archaeology, it was instead a dull, tired look at dead objects with monotone narrators and stilted music. More often than not, legitimate science was restricted to the low-rated and little-watched Public Broadcasting Service, the science channels on cable long ago having surrendered to the mass appeal of pseudoscience and sensationalized versions of archaeology.

Also, there were few books that popularized legitimate archaeology; the archaeologists spent their time producing technical articles for the publish-or-perish university tenure system. To fill the void, "alternative archaeology" and the ancient-astronaut theory would become the archaeological literature for the forgotten masses.

The result was as predictable as it was preventable: the

public at large had come to distrust the archaeologists it had rarely heard from and embraced the personable figures who presented them with a solution for all their questions. There was only one answer for every question in this version of archaeology. Depending on your beliefs, the answer was either aliens or a lost civilization. And the believers were rarely troubled by the implication in the ancient-astronaut theory that primitive peoples were unable to create their own civilizations, monuments, or wonders. Reproducing one of the worst vices of Lovecraft, his racism, these theories speculated that minorities, especially Native Americans, were incapable of building pyramids and temples or developing a sophisticated religion. Instead, they were as children waiting for the great tutors from space (or Atlantis) to come show them the way. Though few of the authors in the genre were overtly racist, the unintended consequence of their theories was to devalue the contributions of native and indigenous people to world culture and civilization.

With a public convinced that it was possible that aliens had given rise to civilization and possibly humanity itself, it was easy to see how H. P. Lovecraft, accidental father of the ancient-astronaut theory, could end up a victim of the belief system he inadvertently created. The fictional stories he wrote increasingly came to be seen as true. Some cult groups who embraced the false versions of the *Necronomicon* as real magical texts argued that Lovecraft had channeled the Old Ones from dimensions beyond time. They believed that his fiction was in fact true, that he had written the cosmic truths in the form of fiction to hide in plain sight his esoteric knowledge that only the elect should be privy to the reality of Cthulhu.

But the same process that created the ancient-astronaut theory from Lovecraft's fiction continues to operate today, though on a much smaller scale. In May 2003, a UFO newsletter called *UFO Roundup* sent out to believers in extraterrestrial visitation ran the following article:

RUINS OF KADATH FOUND IN ANTARCTICA?

A California TV crew missing since November 2002, a video they left behind and a mission by U.S. Navy SEALs are the key elements in a story that claims extensive prehistoric ruins have been found under the ice of Antarctica . . . The AtlantisTV [sic] production crew that shot the video is still missing . . .

"Two Navy officers who saw the tape . . . said it showed spectacular ruins and other things they couldn't go into," an NSF scientist reported. "We chalked it up to some kind of sub-zero-induced delusion until a chopper . . . full of Navy SEALs landed and picked them up and took off. Now, we're scratching our heads . . . "

Science fiction author Howard Phillips Lovecraft (1890–1937) claimed in several stories that a prehistoric city existed in Antarctica called "Kadath of the Cold Waste."

Lovecraft described its "discovery" in his novel *At the Mountains of Madness*, written between January and March 1931. Incredibly, one of his passages is a precise description of a scene in the AtlantisTV [sic] video . . .[7]

The newsletter reported a "news release" originally found on the @lantisTV Web site, which claimed to provide the secret truth about an archaeological dig in Antarctica. Though the @lantisTV Web site clearly says that the dig is "fictional" and that @lantisTV is "earth's coolest entertainment" combining "fantasy and reality," many believed the hype.[8] Even though dozens of skeptical readers wrote to *UFO Roundup* to protest that the article was clearly fictional, it was clear that even more were ready to entertain the idea that Lovecraft's Ancient Ones really were waiting in the icy wastes of Antarctica. I wrote to Joseph Trainor, the editor of *UFO Roundup*, to find out what happened. He told me that the article "was a case in which Lovecraft's fiction, recycled through a source in Europe unaware of the entertainment Web site's purpose, came back to the USA as a supposed 'fact.'"[9]

As we have seen, this selfsame process led from Lovecraft's postwar success in France to the creation of the ancient-astronaut theory. Once again Lovecraft had made the circuit from fiction to fact. This time, however, readers quickly picked up on the mistake and by the next week a wave of reader response prompted *UFO Roundup* to retract the story. All this was made possible by Lovecraft's increased visibility and popularity in the 1990s and early twenty-first century.

Aside from the cultists chanting paeans to Lovecraftian "gods" like Yog-Sothoth and Nyarlathotep, Lovecraft had become a big business. Thousands indulged in Chaosium's "Call of Cthulhu" role-playing game, and millions watched a new slate of Lovecraft-themed movies, the best of which, in my opinion, was *Dagon* (2001), based on "The Shadow Over Innsmouth." A toy company even put out a line of stuffed animals based on monsters from the Lovecraft pantheon. By 2005 one could order a stuffed Cthulhu wearing a Santa outfit or spy gear or dressed in beachwear—"Summer Fun Cthulhu." Besides the numerous editions of Lovecraft's works pouring out of several major publishers—from Del Rey to Penguin—several small publishing houses now produce exclusively Cthulhu Mythos fiction, including Hippocampus and Chaosium. The vast majority of the modern Cthulhu Mythos fiction does not live up to the high standards Lovecraft set in his own work.

Chances are that if he were alive to see all of this, H. P. Lovecraft would have been appalled. He considered his stories to be his art; to see Great Cthulhu, his embodiment of cosmic indifference, turned into a cuddly children's toy would likely have broken his heart. A lifelong scientific materialist, he would also take great umbrage that his literary legacy had spawned a debate over whether aliens had visited earth in the distant past and left their legacy in civilization and human DNA. When

Charles Fort made passing mention of the idea in 1919, Lovecraft called his work "nonsense." When he developed the concept in his own literature, he told anyone who asked that he did not want to mislead them; it was merely fiction.

The greatest irony, of course, is that, in essence, the ancient-astronaut belief of today is not Lovecraft's mythos at all. Lovecraft preached a cosmic indifference, where the aliens were utterly unconcerned with mankind, where humanity was simply a cog in the great machine that was the mindless cosmos. Instead, the ancient-astronaut theory has gradually humanized these indifferent aliens, adopting August Derleth's early revision, which divided the aliens into Good and Evil. Like the Christian host of heaven, the extraterrestrials in man's past have become beneficent angels, tempering the harsh truths concealed within Lovecraft's atheist mythology in favor of a neo-Christian view that replaced angels with aliens. Erich von Däniken started this process, bequeathing to the aliens the trappings once reserved for God. For him they are still an unknowable force, but unlike Lovecraft, these aliens are *directly interested* in mankind. Zecharia Sitchin broke further away, giving the "gods" names and human personalities. The UFO cults completed the transformation, rendering the aliens into a force of cosmic good. On the other extreme, Satanic *Necronomicon* cults transformed the aliens into personifications of cosmic evil. Either way, we are not in Lovecraft country anymore . . .

In a monument to the age we live in, the *New York Times* ran a story in November 2003 asking "Does Science Matter?" The newspaper reported that the public, disillusioned by institutional science's failure to produce the utopia promised in the mid-twentieth century visions of the golden future age, has turned against science. Increasingly, average people see science as useful only for "new gadgets and drugs."[10] In an age of relativism, many no longer believe that science can find transcendental truth, and if it can, they would prefer not to know, lest it rock the boat.

Pseudoscience provided a more comforting and safer alternative than the cold, abstract science of the white-coated priesthood. Ancient-astronaut theories and cult archaeology were accessible and personable ways to seize back power from unseen academies that arbitrarily directed our lives with contradictory dictates from on high about every life process, from diet to mortality to morality. This produced much of the absurdity of modern life: Will day care harm your child? Only if more than half of social scientists agree. Is an egg good for you or will it kill you? Depends on who conducted the study. Should you eat fewer carbohydrates? It must be Monday.

The Age of Relativity made it hard to stick to any firm convictions. Coupled with the rapid, unchecked development of technology—especially communications technology—the bedrocks of modern society broke loose. Postmodern philosophy preached that all beliefs were equal. It destroyed the foundations of previous belief systems but set up none of its own. Testament to the bankruptcy of its ideas, proponents could not even think of a name for their system except that it "came after modernism," which was the last coherent philosophy. Social mores fell by the wayside in the wake of the sexual revolution and the constant interruption of cell phones, while no new rules of etiquette took their place. Following the major events of the early twenty-first century, revisionists were already rewriting history before the ink was dry. The terrorist attacks in New York and Washington on September 11, 2001, spawned hundreds of conspiracy theories, and the pervasive questions about the US government's motives for invading Iraq two years later left nearly everyone unsure about what was really going on. Everything was open to interpretation. There were no right answers. Something was correct only it if were true for you. Every group was now entitled to its own history:

black history, women's history, and gay history. There was no longer human history.

And so we can see the appeal of ancient-astronaut and lost-civilization theories. They provide one answer with no questions asked. There is nothing to discuss, no weighing of competing truths. There is only the one Truth: extraterrestrials. It is the secular version of fundamentalist religion, and it is a reaction against the scientific order that helped to drive apart Western civilization. In its own way, cult archaeology is on the cutting edge of social development, paving the way for the final dissolution of the authoritarian, authoritative scientific order of the past three centuries.

In this we can also see the appeal of H. P. Lovecraft to our modern sensibilities. Though he wrote his tales three-quarters of a century ago, he provided a compelling and terrifying vision of a society in terminal decay and living on the brink of destruction. Lurking underneath the veneer of civilization lie monstrous reminders of man's barbaric past and his empty place in a cold, unfeeling cosmos. Everywhere, powerful, impersonal forces from Outside conspire to destroy the sane order of human society.

The Western world is now adrift amid its own decadence and decline, and it is Lovecraft who provides the mythology that helps us to understand the barbaric monsters whose visages peer at us from the tattered fabric of our society. Forces from Outside, totalitarianism, genocide, terrorism: these are our monsters, no less comprehensible than the pulsing and quivering of Cthulhu's gelatinous body or the non-Euclidean architecture of his sunken city of R'lyeh. The age-old battle between science and pseudoscience, between reason and irrationalism, between the Enlightenment and the Romantics will continue, with first one, then the other gaining the upper hand. Eventually, in the eternal cycle, this phase of irrational Romanticism will also pass and a new Age of Reason will be born. It has happened again and again in the course of Western civilization, and there is no reason to believe this cycle will stop anytime soon.

And when the stars come 'round again and the figurative monster rises from his tomb beneath the sea, the detritus of the old order will be swept away:

> Then in the slow creeping course of eternity, the utmost cycle of the cosmos churned itself into another futile completion, and all things became as they were unreckoned kalpas before. Matter and light were born anew as space once had known them; and comets, suns and worlds sprang flaming into life, though nothing survived to tell that they had been and gone, been and gone, always and always, back to no first beginning.[11]

APPENDIX

A CONTINUUM OF BELIEF

This continuum represents the range of beliefs chronicled in this book. The categories are not, however, mutually exclusive, and some of the advocates listed under each could appear in more than one place. For example, Erich von Däniken has fluctuated between extraterrestrial genesis and ancient astronauts. I have placed him under ancient astronauts because I tried to list names in the category with which they are most closely associated, but these categories are fluid and the reader is invited to draw new lines between them as desired.

EXTRATERRESTRIAL GENESIS

The belief that aliens genetically engineered humanity and are responsible for its civilization and ancient achievements. Because of their technological powers, these beings were mistaken for gods.

Advocates: Zecharia Sitchin
              Alan Alford
              Raëlian Revolution
              Louis Pauwles and Jacques Bergier

ANCIENT ASTRONAUTS

The belief that extraterrestrials visited Earth in the distant past and were responsible for planning or creating ancient monuments and religious traditions. These believers do not necessarily subscribe to extraterrestrial genesis.

Advocates: Erich von Däniken
Robert Temple
David Hatcher Childress
Laurence Gardner
Robert Charroux

LOST CIVILIZATION/HYPERDIFFUSIONISM

The belief that an advanced civilization once existed, and it bequeathed technology and ideology to ancient cultures we know today. Similar to ancient astronauts but without the aliens, hyperdiffusionists believe that some ancient gods are really memories of refugees from the lost civilization after its destruction.

Advocates: Graham Hancock
Robert Bauval
John Anthony West
Ignatius Donnelly
James Churchward
Helena Blavatsky

DIFFUSIONISM

The belief that ancient civilizations were in contact with one another and shared cultural or technological secrets. Similar to hyperdiffusionism, this belief does not need a third party to bequeath civilization.

Advocates: Mound builder mythmakers
               Other nineteenth-century scholars

MAINSTREAM CONSENSUS

The belief that most ancient civilizations developed on their own with only occasional contact with other ancient cultures who were not their direct neighbors. Some limited diffusion likely occurred, but there is no advanced lost civilization or extraterrestrial intervention.

Advocates: Mainstream archaeologists

SCIENTIFIC MATERIALISM

The belief that all that exists is matter and that the laws of physics are the only ultimate truths. Similar to the mainstream consensus, this belief holds that not only was there no advanced lost civilization and no alien intervention, but also such things are virtually impossible.

Advocates: H. P. Lovecraft

NOTES

CHAPTER 1

1. *Rod Serling's Night Gallery*, http://www.nightgallery.net (accessed May 25, 2004).

2. Martin H. Greenberg, Richard Matheson, and Charles G. Waugh, eds., *The Twilight Zone: The Original Stories* (New York: MJF, 1985), p. 1.

3. Rod Serling, foreword to *In Search of Ancient Mysteries*, by Alan Landsburg and Sally Landsburg (New York: Bantam, 1973), p. viii.

4. Ibid.

5. Ibid., pp. viii–ix.

6. Landsburg and Landsburg, *In Search of Ancient Mysteries*, p. 6.

7. Archaeologists use the spelling "Nasca" to refer to the culture that inhabited the Nazca desert.

8. Serling, foreword to *In Search of Ancient Mysteries*, p. viii.

9. Kenneth L. Feder, "Ten Years After: Surveying Misconceptions about the Human Past," *Cultural Resource Management* 18, no. 3 (1995): 11–14.

10. H. P. Lovecraft, *The Horror in the Museum and Other Revisions* (New York: Carroll & Graf, 1997), cover.

11. H. P. Lovecraft, "The Call of Cthulhu," in *Tales* (New York: Library of America, 2005), p. 182. I have tried to cite the most easily obtainable editions for the general reader. The scholar of Lovecraft is

directed to the authoritative but comparatively rare (and expensive) Arkham House editions for the modern corrected texts.

12. Walter E. A. van Beek, "Dogon Restudied: A Field Evaluation of the Work of Marcel Griaule," *Current Anthropology* 32 (1992): 157.

13. Robert Bauval and Adrien Gilbert, *The Orion Mystery* (New York: Three Rivers Press, 1994), pp. 7–9.

14. Ibid., p. 82.

15. Robert Bauval, message board posting to author via Graham Hancock Web site, http://www.grahamhancock.com, April 8, 2001.

CHAPTER 2

1. David E. Schultz and S. T. Joshi, introduction to *From the Pest Zone: Stories from New York*, by H. P. Lovecraft (New York: Hippocampus, 2003), pp. 7–31; S. T. Joshi, *Lovecraft: A Life* (West Warwick, RI: Necronomicon Press, 1996; reprint, 2004), pp. 353–412.

2. L. Sprague de Camp, *Lovecraft: A Biography* (New York: Barnes & Noble, 1996), p. 48.

3. Ibid., p. 50.

4. Ibid., pp. 270–73; Joshi, *Lovecraft: A Life*, p. 428.

5. Morton Klass, *Ordered Universes: Approaches to the Anthropology of Religion* (Boulder, CO: Westview Press, 1995), p. 151.

6. The opposite of materialism is idealism, the belief that all is spirit. Idealism went out of fashion long ago, and in a testament to the success of science, today virtually no major philosopher supports idealism.

7. Brian Fagan, *Ancient North America*, 3rd ed. (New York: Thames and Hudson, 2000), p. 32.

8. Ibid., p. 35.

9. Ignatius Donnelly, *Atlantis: The Antediluvian World* (Project Gutenberg, 2003), http://www.gutenberg.net/etext03/7ataw11.txt (accessed August 17, 2003).

10. Ibid.

11. Ibid. Of course this is not too far different from the more recent idea of the rule by "divine right" or the idea that God ordained a leader.

12. L. Sprague de Camp, *Lost Continents: The Atlantis Theme in History, Science, and Literature* (New York: Dover, 1970), pp. 51–55; Karl P. N. Shuker, *The Unexplained* (Dubai: Carlton Books, 1996), p. 89.

13. Ibid.

14. Theosophical Society in America Web site, http://www.theosophical.org (accessed August 9, 2003).

15. Daniel Caldwell, *The Esoteric World of Madam Blavatsky: Reminiscences and Impressions by Those Who Knew Her*, 2nd ed. preprint (Wheaton, IL: Theosophical Society, 2002), chap. 5, http://www.theosophical.org/theosophy/books/esotericworld/index.html (accessed August 10, 2003).

16. Ithaca, New York, has a reputation as one of America's most liberal cities. Among its attractions are Cornell University and Ithaca College, where Rod Serling taught television courses in the 1970s. Much of the economy is geared to students, who make up half its population during the school year, and the town has businesses devoted to hemp, alternative therapies, or quartz and crystal sexual aids.

17. Caldwell, *Esoteric World*, chap. 7a.

18. Theosophical Society in America Web site.

19. De Camp, *Lost Continents*, pp. 54–58; de Camp, *Lovecraft*, p. 167.

20. Shuker, *Unexplained*, p. 89. Atlantis and Mu were two other lost continents said to have been destroyed by volcanoes. Perhaps the catastrophic 1883 eruption of Krakatau in the Dutch East Indies, which was felt worldwide and claimed more than 36,000 lives, had influenced this choice of destructive agent. See de Camp's *Lost Continents* for more on this theme.

21. Caldwell, *Esoteric World*, chap. 20a.

22. Erich von Däniken, *Gods from Outer Space*, trans. Michael Heron (New York: Bantam, 1972), p. 137.

23. Shuker, *Unexplained*, p. 214; de Camp, *Lost Continents*, pp. 47–50.

24. Charles Fort, *The Book of the Damned* (New York: Horace Liveright, 1931), p. 164.

25. De Camp, *Lovecraft*, pp. 221–22.

CHAPTER 3

1. Noel Carroll, "The Nature of Horror," *Journal of Aesthetics and Art Criticism* 14, no. 1 (1987): 57.

2. Ibid.

3. Jacques Barzun, *From Dawn to Decadence: 500 Years of Western Cultural Life* (New York: HarperCollins, 2000), p. 218.

4. H. P. Lovecraft, *The Annotated Supernatural Horror in Literature*, ed. S. T. Joshi (New York: Hippocampus, 2000), p. 21.

5. Ibid., p. 31.

6. Mary Shelley, *Frankenstein* (New York: Ballantine Classic, 1991), pp. xxii–xxv.

7. Wilbur S. Scott, introduction to *Complete Tales and Poems*, by Edgar Allan Poe (Edison, NJ: Castle Books, 2001), pp. II–III.

8. Poe, *Complete Tales and Poems*, p. 784.

9. Susan J. Navarette, *The Shape of Fear: Horror and the Fin de Siècle Culture of Decadence* (Lexington: University of Kentucky Press, 1998), p. 112.

10. Allen W. Grove, "Rontgen's Ghosts: Photography, X-Rays, and the Victorian Imagination," *Literature and Medicine* 16, no. 2 (1997), http://muse.jhu.edu/ (accessed November 24, 2002).

CHAPTER 4

1. See discussion in Philip A. Shreffler, *The H. P. Lovecraft Companion* (Westport, CT: Greenwood Press, 1977). See S. T. Joshi, *Lovecraft: A Life* (West Warwick, RI: Necronomicon Press, 1996; reprint, 2004), pp. 399–401, for a discussion of Lovecraft's other influences.

2. H. P. Lovecraft, "The Call of Cthulhu," in *Tales* (New York: Library of America, 2005), pp. 182–83.

3. S. T. Joshi, "Howard Phillips Lovecraft: The Life of a Gentleman of Providence," H. P. Lovecraft Archive, http://www.hplovecraft.com (accessed April 3, 2002).

4. L. Sprague de Camp, *H. P. Lovecraft: A Biography* (New York: Barnes & Noble, 1996), p. 98.

5. Lovecraft, *Tales*, p. 181.

6. H. P. Lovecraft, *At the Mountains of Madness*, in *Tales*, p. 541.

7. Joshi, "Howard Phillips Lovecraft." See the author's further discussion in *H. P. Lovecraft: A Life*, chaps. 14 and 15.

8. H. P. Lovecraft, "The Horror at Red Hook," in *Tales*, p. 128.

9. Joshi, "Howard Phillips Lovecraft." See full discussion in Joshi's *Lovecraft: A Life*, chap. 23.

10. For example, I Samuel 5:1–8.

11. H. P. Lovecraft, "Dagon," in *The Transition of H. P. Lovecraft: The Road to Madness* (New York: Del Rey, 1996), p. 40.

12. Ibid.

13. H. P. Lovecraft, "The Temple," in *The Transition of H. P. Lovecraft: The Road to Madness*, p. 75.

14. H. P. Lovecraft, "The Nameless City," in *The Dream Cycle of H. P. Lovecraft: Dreams of Terror and Death* (New York: Del Rey, 1995), p. 63.

15. Ibid., p. 65.

16. Lovecraft, *Tales*, p. 167.

17. Ibid., p. 181. Note, too, the intentionally biblical cadence of the passage, reminiscent of the King James Version.

18. Ibid., p. 183.

19. De Camp, *H. P. Lovecraft: A Biography*, p. 333; cf. Joshi, *H. P. Lovecraft: A Life*, pp. 401–406.

20. To avoid confusion, I have used "Old Ones" to refer to the cosmic beings and "Ancient Ones" to refer to the aliens in Antarctica. Lovecraft used terms like "Old Ones," "Ancient Ones," and "Elder Ones/Things" interchangeably in his stories. Later authors attempted to codify which were which with varying degrees of success.

21. Erik Davis, "Calling Cthulhu," *Gnosis* (1995), http://www.levity.com (accessed August 3, 2002).

22. H. P. Lovecraft, "Quotes about the Necronomicon," H. P. Lovecraft Archive, http://www.hplovecraft.com (accessed August 4, 2003).

CHAPTER 5

1. *Weird Tales* was revived twice more, first in the 1970s and recently by DNA Publications, but never matched the quality of the original.

2. S. T. Joshi, *H. P. Lovecraft: A Life* (West Warwick, RI: Necronomicon Press, 1996; reprint, 2004), p. 298; L. Sprague de Camp, *H. P. Lovecraft: A Biography* (New York: Barnes & Noble, 1996), p. 212.

3. C. M. Eddy, "The Loved Dead," in *The Loved Dead and Other Revisions*, H. P. Lovecraft et al. (New York: Carroll & Graf, 1997), p. 154. The following account of the outrage over "The Loved Dead" is disputed. See discussion in Joshi, *H. P. Lovecraft: A Life*, p. 331.

4. See the recent popularity of Sylvia Browne, John Edward, and others.

5. Joshi, *H. P. Lovecraft: A Life*, pp. 329–31; de Camp, *H. P. Lovecraft: A Biography*, p. 186.

6. Also known as "Under the Pyramids."

7. Hazel Heald, "Winged Death," in *The Horror in the Museum and Other Revisions*, H. P. Lovecraft et al. (New York: Carroll & Graf, 1997), p. 22.

8. William Lumley, "The Diary of Alonzo Typer," in *The Horror in the Museum and Other Revisions*, p. 86.

9. De Camp, *H. P. Lovecraft: A Biography*, p. 113.

10. Chris Jarocha-Ernst, "Klarkash-Ton and the Cthulhu Mythos," *Clark Ashton Smith: Master of Fantasy*, http://www.oceanstar.com/cas/cjetext.htm (accessed August 27, 2003).

11. Clark Ashton Smith, "Return of the Sorcerer," in *Tales of the Cthulhu Mythos*, H. P. Lovecraft et al. (New York: Del Rey, 1998), p. 29.

12. The other *Night Gallery* tales based on Lovecraftian fiction were "Pickman's Model" and "Cool Air," based on minor stories by Lovecraft, and the (supposedly) comic vignettes "Miss Lovecraft Sent Me" and "Professor Peabody's Last Lecture," both of which were pure creations of *Night Gallery* staff independent of Lovecraft's texts.

13. Clark Ashton Smith, "The Tale of Satampra Zeiros," *The Eldritch Dark: The Sanctum of Clark Ashton Smith*, http://www.eldritchdark.com/ (accessed August 17, 2003).

14. Jarocha-Ernst, "Klarkash-Ton."

15. Robert M. Price, introduction to *Nameless Cults: The Cthulhu Mythos Fiction of Robert E. Howard*, by Robert E. Howard (Hayward, CA: Chaosium, 2001), p. xvii; de Camp, *H. P. Lovecraft: A Biography*, p. 145.

16. H. P. Lovecraft, "The Call of Cthulhu," in *Tales* (New York: Library of America, 2005), p. 182.

17. Robert E. Howard, "Skull Face," in *Nameless Cults: The Cthulhu Mythos Fiction of Robert E. Howard*, p. 316.

18. Howard, *Nameless Cults*, p. 252.

19. Ibid.

20. De Camp, *H. P. Lovecraft: A Biography*, p. 114.

21. Ibid, p. 414; Joshi, *H. P. Lovecraft: A Life*, p. 612.

22. Price, introduction to *Nameless Cults*, p. xiii. Unbeknownst to me when I began this book, Price also authored an article that speculated about the connection between Lovecraft and the theory of ancient astronauts. See Robert M. Price and Charles Garofalo, "Chariots of the Old Ones," in *Black, Forbidden Things: Cryptical Secrets from the "Crypt of Cthulhu,"* ed. Robert M. Price (Mercer Island, WA: Starmont House, 1992), pp. 86–87.

23. De Camp, *H. P. Lovecraft: A Biography*, p. 318.

24. Perry M. Grayson, "Frank Belknap Long, Jr.: Fantasist of Multiple Dimensions, A Preliminary Critical and Historical Overview," *Peregrine's Realm*, http://www.thevine.net/~fortress/fblhist.htm (accessed August 28, 2003).

25. Michael G. Pfefferkorn, "The Shambler from Wisconsin," *The Bat Is My Brother: The Unofficial Robert Bloch*, http://mgpfeff.home.sprynet.com/bloch.html (accessed August 28, 2003).

26. John Howard, "The August Derleth Papers," Walden East, http://www.waldeneast.fsnet.co.uk/adpcontents.htm (accessed September 4, 2003).

27. August Derleth, "An Autobiography," August Derleth Society, http://www.derleth.org (accessed September 6, 2003).

28. De Camp, *H. P. Lovecraft: A Biography*, pp. 431–32.

29. Robert Bloch, introduction to *The Best of H. P. Lovecraft: Bloodcurdling Tales of Horror and the Macabre*, by H. P. Lovecraft (New York:

Del Rey/Ballantine, 1982), p. 9. See also Joshi, *H. P. Lovecraft: A Life*, chap. 25, for discussion.

30. An Internet petition circulated, asking publisher Carroll & Graf to remove Lovecraft's name from these books, but today Lovecraft's name remains.

31. H. P. Lovecraft, *Tales*, p. 183.

32. Derleth, "Autobiography."

33. Bloch, introduction to *The Best of H. P. Lovecraft*, p. 9.

34. John Jamieson, "Books and the Soldier," *Public Opinion Quarterly* 9, no. 3 (Autumn 1945): 320.

35. Ibid, p. 325.

36. Bloch, introduction to *The Best of H. P. Lovecraft*, p. 9; Joshi, *H. P. Lovecraft: A Life*, pp. 637–38.

CHAPTER 6

1. Richard Dolan, *UFOs and the National Security State: Chronology of a Coverup, 1941–1973* (Charlottesville, VA: Hampton Roads, 2002), p. 18; Karl P. N. Shuker, *The Unexplained* (Dubai: Carlton Books, 1996), p. 135.

2. Dolan, *UFOs and the National Security State*, pp. 18–19.

3. Kal K. Korff, *The Roswell UFO Crash: What They Don't Want You to Know* (Amherst, NY: Prometheus Books, 1997; reprint, New York: Dell Publications, 2000), pp. 17–19.

4. Valerii I. Sanarov, "On the Nature and Origin of Flying Saucers and Little Green Men," *Current Anthropology* 22, no. 2 (April 1981): 163–64.

5. Matthew Sweet, *Inventing the Victorians: What We Think We Know about Them and Why We're Wrong* (New York: St. Martin's Press, 2001), p. 23.

6. Shuker, *The Unexplained*, p. 136.

7. As will be seen, the Martian character laid bare the developing equation between extraterrestrials and communists. It was, after all, the *Red* Planet.

8. Shuker, *The Unexplained*, p. 137.

9. Ibid, p. 138.

10. Thomas E. Bullard, "UFO Abduction Reports: The Supernatural Kidnap Narrative Returns in Technological Guise," *Journal of American Folklore* 102, no. 404 (April–June 1989): 164.

11. "Duck Dodgers in the 24½th Century," *Looney Tunes Golden Collection*, DVD, directed by Chuck Jones (1953; Burbank, CA: Warner Home Video, 2003).

12. Thomas Shaw, "Martyrs, Miracles, and Martians: Religion and Cold War Cinematic Propaganda in the 1950s," *Journal of Cold War Studies* 4, no. 2 (Spring 2002): 3.

13. Tom Shippey, introduction to *The Oxford Book of Science Fiction Stories* (New York: Oxford University Press, 1992), pp. xxii–xxiii.

14. Paul Johnson, ed., *Sci.Skeptic FAQ*, sec. 3.8, http://home.xnet.com/~blatura/skeptic.html (accessed September 9, 2003).

15. Bullard, "UFO Abduction Reports," pp. 148–49.

16. Johnson, *Sci.Skeptic FAQ*, sec. 3.8.

17. Bullard, "UFO Abduction Reports," p. 164.

CHAPTER 7

1. Richard I. Jobs, "Tarzan under Attack: Youth, Comics, and Cultural Reconstruction in Postwar France," *French Historical Studies* 26, no. 4 (Fall 2003): 688.

2. Ibid., p. 693.

3. Ibid., pp. 721–22.

4. George Slusser, "Science Fiction in France: An Introduction," *Science Fiction Studies* 16, no. 49 (November 1989), http://www.depauw.edu/sfs/covers/cov49.htm (accessed August 2, 2003).

5. Peter Fitting, "SF Criticism in France," *Science Fiction Studies* 1, no. 3 (Spring 1974), http://www.depauw.edu/sfs/backissues/3/fitting3art.htm (accessed August 2, 2003).

6. R. T. Gault, "The Quixotic Dialectical Metaphysical Manifesto: Morning of the Magicians," *Absolute Elsewhere*, http://www.cafes.net/ditch/motm1.htm (accessed July 27, 2003).

7. Erik Davis, "Calling Cthulhu," *Gnosis* (1995), http://www

.levity.com (accessed August 3, 2002); see also S. T. Joshi, *H. P. Lovecraft: A Life* (West Warwick, RI: Necronomicon Press, 1996; reprint, 2004), p. 623, for an account of Bergier's early enthusiasm for Lovecraft, and Michel Houllebecq, *H. P. Lovecraft: Against the World, Against Life* (San Francisco: Believer Books, 2005), for a French take on Lovecraft's appeal. A 2005 Houllebecq novel defended Raëlianism and cloning, discussed in chapter 16.

8. Fitting, "SF Criticism in France."

9. Marc Angenot, "Following the Thread," review of *Science-Fiction et psychanalyse: L'imaginaire social de la S. F.* by Marcel Thaon et al., *Science Fiction Studies* 8, no. 16 (July 1989), http://www.depauw.edu/sfs/reviews_pages/r48.htm#a48 (accessed August 30, 2003).

10. Colin Wilson and Damon Wilson, *The Mammoth Encyclopedia of the Unsolved* (New York: Carroll & Graf, 2000), p. 149.

11. Ibid., p. 148; David Frum, *How We Got Here: The 70's: The Decade That Brought You Modern Life—For Better or Worse* (New York: Basic Books, 2000), p. 134.

12. Gault, "Quixotic Dialectical Metaphysical Manifesto."

13. Ibid.

14. David Dutton, *Neville Chamberlain* (London: Edward Arnold, 2001), p. 22.

15. Wilson and Wilson, *Mammoth Encyclopedia of the Unknown*, p. 52.

16. Gault, "Quixotic Dialectical Metaphysical Manifesto."

17. Wilson and Wilson, *Mammoth Encyclopedia of the Unknown*, pp. 121–22.

18. Gault, "Quixotic Dialectical Metaphysical Manifesto."

19. Michael Coe, *Mexico: From the Olmecs to the Aztecs*, 4th ed. (Singapore: Thames & Hudson, 1994; reprint, 2000), pp. 62, 68.

20. Theodore Schick Jr. and Lewis Vaughn, *How to Think about Weird Things: Critical Thinking for a New Age*, 2nd ed. (Mountainview, CA: Mayfield Publishing, 1999), p. 203.

CHAPTER 8

1. Erich von Däniken, *Chariots of the Gods?* trans. Michael Heron (New York: Bantam, 1973), p. 154.

2. Gavin Souter, "The Disappointing but Profitable Mysteries of Erich von Däniken," *Advertiser* (March 31, 1973); reprinted in *Investigator* 13 (July 1990).

3. Robert Shaeffer, "Erich von Däniken's 'Chariots of the Gods?': Science of Charlatanism?" *NICAP UFO Investigator* (October/November 1974).

4. Colin Wilson and Damon Wilson, *The Mammoth Encyclopedia of the Unknown* (New York: Carroll & Graf, 2000), p. 123.

5. Von Däniken, *Chariots of the Gods?* p. viii.

6. David Frum, *How We Got Here: The 70's: The Decade That Brought You Modern Life—For Better or Worse* (New York: Basic Books), p. 134.

7. Erich von Däniken, "Welcome to the World of Mysteries of Erich von Däniken," May 28, 2004, http://www.daeniken.com (May 29, 2004).

8. Schaeffer, "Erich von Däniken."

9. H. E. Legrand and Wayne E. Bosse, *"Chariots of the Gods?* and All That: Pseudo-History in the Classroom," *History Teacher* 8, no. 3 (May 1975): 359–70.

10. Von Däniken, *Chariots of the Gods?* cover.

11. Ibid., p. vii.

12. Ibid., p. 3.

13. Paul V. Heinrich, The Wild Side of Geoarchaeology Page, http://www.intersurf.com/~chalcedony/wildside.shtml (accessed October 2, 2003).

14. James B. Richardson III, *People of the Andes* (Washington, DC: Smithsonian Books, 1994), pp. 117–19.

15. Von Däniken, *Chariots of the Gods?* p. 16.

16. Richardson, *People of the Andes*, p. 117.

17. Von Däniken, *Chariots of the Gods?* p. 30.

18. Ibid., p. 36.

19. Ibid., p. 40.

20. Brian Fagan, *Egypt of the Pharaohs* (Washington, DC: National Geographic, 2001), pp. 87–88.

21. Von Däniken, *Chariots of the Gods?* p. 77.

22. Ibid.

23. Ibid., p. 153.

24. Frum, *How We Got Here*, p. 134

25. Legrand and Boese, "*Chariots of the Gods?* and All That." Of course, the situation did not improve as the years went by.

26. Erich von Däniken, *Gods from Outer Space*, trans. Michael Heron (New York: Bantam, 1972), p. vii.

27. Ibid., p. x.

28. Ibid., p. 114.

29. In 2000 Adrienne Mayor plausibly proposed that the ancients derived their ideas about hybrids from interpreting fossils from the Pleistocene. See Adrienne Mayor, *The First Fossil Hunters* (Princeton, NJ: Princeton University Press, 2000).

30. Erich von Däniken, *The Gold of the Gods*, trans. Michael Heron (New York: Putnam, 1973), front flap.

31. Ibid., p. 99.

32. Ibid., p. 1.

33. Ibid., p. 6.

34. Ibid.

35. Ibid., p. 7.

36. Ibid., p. 9.

37. Ibid., p. 10.

38. Ibid., pp. 16–17.

39. Ibid., p. 11.

40. Erich von Däniken, *In Search of Ancient Gods: My Pictorial Evidence for the Impossible*, trans. Michael Heron (New York: Bantam, 1975), p. 145.

41. Souter, "The Disappointing but Profitable Mysteries of Erich von Däniken."

42. Ibid.

43. Anonymous [pseud.], "Erich von Däniken," *Investigator* 13 (July 1990).

44. Wilson and Wilson, *Mammoth Encyclopedia of the Unknown*, p. 123.

45. Erich von Däniken, *Signs of the Gods?* trans. Michael Heron (New York: Berkley, 1983), p. 127.

46. Erich von Däniken, *The Eyes of the Sphinx: The Newest Evidence of Extraterrestrial Contact in Ancient Egypt* (New York: Berkley, 1996), p. 278.

47. Von Däniken, *Eyes of the Sphinx*, pp. 242–70; Erich von Däniken, *The Return of the Gods: Evidence of Extraterrestrial Visitations*, trans. Matthew Barton (Shaftesbury, UK: Element, 1997), pp. 144–64.

48. Erich von Däniken, *Odyssey of the Gods: The Alien History of Ancient Greece* (Shaftesbury, UK: Element, 2000).

49. Giorgio Tsoukalos, e-mail to author, July 29, 2003. Mr. Tsoukalos and I had met before when I interviewed him for a student television news story in 2002. Mr. Tsoukalos disliked my skeptical questions. The story was plagued with technical problems, and the tape with his interview was accidentally erased. Tsoukalos accused me of acting in bad faith for not providing him with a copy of the finished project, though as I explained, there was no tape. The story never aired.

50. Ibid.

51. Mystery Park, http://www.mysterypark.ch (accessed October 4, 2003).

CHAPTER 9

1. Anonymous [pseud.], "Erich von Däniken," *Investigator* 13 (July 1990).

2. R. T. Gault, *The Absolute Elsewhere: Fantastic, Visionary, and Esoteric Literature in the 1960s and 1970s*, http://www.cafes.net/ditch/Elsewhere.htm (accessed May 29, 2004).

3. Ibid.

4. *Alien*, directed by Ridley Scott (Burbank, CA: Twentieth Century Fox, 1979).

5. Robert M. Price, ed., *The Necronomicon: Selected Stories and Essays Concerning the Blasphemous Tome of the Mad Arab* (Hayward, CA: Chaosium, 1996), p. 123.

6. Daniel Harms and John William Gonce III, Necronomicon Files On-Line, http://www.necfiles.org (accessed October 9, 2003).

7. Dan Clore, "The Lurker on the Threshold of Interpretation: Hoax *Necronomicons* and Paratextual Noise," Dan Clore Necronomicon Page, http://www.geocities.com/SoHo/9879/lurker.htm (accessed July 5, 2002).

8. Harms and Gonce, Necronomicon Files On-Line.

9. Khem Caigan, "The Simonomicon," Khem Caigan Official Site, http://home.flash.net/~khem/Simonomicon.html (accessed June 2, 2002).

10. Clore, "Lurker on the Threshold of Interpretation."

11. Alan Cabal, "The Doom That Came to Chelsea," *New York Press* 16, no. 23 (2004), http://www.nypress.com/inside.cfm?content _id=8374&return (accessed May 29, 2004).

12. Peter H. Gilmore, "The *Necronomicon*: Some Facts about Fiction," Church of Satan, http://www.churchofsatan.com/Pages/FAQ necronomicon.html (accessed November 1, 2003).

13. Barry R. Parker, *Alien Life: The Search for Extraterrestrials and Beyond* (New York: Perseus, 1998), p. 223.

14. *Public Papers of the Presidents of the United States: Jimmy Carter 1979, Book II* (Washington, DC: Government Printing Office, 1980), pp. 1235–41.

15. John R. Clarke, *Roman Sex: 100 BC–AD 250* (New York: Harry N. Abrams, 2003).

16. Parker, *Alien Life*, p. 223.

17. See A. N. Wilson, *God's Funeral: The Decline of Faith in Western Civilization* (New York: W. W. Norton, 1999).

18. Edward A. Tiryakian, "Toward the Sociology of Esoteric Culture," *American Journal of Sociology* 78, no. 3 (November 1972): 491–512.

19. Michael Cuneo, *American Exorcism: Expelling Demons in the Land of Plenty* (New York: Broadway Books, 2002).

20. Thomas E. Bullard, "UFO Abduction Reports: The Supernatural Kidnap Narrative Returns in Technological Guise," *Journal of American Folklore* 102, no. 404 (April–June 1989): 149.

21. Ibid., p. 168.

22. Of course this does not preclude the possibility, however remote, that some alien abductions may be real, but it does suggest that the majority of such reports are more influenced by cultural representations of these events.

23. Tiryakian, "Toward the Sociology of Esoteric Culture," p. 491.

24. Ibid., p. 494.

25. Ibid., p. 510.

26. H. E. Legrand and Wayne E. Boese, "*Chariots of the Gods?* and All That: Pseudo-History in the Classroom," *History Teacher* 8, no. 3 (May 1975): 359–60.

27. Ibid., p. 368.

28. Ibid., p. 360.

29. Neal Gabler, *Life the Movie: How Entertainment Conquered Reality* (New York: Alfred A. Knopf, 1998), pp. 128–29.

CHAPTER 10

1. Robert Temple, *The Sirius Mystery: New Scientific Evidence of Alien Contact 5,000 Years Ago*, rev. ed. (Rochester, VT: Destiny Books, 1998), p. 14.

2. Charles E. Orser Jr., "The 15,000-Year Mistake: When the Facts Don't Fit, Blame the Sun," *Scientific American Discovering Archaeology* (January 31, 2001), http://www.discoveringarchaeology.com/articles/013101-15,000mistake (accessed April 30, 2001).

3. Filip Coppens, "Dogon Shame," *Fortean Times* 140 (November 2000), http://www.forteantimes.com/articles/140_dogonshame.shtml (accessed April 27, 2005). The source for the claims about the creator-gods was Lynn Picknett and Clive Prince's *The Stargate Conspiracy* (New York: Berkley Books, 2001), which argued that ufology, the paranormal, and alternative archaeology were all part of a grand conspiracy fifty years in the making to ready the world for the return of the ancient astronauts through what amounted to mind control. The book was the natural result of taking ideas like Lovecraft's Cthulhu cult too literally.

4. Temple, *Sirius Mystery*, pp. 40–41.

5. Ibid., p. 41.

6. After the moon, Venus is the brightest object, but it is a planet. Sirius follows Venus in the order of brightness.

7. Clarke authored a parody of Lovecraft's *At the Mountains of Madness* called "At the Mountains of Murkiness" when he was young. Lovecraft's work had a clear influence on Clarke's best-known creation, *2001: A Space Odyssey*.

8. Temple, *Sirius Mystery*, pp. 40–48.

9. Ibid., p. 44.

10. Ibid., pp. 75–76.

11. Ibid., p. 44.

12. Ibid., pp. 161–62.

13. The Egyptians had many gods that varied in importance over the three thousand years of their civilization. Ammon was often considered one of the most important, but he vied for the title with Ra, Horus, and Osiris. Later, a composite Amun-Ra held the post.

14. Temple, *Sirius Mystery*, p. 309.

15. Ibid., back cover.

16. Ibid.

17. James Oberg, "The Sirius Mystery," in *UFOs and Outer Space Mysteries* (Virginia Beach: Donning Press, 1982), reprinted at http://www.debunker.com/texts/dogon.html (accessed October 12, 2003).

18. Temple, *Sirius Mystery*, p. 5.

19. Ibid., p. 4.

20. Ian Ridpath, "Investigating the Sirius 'Mystery,'" *Skeptical Inquirer* 3, no. 1 (Fall 1978): 56–62.

21. Temple, *Sirius Mystery*, p. 6.

22. Bernard Ortiz de Montellano, "The Dogon Revisited," Doug's Archaeology Page, http://www.ramtops.demon.co.uk/dogon.html (accessed October 16, 2003).

23. See Twain's story "Captain Stormfield's Visit to Heaven."

24. Temple, *Sirius Mystery*, p. 7.

25. Ibid., p. 8.

26. Ibid., p. 9.

27. Ibid., pp. 9–11.

28. Oberg, "The Sirius Mystery."

29. Walter E. A. van Beek, "Dogon Restudied: A Field Evaluation of the Work of Marcel Griaule," *Current Anthropology* 32 (1992): 153.

30. Ortiz de Montellano, "Dogon Revisited."

31. Van Beek, "Dogon Restudied," p. 139.

32. Ibid., p. 142.

33. Ibid., p. 148.

34. Ibid., pp. 156–57.

35. Ibid., pp. 150–51.

36. Ibid., pp. 153–54.

37. Ibid., p. 157.

CHAPTER 11

1. Robert Bauval and Adrian Gilbert, *The Orion Mystery* (New York: Three Rivers Press, 1994), p. 8.

2. Ibid., p. 9.

3. Ibid., p. 8.

4. Ibid., p. 9.

5. Ibid., p. 107.

6. Ibid., p. 109.

7. Ibid., p. 116.

8. Ibid., p. 122.

9. Ibid., pp. 140–60.

10. Ibid.

11. Robert Bauval, "The Great Pyramids as Stellar Representation of Orion's Belt," Official Graham Hancock Web site, December 2000, http://www.grahamhancock.com (accessed December 29, 2000).

12. Bauval and Gilbert, *The Orion Mystery*, pp. 125–26.

13. Ibid., pp. 128–29.

14. Ibid., p. 137.

15. John Anthony West, *The Serpent in the Sky: The High Wisdom of Ancient Egypt* (London: Wildwood House, 1979), pp. 229–30; quoted in Robert Temple, *The Sirius Mystery: New Evidence of Alien Contact 5,000 Years Ago* (Rochester, VT: Destiny Books, 1998), p. 13.

16. Gary Lachman, "René Schwaller de Lubicz and the Intelligence

of the Heart," *Quest Magazine* (January–February 2000), reprinted by the Theosophical Society of America, http://www.theosophical.org (accessed October 20, 2003).

17. Ibid.

18. John Anthony West, "The Wisdom of Ancient Egypt," *Quest Magazine* (January–February 2000), reprinted by the Theosophical Society of America, http://www.theosophical.org (accessed October 20, 2003).

19. Temple, *Sirius Mystery*, p. 12.

20. Ibid., p. 14.

21. John Anthony West, e-mail to author, November 14, 2003.

22. Erich von Däniken, *The Eyes of the Sphinx: The Newest Evidence of Extraterrestrial Contact in Ancient Egypt* (New York: Berkley Books, 1996).

23. Adrian Gilbert and Maurice Cotterell, *The Mayan Prophecies: Unlocking the Secrets of a Lost Civilization* (New York: Barnes & Noble, 1996).

24. Adrian Gilbert, *Signs in the Sky: The Astrological and Archaeological Evidence for the Birth of a New Age* (New York: Three Rivers Press, 2001), pp. 251–53.

25. Ibid., p. 304.

26. Giorgio de Santillana and Hertha von Dechend, *Hamlet's Mill: An Essay Investigating the Origins of Human Knowledge and Its Transmission through Myth* (Boston: Nonpareil Books, 1998), p. 451.

27. Bauval and Gilbert, *The Orion Mystery*, p. 209, diagram.

28. Ibid., p. 192.

29. Ed Krupp, "Astronomical Integrity at Giza," In the Hall of Ma'at: Weighing the Evidence for Alternative History, October 2001, http://www.hallofmaat.com (accessed October 31, 2003).

30. The 1994 documentary was among the first "alternative history" documentaries I ever saw, and it helped spark my interest in the genre.

31. Robert Bauval, "The Mystery of the Upside-Down Pyramids: The Case of the BBC *Horizon* 'Atlantis Reborn' Programme," Official Graham Hancock Web site, http://www.grahamhancock.com (accessed October 31, 2003).

32. Robert Bauval, message board postings, Official Graham Hancock Web site, April 8, 2001, http://www.grahamhancock.com (accessed April 8, 2001).

CHAPTER 12

1. Graham Hancock, *Fingerprints of the Gods* (New York: Crown, 1995).

2. Graham Hancock, *The Sign and the Seal* (New York: Touchstone, 1992), pp. 8–9.

3. Graham Hancock, "Writing about Outrageous Hypotheses and Extraordinary Possibilities: A View from the Trenches," Official Graham Hancock Web site, http://www.grahamhancock.com (accessed October 28, 2003).

4. Hancock, *Sign and the Seal*, pp. 88, 339.

5. Hancock, "Writing about Outrageous Hypotheses."

6. Although the terms are imprecise, I am using "alternative history" to mean radical theories of the past like lost-civilization hypotheses and Afrocentrism that do not include ancient astronauts.

7. Paul V. Heinrich, The Wild Side of Geoarchaeology Page, http://www.intersurf.com/~chalcedony/wildside.shtml (accessed October 2, 2003).

8. Katherine Reece, "The Spanish Imposition," In the Hall of Ma'at: Weighing the Evidence for Alternative History, http://www.hallofmaat.com (accessed November 1, 2003).

9. Catherine Yronwode, "Notes on a Lecture by Graham Hancock," Lucky Mojo, http://www.luckymojo.com/hancocklecture.html (accessed April 2, 2001).

10. Hancock, *Fingerprints of the Gods*, p. 78.

11. Graham Hancock, *Heaven's Mirror: The Quest for the Lost Civilization* (New York: Crown, 1998), p. 304.

12. James B. Richardson III, *People of the Andes* (Washington, DC: Smithsonian Books, 1995).

13. Charles E. Orser Jr., "The 15,000-Year Mistake: When the Facts Don't Fit, Blame the Sun," *Scientific American Discovering Archaeology* (January 31, 2001), http://www.discoveringarchaeology.com/articles/013101-15,000mistake (accessed April 30, 2001).

14. For example, the Asian epicanthic eye folds found in Mexican natives and the Olmec heads are absent in African populations. See G. Haslip-Viera, B. Ortiz de Montellano, and W. Barbour, "CA Forum

on Anthropology in Public: Robbing Native American Cultures: Van Sertima's Afrocentricity and the Olmec," *Current Anthropology* 38 (1997): 423.

15. Hancock, *Fingerprints of the Gods*, p. 137.

16. Ibid.

17. The famed Mesoamerican scholar Michael Coe says that knowledge of this paper-making method "was diffused from eastern Indonesia to Mesoamerica at a very early date." He further argues that since bark paper was used to make books, information may have been exchanged between Pacific and Mesoamerican peoples. Of course, he held that "it should be categorically emphasized that *no* objects manufactured in the Old World have been identified in any Maya site," though he believes some isolated travelers may have ventured to Mexico a few times. Michael Coe, *The Maya*, 6th ed. (Singapore: Thames and Hudson, 2001), p. 58.

18. Hancock, *Fingerprints of the Gods*, p. 137.

19. Ibid., p. 151.

20. Erich von Däniken, *Chariots of the Gods?* trans. Michael Heron (New York: Bantam, 1973), p. 100.

21. Hancock, *Fingerprints of the Gods*, p. 115.

22. Heinrich, Wild Side of Geoarchaeology Page.

23. Published as *Keeper of Genesis* in the United Kingdom.

24. Graham Hancock and Robert Bauval, *Mystery of the Sphinx: A Quest for the Hidden Legacy of Mankind* (New York: Crown, 1996), p. 21.

25. August Matthusen, posting to sci.anthropology newsgroup January 9, 1997, http://www.anatomy.usyd.edu.au/danny/anthropology/sci.anthropology/archive/january-1997/0231.html (accessed November 1, 2003). Geologist August Matthusen is among Schoch's staunchest critics. He argued that Schoch's idea that rain produced a distinct pattern in the rocks was unsupportable because Schoch had not tested whether wind and water truly erode different patterns on the Sphinx limestone. Matthusen claims that different densities of the layers of Giza limestone account for the weathering pattern.

26. West, e-mail to author, November 14, 2003.

27. Hancock, *Heaven's Mirror*, pp. 124–27.

28. For example, Jaromir Malek, review of *Fingerprints of the Gods*,

by Graham Hancock, *Discussions in Egyptology* 34 (1996), reprinted on In the Hall of Ma'at: Weighing the Evidence for Alternative History, http://www.hallofmaat.com (accessed October 30, 2003).

29. Hancock, "Writing about Outrageous Hypotheses."

30. Richard Highfield, "BBC Reedits Horizon after Watchdog's Attack," *Daily Telegraph* (London), December 11, 2001.

CHAPTER 13

1. Michael Cuneo, *American Exorcism: Expelling Demons in the Land of Plenty* (New York: Broadway Books, 2002); Morton Klass, *Ordered Universes: Approaches to the Anthropology of Religion* (Boulder, CO: Westview Press, 1995), chap. 19.

2. Klass, *Ordered Universes*, p. 156 and note 4.

3. Ibid., pp. 150–51.

4. Graham Hancock and Robert Bauval, *The Message of the Sphinx: A Quest for the Hidden Legacy of Mankind* (New York: Crown, 1996).

5. Ibid., pp. 292–93.

6. Ibid., pp. 93–96.

7. Ibid., p. 293.

8. Ibid., p. 203.

9. Ibid., pp. 266–67.

10. Kenneth L. Feder, "Ten Years After: Surveying Misconceptions about the Human Past," *Cultural Resource Management* 18, no. 3 (1995): 11.

11. CSICOP is part of the Center for Inquiry, parent company of Prometheus Books, the publisher of this book. Though I subscribe to CSICOP's *Skeptical Inquirer* and am a so-called associate member (a glorified magazine subscription), I am not professionally affiliated with CSICOP.

12. The Discovery Channel has since switched to programs about large motorcycles, TLC to decorating and makeover shows, and the Travel Channel to televised poker tournaments, haunted hotels, and tours of Las Vegas. Discovery Communications launched a new Science Channel to take up some of the slack.

13. Feder, "Ten Years After," pp. 12–14.

14. Richard Brooks and Niklas Rasche, "Book on 'Lost Tribe' Shelved in Plagiarism Row; Rivals Claim Para-Science Author Copied Theories on Egypt," *Sunday Observer* (UK), June 14, 1998.

15. Mark Wells and Richard Wells, "The Theory of the Chinese Pyramids," *Earth Quest* (November 2000), http://www.earthquest.co.uk/articles/theory.html (accessed November 7, 2003).

16. Robert Bauval and Graham Hancock, "The Mysterious Structures That May Upstage NASA's Evidence of Martian Life," *Daily Mail* (London), August 17–19, 1996.

17. Ibid.

18. Graham Hancock, Robert Bauval, and John Grigsby, *The Mars Mystery* (New York: Crown, 1998).

19. Ibid., p. 260.

20. Ibid.

21. Ibid, p. 282.

22. Graham Hancock, *Underworld* (London: Michael Joseph, 2002).

23. Jason Colavito, "Diving for Answers," review of *Underword*, by Graham Hancock, Lost Civilizations Uncovered, March 2002, http://www.thelostcivilizations.com (accessed April 28, 2005).

24. Brett Hilton-Barber, "A Restless Soul," *Sunday Times* (South Africa), June 2, 2002.

25. Ibid.

26. Graham Hancock, e-mail to author, August 9, 2003.

27. The Official Web site of Talisman, http://www.talismanthebook.com (accessed May 30, 2004).

28. Robert Bauval, introduction to *Talisman: Sacred Cities, Secret Faith*, by Graham Hancock and Robert Bauval (London: Michael Joseph, 2004), reprinted on Official Web site of Talisman, http://www.talismanthebook.com (accessed May 30, 2004).

29. Robert Bauval, message board posting on http://www.robertbauval.com, February 10, 2003.

CHAPTER 14

1. Tim Hunker, http://homepage2.nifty.com/88/jyunbi0/hunker .htm (accessed April 2, 2001).

2. Ibid.

3. Graham Hancock and Robert Bauval, *The Message of the Sphinx: A Quest for the Hidden Legacy of Mankind* (New York: Crown, 1996), p. 104.

4. Ibid.

5. Ibid.

6. Ibid., p. 320.

7. Ian Lawton, "A Refutation of the Theories of Zecharia Sitchin," May 1, 2000, http://www.ianlawton.com (accessed April 2, 2001). Lawton later developed his own alternative history theories, but these should not detract from his criticism of Sitchin.

8. Zecharia Sitchin, "Forging the Pharaoh's Name," *Ancient Skies* 8, no. 2 (1981).

9. Erich von Däniken, *The Eyes of the Sphinx: The Newest Evidence of Extraterrestrial Contact in Ancient Egypt* (New York: Berkley Books, 1996), pp. 263–64.

10. Graham Hancock, "Position Statement by Graham Hancock on the Antiquity and Meaning of the Giza Monuments," Official Graham Hancock Web site, July 22, 1998, http://www.grahamhancock.com (accessed July 23, 1998).

11. Ibid.

12. Surveyed using search terms "Vyse" and "quarry marks," May 31, 2004. More reassuringly, there were several pages of refutations of the Sitchin theory listed, too.

13. Lawton, "Refutation."

14. Zecharia Sitchin, "Interview with Zecharia Sitchin," *Connecting Link* 17 (July 1993), http://www.metatron.se/asitch.html (accessed May 31, 2004).

15. Zecharia Sitchin, *Twelfth Planet* (New York: Avon Books, 1979). Of course, the Mesopotamians could not have known about the outer planets, invisible without sophisticated telescopes. Sitchin believes the aliens were responsible for providing such anomalous knowledge.

16. Sitchin, "Interview."

17. Also spelled Nephilim and translated in the King James Bible as "giants."

18. Sitchin, "Interview."

19. *Science*, April 6, 2001, quoted in Zecharia Sitchin, "The Case of the Lurking Planet," Official Zecharia Sitchin Homepage, May 2001, http://www.sitchin.com (accessed May 31, 2004).

20. Sitchin, "The Case of the Lurking Planet."

21. Lawton, "Refutation."

22. Robert Todd Carroll, "Zecharia Sitchin," *The Skeptic's Dictionary*, April 26, 2001, http://skepdic.com/sitchin.html (accessed April 30, 2001).

23. Ibid.

24. See examples in the "Seminar Reports" of Sitchin's Web site, http://www.sitchin.com.

25. Rob Hafernik, "Sitchin's Twelfth Planet," June 1996, http://www.geocities.com/Area51/Corridor/8148/hafernik.html (accessed April 2, 2001).

26. Ibid.

27. Ibid.

28. Sitchin, *Twelfth Planet*, p. 163.

29. Hafernik, "Sitchin's Twelfth Planet."

30. William Saylor, "Akkadian Seal," http://members.tripod.com/wlsaylor/akkadian_seal.htm (accessed April 2, 2001).

31. Ibid.

32. Zecharia Sitchin, "Philadelphia," 2003, Official Web site of Zecharia Sitchin, http://www.sitchin.com/philadelphia.htm (accessed October 12, 2003).

33. Zecharia Sitchin, Official Web site of Zecharia Sitchin, http://www.sitchin.com (accessed October 12, 2003).

34. Lawton, "Refutation."

35. Surveyed using search term "Sitchin," May 31, 2004.

36. Sitchin, "Interview."

37. David Greenbaum, "Los Angeles Seminar Hailed as 'The Best,'" Official Web site of Zecharia Sitchin, http://www.sitchin.com/losangeles.htm (accessed October 2, 2003).

38. Hafernik, "Sitchin's Twelfth Planet."
39. Billed as "a fun and easy way to expose your friends and family to Zecharia Sitchin's work," the cards feature Sumerian pictures with Sitchin Studies trivia facts. "The Winged Disk," 2003, http://www.wingeddisk.com/ (accessed May 31, 2004).

CHAPTER 15

1. Giorgio Tsoukalos, e-mail to author, July 29, 2003.
2. Peter Hay, "Fabulous Secret Said Discovered in Grand Canyon 90 Years Ago," *Sightings*, http://www.rense.com/earthchanges/grand canyon_e.htm (accessed October 3, 2003).
3. David Hatcher Childress, "The Evidence for Ancient Atomic Warfare Part One," *Nexus* 7, no. 5 (September–October 2000), and "The Evidence for Ancient Atomic Warfare Part Two," *Nexus* 7, no. 6 (November–December 2000), http://www.nexusmagazine.com (accessed October 3, 2003).
4. Duncan Roads, "Frequently Asked Questions," *Nexus* 2, no. 27 (August–September 1995), http://www.nexusmagazine.com (accessed October 3, 2003).
5. Childress, "The Evidence for Anicent Atomic Warfare Part One."
6. Ibid.
7. Erich von Däniken, *Chariots of the Gods?* trans. Michael Heron (New York: Bantam, 1973), p. 36.
8. Erich von Däniken, *Gods from Outer Space*, trans. Michael Heron (New York: Bantam, 1972), p. 131.
9. Childress, "The Evidence for Ancient Atomic Warfare Part Two."
10. Ibid.
11. Ibid.
12. Ibid.
13. Childress, "The Evidence for Ancient Atomic Warfare Part One."
14. Childress, "The Evidence for Ancient Atomic Warfare Part Two."
15. Ibid.
16. Ibid.
17. Alan F. Alford, e-mail to author, November 14, 2003.

18. Alan F. Alford, "Let There Be Light": The Official Web site of Alan F. Alford, http://www.eridu.co.uk/ (accessed November 2, 2003).

19. Ibid.

20. Ibid.

21. Ibid.

22. Ibid. Interestingly, Alford is not the only author in the genre to be so interested in sexuality as a sign of the aliens. In *Gods from Outer Space* von Däniken devotes a full chapter to the "perversions of our ancestors," and as will be seen, Laurence Gardner believes menstrual blood to be part of the alien diet. Many authors, too, seem obsessed with discovering which groups mated with one another to produce today's populations. I leave it for the reader to decide what these sexual ideas mean.

23. "Speaker Biography: Desmond Morris," 2003, Celebrity Speakers Limited, http://www.speakers.co.uk/Retro/SubPages/Speakers/5017.htm (accessed November 3, 2003).

24. Alford, "Let There Be Light": The Official Web site of Alan F. Alford.

25. Ibid.

26. Ibid.

27. Ibid.

28. Alford, e-mail to author.

29. Both derived the idea from Baigent, Leigh, and Lincoln's *Holy Blood, Holy Grail*, a monumental work of pseudoscience whose lack of extraterrestrial content places it outside the scope of this book.

30. Laurence Gardner, *Bloodline of the Holy Grail* (New York: Barnes & Noble, 1997).

31. Ibid., p. 249. However, the pun is a later invention and was not actually used in medieval times.

32. Ibid., chap. 16.

33. Sean Murphy, "Report on the Pedigree of Michael Lafosse, Styled Prince Michael of Albany," *Irish Chiefs*, Centre for Irish Genealogical and Historical Studies, October 31, 2002, http://homepage.tinet.ie/~seanj murphy/chiefs/lafosse.htm (accessed November 4, 2003).

34. Gardner, *Bloodline of the Holy Grail*, chap. 3.

35. Ibid., pp. 458, 469.

36. Laurence Gardner, e-mail to author, January 19, 2004.

37. Laurence Gardner, "Genesis of the Grail Kings Lecture Transcript," http://www.karenlyster.com/genesis.html (accessed October 27, 2003).

38. Ibid.

39. Ibid.

40. Ibid.

41. Ibid.

42. Ibid.

43. Gardner, e-mail to author.

44. Ibid.

45. Ibid.

46. Gardner, *Bloodline of the Holy Grail*, p. 5.

47. Gardner, e-mail to author.

CHAPTER 16

1. Chris Lehman, "The Deep Roots of Heaven's Gate," *Harper's*, June 1997, p. 15, in Expanded Academic ASAP, http://www.galegroup.com/tlist/sb5019.html (accessed May 31, 2004).

2. Elizabeth Gleick, "The Marker We've Been . . . Waiting For," *Time*, April 7, 1997, pp. 28–36, in Expanded Academic ASAP, http://www.galegroup.com/tlist/sb5019.html (accessed May 31, 2004).

3. Ibid.

4. Ibid.

5. Ibid.

6. Ibid.

7. H. P. Lovecraft, "The Whisperer in Darkness," in *Tales* (New York: Library of America, 2005), p. 425.

8. Ibid., p. 435.

9. Ibid., p. 479.

10. Irving Hexham and Karla Poewe, "UFO Religion," *Christian Century* 114 (May 7, 1997): 439–40.

11. Unarius Academy of Science Web site, http://www.unarius.org/start.html (accessed November 5, 2003).

12. Ross Hoffman, "Unarias Academy of Science," The Religious Movements Homepage Project, University of Virginia, 1998, http://religiousmovements.lib.virginia.edu/nrms/unarius.html (accessed November 5, 2003).

13. Greg Brown, "Unarias Academy of Science: Spaceships Arriving 2001," Roadside America, http://www.roadsideamerica.com /attract/CAELCunarius.html (accessed November 5, 2003).

14. Hoffman, "Unarias Academy of Science."

15. Ibid.

16. Unarias Academy of Science Web site.

17. Brown, "Unarias Academy of Science."

18. Ibid.

19. Ryan J. Cook, "Discussion," UFOs & Anthropology, Center for Anthroufology, 2002, http://home.uchicago.edu/~ryancook/un-nwtxt .htm (accessed November 8, 2003).

20. Ibid.

21. Rick Ross, "Nuwaubians," Ross Institute for the Study of Destructive Cults, Controversial Groups and Movements, http:// www.rickross.com (accessed November 8, 2003).

22. Faye Whittemore, "International Raëlian Religion," The Religious Movements Homepage Project, University of Virginia, 1998, http://religiousmovements.lib.virginia.edu/nrms/rael.html (accessed November 9, 2003).

23. Ibid.

24. Raëlian Movement, "The Raëlian Revolution," http://www .rael.org (accessed April 2, 2001).

25. Ricky Roehr, e-mail to author, November 13, 2003.

26. Raël (Claude Vorilhon), The Message Given by Extra-Terrestrials (Raëlian Movement, 1998).

27. Whittemore, "International Raëlian Religion."

28. Ibid.

29. Ibid.

30. Dennis Roddy, "Prophet Sounds as If He Came from Another Planet," Pittsburgh Post-Gazette, November 17, 2001.

31. Ibid.

32. Whittemore, "International Raëlian Religion."

33. Raëlian Movement, "The Raëlian Revolution."

34. Roehr, e-mail to author.

35. Nell Boyce and James M. Pethokoukis, "Clowns or Cloners?" *US News & World Report*, January 13, 2003, pp. 48–50.

36. Whittemore, "International Raëlian Religion."

37. Ibid.

38. Ibid.

39. Erich von Däniken, *Chariots of the Gods?* trans. Michael Heron (New York: Bantam, 1973), pp. 51–52.

40. Erich von Däniken, *Gods from Outer Space*, trans. Michael Heron (New York: Bantam, 1972), p. 12.

41. Boyce and Pethokoukis, "Clowns or Cloners?"

42. Whittemore, "International Raëlian Religion."

43. Virginia Morell, "A Clone of One's Own," *Discover* 19, no. 5 (May 1998): 82–89.

44. Ibid.

45. "Abducting the Cloning Debate," *Time*, January 13, 2003, pp. 46–49.

46. Morell, "A Clone of One's Own."

47. Roehr, e-mail to author.

48. Boyce and Pethoukokis, "Clowns or Cloners?"

49. Nell Boyce, David E. Kaplan, and Douglas Pasternak, "The God Game No More," *US News & World Report*, July 9, 2001, pp. 20–21.

50. Boyce and Pethoukokis, "Clowns or Cloners?"

51. Ibid.

52. "Raelian Leader Says Cloning First Step to Immortality," CNN.com, December 27, 2002, http://www.cnn.com/2002/HEALTH/12/27/human.cloning/ (accessed December 28, 2002).

53. Ibid.

54. Roehr, e-mail to author.

55. "Raelian Leader Says Cloning First Step to Immortality."

56. Boyce and Pethokoukis, "Clowns or Cloners?"

57. Roehr, e-mail to author.

58. Ibid.

59. James Langton, "Cult Finds Eternal Youth Formula," *Evening Standard* (London), November 14, 2003.

60. H. P. Lovecraft, "The Nameless City," in *The Dream Cycle of H. P. Lovecraft: Dreams of Terror and Death* (New York: Del Rey, 1995), p. 65.

CHAPTER 17

1. H. P. Lovecraft, "The Call of Cthulhu," in *Tales* (New York: Library of America, 2005), p. 167.

2. Jacques Barzun, *From Dawn to Decadence: 500 Years of Western Cultural Life* (New York: HarperCollins, 2000), p. 798.

3. James A. Herrick, *The Making of the New Spirituality: The Eclipse of the Western Religious Tradition* (Downers Grove, IL: InterVarsity Press, 2003), p. 263.

4. Associated Press, "Adults Are Taking Back Halloween," October 28, 2003, MSNBC.com (accessed October 28, 2003).

5. Part of that might be a perception problem on the part of modern people; after all Grover Cleveland had to discuss his extra-marital affair during the 1888 election.

6. "At Top Ten Liberal Arts Colleges, Liberal Arts Is Dying, Concludes Special Report from IWF," Independent Women's Forum, October 27, 2003, http://www.iwf.org/news/031027a.shtml (accessed October 28, 2003).

7. Joseph Trainor, "Ruins of Kadath Found in Antarctica?" *UFO Roundup* 8, no. 19 (May 14, 2003), http://www.ufoinfo.com/roundup/v08/rnd0819.shtml (accessed November 12, 2003). Article excerpt appears by permission of Joseph Trainor.

8. @lantis.tv: Earth's Coolest Entertainment, http://lantis.tv/ (accessed May 31, 2004).

9. Joseph Trainor, e-mail to author, November 14, 2003.

10. William J. Broad and James Glanz, "Does Science Matter?" *New York Times*, November 11, 2003.

11. H. P. Lovecraft, *The Dream Quest of Unknown Kadath*, in *The Dream Cycle of H. P. Lovecraft: Dreams of Terror and Death* (New York: Del Rey, 1995), p. 192.

SELECT BIBLIOGRAPHY

Alford, Alan. Official Web site of Alan F. Alford. http://www.eridu.co.uk/.

Angenot, Marc. "Following the Thread." Review of *Science-fiction et psychanalyse: L'imaginaire social de la S.F.* by Marcel Thaon et al. *Science Fiction Studies* 8, no. 16 (July 1989). http://www.depauw .edu/sfs/reviews_pages/r48.htm#a48.

Anonymous [pseud.]. "Erich von Däniken." *Investigator* 13 (July 1990).

Barzun, Jacques. *From Dawn to Decadence: 500 Years of Western Cultural Life.* New York: HarperCollins, 2000.

Bauval, Robert, and Adrian Gilbert. *The Orion Mystery.* New York: Three Rivers Press, 1994.

Bullard, Thomas E. "UFO Abduction Reports: The Supernatural Kidnap Narrative Returns in Technological Guise." *Journal of American Folklore* 102, no. 404 (April–June, 1989): 147–70.

Caldwell, Daniel. *The Esoteric World of Madam Blavatsky: Reminiscences and Impressions by Those Who Knew Her.* 2nd ed. Preprint. Theo- sophical Society. http://www.theosophical.org/theosophy/books /esotericworld/index.html.

Caroll, Robert Todd. *The Skeptic's Dictionary.* http://skepdic.com/.

Carroll, Noel. "The Nature of Horror." *Journal of Aesthetics and Art Criticism* 46, no. 1 (Autumn 1987): 51–59.

Childress, David Hatcher. "The Evidence for Ancient Atomic Warfare Part One." *Nexus* 7, no. 5 (September–October 2000). http://www .nexusmagazine.com.

———. "The Evidence for Ancient Atomic Warfare Part Two." *Nexus* 7, no. 6 (November–December 2000). http://www.nexusmagazine.com.

Clarke, John R. *Roman Sex: 100 BC–AD 250*. New York: Harry N. Abrams, 2003.

Clore, Dan. "The Lurker on the Threshold of Interpretation: Hoax *Necronomicons* and Paratextual Noise." Dan Clore Necronomicon Page. http://www.geocities.com/SoHo/9879/lurker.htm.

Coe, Michael. *The Maya*. 6th ed. 1999. Reprint, Singapore: Thames and Hudson, 2001.

———. *Mexico: From the Olmecs to the Aztecs*. 4th ed. 1994. Reprint, Singapore: Thames & Hudson, 2000.

Cook, Ryan J. "Discussion." UFOs and Anthropology. Center for Anthroufology. http://home.uchicago.edu/~ryancook/un-nwtxt.htm.

Coppens, Filip. "Dogon Shame." *Fortean Times*. November 2000. http://www.forteantimes.com/articles/140_dogonshame.shtml.

Cuneo, Michael. *American Exorcism: Expelling Demons in the Land of Plenty*. New York: Broadway Books, 2002.

Däniken, Erich von. *Chariots of the Gods?* Translated by Michael Heron. New York: Bantam, 1973.

———. *Gods from Outer Space*. Translated by Michael Heron. New York: Bantam, 1973.

———. *The Gold of the Gods*. Translated by Michael Heron. New York: Putnam, 1973.

———. *The Eyes of the Sphinx: The Newest Evidence of Extraterrestrial Contact in Ancient Egypt*. New York: Berkley, 1996.

———. *Odyssey of the Gods: The Alien History of Ancient Greece*. Shaftesbury, UK: Element, 2000.

———. *The Return of the Gods: Evidence of Extraterrestrial Visitations*. Translated by Matthew Barton. Shaftesbury, UK: Element, 1997.

———. *In Search of Ancient Gods: My Pictorial Evidence for the Impossible*. Translated by Michael Heron. New York: Bantam, 1975.

———. *Signs of the Gods?* Translated by Michael Heron. New York: Berkley, 1983.

———. Welcome to the World of Mysteries of Erich von Däniken. http://www.daeniken.com.

Davis, Erik. "Calling Cthulhu," *Gnosis* (1995). http://www.levity.com.

de Camp, L. Sprague. *H. P. Lovecraft: A Biography*. New York: Barnes & Noble, 1996.

———. *Lost Continents: The Atlantis Theme in History, Science, and Literature*. New York: Dover, 1970.

Derleth, August. "An Autobiography." August Derleth Society. http://www.derleth.org.

Dolan, Richard. *UFOs and the National Security State: Chronology of a Coverup, 1941–1973*. Hampton Roads, 2002.

Donnelly, Ignatius. *Atlantis: The Antediluvian World*. Project Gutenberg. http://www.gutenberg.net/etext03/7ataw11.txt.

Dutton, David. *Neville Chamberlain*. London: Edward Arnold, 2001.

Fagan, Brian. *Ancient North America*. 3rd ed. New York: Thames and Hudson, 2000.

———. *Egypt of the Pharaohs*. Washington, DC: National Geographic, 2001.

Feder, Kenneth L. "Ten Years After: Surveying Misconceptions about the Human Past." *Cultural Resource Management* 18, no. 3 (1995): 11–14.

Fitting, Peter. "SF Criticism in France." *Science Fiction Studies* 1, no. 3 (Spring 1974). http://www.depauw.edu/sfs/backissues/3/fitting 3art.htm.

Fort, Charles. *The Book of the Damned*. New York: Horace Liveright, 1931.

Frum, David. *How We Got Here: The 70's: The Decade That Brought You Modern Life—For Better or Worse*. New York: Basic Books, 2000.

Gardner, Laurence. *Bloodline of the Holy Grail*. New York: Barnes & Noble, 1997.

———. "Genesis of the Grail Kings Lecture Transcript." http://www.karenlyster.com/genesis.html.

Gault, R. T. "The Absolute Elsewhere: Fantastic, Visionary, and Esoteric Literature in the 1960s and 1970s." http://www.cafes.net/ditch/Elsewhere.htm.

Gilbert, Adrian. *Signs in the Sky: The Astrological and Archaeological Evidence for the Birth of a New Age*. New York: Three Rivers Press, 2001.

Gilbert, Adrian, and Maurice Cotterell. *The Mayan Prophecies: Unlocking the Secrets of a Lost Civilization.* New York: Barnes & Noble, 1996.

Grayson, Perry M. "Frank Belknap Long, Jr.: Fantasist of Multiple Dimensions. A Preliminary Critical and Historical Overview." http://www.thevine.net/~fortress/fblhist.htm.

Greenberg, Martin H., Richard Matheson, and Charles G. Waugh, eds. *The Twilight Zone: The Original Stories.* New York: MJF, 1985.

Grove, Allen W. "Rontgen's Ghosts: Photography, X-Rays, and the Victorian Imagination." *Literature and Medicine* 16, no. 2 (1997). http://muse.jhu.edu/.

Hafernik, Rob. "Sitchin's Twelfth Planet." http://www.geocities.com/Area51/Corridor/8148/hafernik.html.

Hancock, Graham. *Fingerprints of the Gods.* New York: Crown, 1995.

———. *Heaven's Mirror: The Quest for the Lost Civilization.* New York: Crown, 1998.

———.Official Graham Hancock Web site. http://www.graham hancock.com.

———. *The Sign and the Seal.* New York: Touchstone, 1992.

———. *Underworld.* London: Michael Joseph/Penguin, 2002.

Hancock, Graham, and Robert Bauval. *The Message of the Sphinx: A Quest for the Hidden Legacy of Mankind.* New York: Crown, 1996.

Hancock, Graham, Robert Bauval, and John Grigsby. *The Mars Mystery.* New York: Crown, 1998.

Harms, Daniel, and John William Gonce III. Necronomicon Files On-Line. http://www.necfiles.org.

Haslip-Viera, G., B. Ortiz de Montellano, and W. Barbour. "CA Forum on Anthropology in Public: Robbing Native American Cultures: Van Sertima's Afrocentricity and the Olmec." *Current Anthropology* 38 (1997): 419–41.

Heinrich, Paul V. Wild Side of Geoarchaeology Page. http://www.inter surf.com/~chalcedony/wildside.shtml.

Herrick, James A. *The Making of the New Spirituality: The Eclipse of the Western Religious Tradition.* Downers Grove, IL: Intervarsity Press, 2003.

Houellebecq, Michel. *H. P. Lovecraft: Against the World, Against Life.* San Francisco: Believer Books, 2005.

Howard, Robert E. *Nameless Cults: The Cthulhu Mythos Fiction of Robert E. Howard*. Edited by Robert M. Price. Oakland, CA: Chaosium, 2001.

In the Hall of Ma'at: Weighing the Evidence for Alternative History. http://www.hallofmaat.com.

Jamieson, John. "Books and the Soldier." *Public Opinion Quarterly* 9, no. 3 (Autumn 1945): 320–32.

Jarocha-Ernst, Chris. "Klarkash-Ton and the Cthulhu Mythos." http://www.oceanstar.com/cas/cjetext.htm.

Jobs, Richard I. "Tarzan under Attack: Youth, Comics, and Cultural Reconstruction in Postwar France." *French Historical Studies* 26, no. 4 (Fall 2003): 687–725.

Johnson, Paul, ed. *Sci.Skeptic FAQ*. http://home.xnet.com/~blatura/skeptic.html.

Joshi, S. T. "Howard Phillips Lovecraft: The Life of a Gentleman of Providence." H. P. Lovecraft Archive. http://www.hplovecraft.com.

———. *H. P. Lovecraft: A Life*. 1996. Reprint, West Warwick, RI: Necronomicon Press, 2004.

Klass, Morton. *Ordered Universes: Approaches to the Anthropology of Religion*. Boulder, CO: Westview Press, 1995.

Korff, Kal K. *The Roswell UFO Crash: What They Don't Want You to Know*. Amherst, NY: Prometheus Books, 1997. Reprint, New York: Dell Publications, 2000.

Lachman, Gary. "René Schwaller de Lubicz and the Intelligence of the Heart." *Quest Magazine*, January–February, 2000. Reprinted at Theosophical Society of America. http://www.theosophical.org.

Landsburg, Alan, and Sally Landsburg. *In Search of Ancient Mysteries*. New York: Bantam, 1974.

———. *The Outer Space Connection*. New York: Bantam, 1975.

Lawton, Ian. "A Refutation of the Theories of Zecharia Sitchin." http://www.ianlawton.com.

Legrand, H. E., and Wayne E. Boese. "*Chariots of the Gods?* and All That: Pseudo-History in the Classroom." *History Teacher* 8, no. 3 (May 1975): 359–70.

Lovecraft, H. P. *The Annotated Supernatural Horror in Literature*. Edited by S. T. Joshi. New York: Hippocampus, 2000.

———. *The Best of H. P. Lovecraft: Bloodcurdling Tales of Horror and the Macabre*. New York: Del Rey, 1982.

———. *The Dream Cycle of H. P. Lovecraft: Dreams of Terror and Death*. New York: Del Rey, 1995.

———. *From the Pest Zone: Stories from New York*. Edited by S. T. Joshi. New York: Hippocampus, 2003.

———. *Tales*. New York: Library of America, 2005.

———. *The Transition of H. P. Lovecraft: The Road to Madness*. New York: Del Rey, 1996.

Lovecraft, H. P., and others. *The Horror in the Museum and Other Revisions*. New York: Carroll and Graf, 1997.

———. *The Loved Dead and Other Revisions*. New York: Carroll and Graf, 1997.

———. *Tales of the Cthulhu Mythos*. New York: Del Rey, 1998.

Navarette, Susan J. *The Shape of Fear: Horror and the Fin de Siècle Culture of Decadence*. Lexington: University of Kentucky Press, 1998.

Oberg, James. "The Sirius Mystery." In *UFOs and Outer Space Mysteries*. Donning Press, 1982. Reprinted at www.debunker.com/texts/dogon.html.

Orser, Charles E., Jr. "The 15,000-Year Mistake: When the Facts Don't Fit, Blame the Sun." *Scientific American Discovering Archaeology*. January 31, 2001. http://www.discoveringarchaeology.com/articles/013101-15,000mistake.

Ortiz de Montellano, Bernard. "The Dogon Revisited." Doug's Archaeology Page. http://www.ramtops.demon.co.uk/dogon.html.

Parker, Barry R. *Alien Life: The Search for Extraterrestrials and Beyond*. New York: Perseus, 1998.

Pfefferkorn, Michael G. "The Shambler from Wisconsin." The Bat Is My Brother: The Unofficial Robert Bloch. http://mgpfeff.home.sprynet.com/bloch.html.

Poe, Edgar Allan. *Complete Tales and Poems*. Edison, NJ: Castle Books, 2001.

Price, Robert M., ed. *Black, Forbidden Things: Cryptical Secrets from the "Crypt of Cthulhu."* Mercer Island, WA: Starmont House, 1992.

———, ed. *The Necronomicon: Selected Stories and Essays concerning the Blasphemous Tome of the Mad Arab*. Oakland, CA: Chaosium, 1996.

Public Papers of the Presidents of the United States: Jimmy Carter 1979, Book II. Washington, DC: Government Printing Office, 1980.

Raël (Claude Vorilhon). *The Message Given by Extra-Terrestrials.* Raëlian Movement, 1998.

Raëlian Movement. *The Raëlian Revolution.* http://www.rael.org.

Richardson, James B., III. *People of the Andes.* Washington, DC: Smithsonian Books, 1994.

Ridpath, Ian. "Investigating the Sirius 'Mystery.'" *Skeptical Inquirer* 3, no. 1 (Fall 1978): 56–62.

Roads, Duncan. "Frequently Asked Questions." *Nexus* 2, no. 27 (August–September 1995). http://www.nexusmagazine.com.

Ross, Rick. "Nuwaubians." Ross Institute for the Study of Destructive Cults, Controversial Groups and Movements. http://www.rickross.com.

Sanarov, Valerii I. "On the Nature and Origin of Flying Saucers and Little Green Men." *Current Anthropology* 22, no. 2 (April 1981): 163–67.

Santillana, Giorgio D., and Hertha von Dechend. *Hamlet's Mill: An Essay Investigating the Origins of Human Knowledge and Its Transmission through Myth.* Boston: Nonpareil Books, 1998.

Schick, Theodore Jr., and Lewis Vaughn. *How to Think about Weird Things: Critical Thinking for a New Age.* 2nd ed. Mountainview, CA: Mayfield Publishing, 1999.

Shaeffer, Robert. "Erich von Däniken's 'Chariots of the Gods?': Science or Charlatanism?" *NICAP UFO Investigator*, October/November 1974.

Shaw, Thomas. "Martyrs, Miracles, and Martians: Religion and Cold War Cinematic Propaganda in the 1950s." *Journal of Cold War Studies* 4, no. 2 (Spring 2002): 3–22.

Shelley, Mary. *Frankenstein.* New York: Bantam Classic, 1991.

Shippey, Tom, ed. *The Oxford Book of Science Fiction Stories.* New York: Oxford University Press, 1992.

Shreffler, Philip A. *The H. P. Lovecraft Companion.* Connecticut: Greenwood Press, 1977.

Shuker, Karl P. N. *The Unexplained.* London: Carlton Books, 1996.

Sitchin, Zecharia. "Forging the Pharaoh's Name." *Ancient Skies* 8, no. 2 (1981).

———. *The Twelfth Planet.* New York: Avon Books, 1979.

———. Zecharia Sitchin's Official Web site. http://www.sitchin.com.

Slusser, George. "Science Fiction in France: An Introduction." *Science Fiction Studies* 16, no. 49 (November 1989). http://www.depauw.edu/sfs/covers/cov49.htm.

Smith, Clark Ashton. The Eldritch Dark: The Sanctum of Clark Ashton Smith. http://www.eldritchdark.com/.

Souter, Gavin. "The Disappointing but Profitable Mysteries of Erich von Däniken." *Advertiser*, March 31, 1973. Reprinted in *Investigator* 13 (July 1990).

Sweet, Matthew. *Inventing the Victorians: What We Think We Know about Them and Why We're Wrong.* New York: St. Martin's Press, 2001.

Temple, Robert. *The Sirius Mystery: New Scientific Evidence of Alien Contact 5,000 Years Ago.* Rochester, VT: Destiny Books, 1998.

Theosophical Society in America Web site. http://www.theosophical.org.

Tiryakian, Edward A. "Toward the Sociology of Esoteric Culture." *American Journal of Sociology* 78, no. 3 (November 1972): 491–512.

Unarius Academy of Science. Unarius Academy of Science Web site. http://www.unarius.org/start.html.

van Beek, Walter E. A. "Dogon Restudied: A Field Evaluation of the Work of Marcel Griaule." *Current Anthropology* 32 (1992): 139–67.

Wells, Mark, and Richard Wells. "The Theory of the Chinese Pyramids." EarthQuest. November 2000 update. http://www.earthquest.co.uk/articales/theory.html.

West, John Anthony. "The Wisdom of Ancient Egypt." *Quest Magazine*. January–February 2000. Reprinted on Theosophical Society of America. http://www.theosophical.org.

Whittemore, Faye. "International Raëlian Religion." Religious Movements Homepage Project. University of Virginia. http://religiousmovements.lib.virginia.edu/nrms/rael.html.

Wilson, A. N. *God's Funeral: The Decline of Faith in Western Civilization.* New York: W. W. Norton, 1999.

Wilson, Colin Wilson, and Damon Wilson. *The Mammoth Encyclopedia of the Unsolved.* New York: Carroll and Graf, 2000.

Yronwode, Catherine. "Notes on a Lecture by Graham Hancock." http://www.luckymojo.com/hancocklecture.html.

INDEX